Second Life
FOR
DUMMIES

Cheat Sheet

Menu Keyboard Shortcuts

Press This	To Do This
Ctrl+F	Open Search menu.
Ctrl+I	Open Inventory window.
Ctrl+M	Open World Map.
Ctrl+Shift+M	Open Mini-Map.
Ctrl+P	Open Preferences menu.
Ctrl+Q	Quit Second Life.
Ctrl+Alt+D	Open/close Debug menu.
Ctrl+Shift+A	Start/stop movie capture to disk.
Ctrl+Alt+1	Hide user interface so it doesn't appear in capture.
Ctrl+Shift+S	Take a snapshot.

Communication Keyboard Shortcuts

Press This	To Do This
Enter	Sends chat typed into the chat window.
/me	Displays the message that follows as a text emote.
Ctrl+Enter	Shout.
Ctrl+T	Instant message.
Ctrl+H	Open chat history.
/*gesture*	Begin the selected gesture.
Ctrl+G	Open Gestures menu.

Navigation Keyboard Shortcuts

Press This	To Do This
↑/↓ (or the W or S key, respectively)	Walk forward or backward.
←/→ (or the L or R key, respectively)	Turn left or right.
F	Fly, when not in Chat mode.
Page Up/Page Down (or the E or C key, respectively)	Fly higher or lower.
Ctrl+R	Run (toggle run on and off).

For Dummies: Bestselling Book Series for Beginners

Second Life
FOR
DUMMIES

Cheat Sheet

Camera Control Keyboard Shortcuts

Press This	To Do This
Esc	Reset view.
M	Toggles to Mouse Look when not in Chat mode.
Alt+click	Focus camera on an object or avatar clicked.
Ctrl+Alt+drag mouse	Orbit camera view.
Ctrl+Shift+Alt+drag mouse	Pan camera view.
Ctrl+0 (zero)	Zoom in.
Ctrl+8	Zoom out.
Ctrl+9	Reset to default zoom.
Ctrl+Alt+M	Control position of the sun with mouse.

Building Keyboard Shortcuts

Press This	To Do This
B	Open Build menu when not in Chat mode.
Ctrl+1	Focus.
Ctrl+2	Move.
Ctrl+3	Edit.
Ctrl+4	Create.
Ctrl+5	Land.
Shift+drag mouse	Copy object when in Edit mode.
Ctrl+Z	Undo when in Edit mode.
Ctrl+L	Link selected objects.
Ctrl+Shift+L	Unlink parts of selected object.
Ctrl+U	Upload image.

For Dummies: Bestselling Book Series for Beginners

Second Life® FOR DUMMIES®

by Sarah Robbins and Mark Bell

BICENTENNIAL
1807
WILEY
2007
BICENTENNIAL

Wiley Publishing, Inc.

Second Life® For Dummies®

Published by

Wiley Publishing, Inc.

111 River Street

Hoboken, NJ 07030-5774

www.wiley.com

For general information on our other products and services, please contact our Customer Care Department within the U.S. at 800-762-2974, outside the U.S. at 317-572-3993, or fax 317-572-4002.

For technical support, please visit www.wiley.com/techsupport.

Wiley also publishes its books in a variety of electronic formats. Some content that appears in print may not be available in electronic books.

Library of Congress Control Number: 2007941626

ISBN: 978-0-470-18025-9

Manufactured in the United States of America

10 9 8 7 6 5 4 3 2 1

WILEY

About the Authors

Sarah "Intellagirl" Robbins is the Director of Emerging Technologies for Media Sauce (**www.mediasauce.com**) in Carmel, Indiana, as well as a Ph.D. candidate in Rhetoric at Ball State University, where she teaches Rhetoric and Composition by using Second Life. She currently spends her time blogging at Ubernoggin.com and researching technology trends for education and marketing. She's frequently on the go, giving talks all over the country about Second Life and Web 2.0 topics.

Sarah is the proud mother of five-year-old triplets (Morrigan, Teagan, and Xander), who recognize her avatar as "Mommy!" When she's not hanging with the munchkins, she's reading a few hundred blogs daily, attending seminars, knitting, and collecting socks. And yes, she does have pink hair in real life, too!

Mark Bell is a Ph.D. student in Telecommunications at Indiana University, where he studies social networks in virtual worlds with the Synthetic Worlds Initiative. Before going back to school, Mark spent 14 years in the software industry as a trainer, a documentation specialist, and an all-about super geek. He is a Canadian transplant in Hoosier Land and gets back across the border north (where they understand "real sports") as often as he can. Mark is the father of Jackson, who is five. Mark blogs at Storygeek.com

In their "free" time, Mark and Sarah run the Second Life Researcher's List (SLRL), throw parties for their starving grad student friends, and play Wii games with four five-year-olds.

Dedication

Sarah's dedication: To my parents, Harold and Kathy, who, even when they cringed at my craziness, have always been encouraging of my off-the-wall endeavors. To my sister, Lara, who can still say she's the "normal" one. To my kids, who are the light of my life and the reason I care so much about the future. And to Mark, love of my life, cream in my coffee, and my "Egg on Toast!!!!"

Mark's dedication: To my mother, Madonna, who constantly gives me strength, encouragement, and love. To the memory of my father, Carl, that is fuel that ceaselessly powers my engine. To my son, Jackson, who I try to always give the best of me. To my siblings: David, Debbie, Terry, and Sharron, and their families, whom I never see enough but I learn lessons from every day. To Sarah, my love. I owe so much to this partner in mind, heart, and spirit. You have challenged me to obtain the highest levels of what I am capable of by being a perfect role model. To Davin and Vince, who I love like brothers.

Authors' Acknowledgments

This book may have been typed by two people, but it was written by thousands. We humbly thank the Second Life community. Without you, your creativity, and your willingness to wear a box on your head, this book would have not been written.

Thanks to Steve Hayes and Blair Pottenger at Wiley for putting up with our delays, hectic lives, and overall nuttiness. Thanks to our tech editor, Ryan Williams, for catching our mistakes and knowing how tough it is to document something that constantly changes. And thanks to our copy editor, Teresa Artman, for not throttling us for our love of commas.

And to a few (okay, a lot) special Second Lifers (as their Second Life names): Fleep Tuque, who is endlessly enthusiastic; Robin Sojourner, the queen of all that is tricky about Second Life; Professor Beliveau, for being a butt-kicker; Milosun Czervik, for asking, "How's the dissertation?"; AJ Brooks, for being our first fan; Akela Talamaska, for talking Sarah off ledges; Buddy Sprocket and Jeremy Kabumpo, for being fearless leaders; Jane Calvert, for rallying the troops for the book cover; Cleon Goff, for being the king of media; Cyrus Huffhines, Man Michinaga, and Rubaiyat Shatner, for bringing art to Second Life; Desideria Stockton, for making literature come alive; JoannaTrail Blazer, for her support and tallness; Larry Pixel, for his fight for quality education; Barry Joseph, for making the world a better place for kids; Marcius Dowding, for asking, "Is it done yet?"; Wendy Widget, for her "Go grrrrl!"; Veritas Veriscan, for her dedication; Wainbrave Bernal, for being brilliant and yet very ugly; Audio Zenith, for making education a great party; Buyers Sellers, for studying Metanomics; LauraMaria Onomatopoeia, for her constant cheerleading; and to Pathfinder Linden, for his help and dedication in the "old days." Thanks to Sarah's students for their willingness to be guinea pigs.

Special thanks to the Center for Media Design at Ball State University, Michael Holmes, Carole Papper, Kris Fleckenstein, and Edward Castronova for not thinking that Second Life was a crazy idea. Thanks to James Cheseboro for recognizing that Second Life is a culture. Thanks to MediaSauce, especially Bryan Gray, for believing that the revolution really is coming.

Thanks to Nick Geidner. This is all your fault! To Betsy Pike, our hope for the future.

Thank you to Linden Lab for making a new world for us to live in.

Most special thanks to our friends and family who understood "We can't. We *have* to write!"

Publisher's Acknowledgments

We're proud of this book; please send us your comments through our online registration form located at `www.dummies.com/register/`.

Some of the people who helped bring this book to market include the following:

Acquisitions, Editorial, and Media Development

Project Editor: Blair J. Pottenger

Executive Editor: Steven Hayes

Acquisitions Editor: Melody Layne

Senior Copy Editor: Teresa Artman

Technical Editor: Ryan Williams

Editorial Manager: Kevin Kirschner

Media Project Supervisor: Laura Moss-Hollister

Media Development Specialist: Angela Denny

Editorial Assistant: Amanda Foxworth

Senior Editorial Assistant: Cherie Case

Cartoons: Rich Tennant (`www.the5thwave.com`)

Composition Services

Senior Project Coordinator: Kristie Rees

Layout and Graphics: Alissa D. Ellet

Proofreaders: John Greenough, Susan Moritz, Sossity R. Smith

Indexer: Steve Rath

Anniversary Logo Design: Richard Pacifico

Publishing and Editorial for Technology Dummies

Richard Swadley, Vice President and Executive Group Publisher

Andy Cummings, Vice President and Publisher

Mary Bednarek, Executive Acquisitions Director

Mary C. Corder, Editorial Director

Publishing for Consumer Dummies

Diane Graves Steele, Vice President and Publisher

Joyce Pepple, Acquisitions Director

Composition Services

Gerry Fahey, Vice President of Production Services

Debbie Stailey, Director of Composition Services

Table of Contents

Introduction

*E*veryone is doing it. Jumping into the exciting world of Second Life (SL) to see what all the buzz is about, to start a business, to catch up with friends, to teach a class, or just to go dancing without having to worry about how uncomfortable those heels are going to get by the end of the night.

Maybe you've only just heard about SL. Maybe you joined, logged in, and got stuck. Maybe you're an SL veteran but want to know more about building, running a business, or another advanced skill. No matter who you are, if you're interested in SL, you've got the right book in your hands. What are you waiting for?! Get going. There are more than nine million people waiting to meet you!

About This Book

Millions of people are converts of the SL experience, but that doesn't mean it's easy. Everyone is a newbie (a *newb*) at some point, but you don't have to look like one. *For Dummies* books aren't written just as guides but as trusted sources of information. We're here, in these pages, to hold your hand, pat your back, and cheer for you as you try out this new reality. No need to be scared or uptight. Second Life is fun when you know what you're doing, and you soon will.

If you've read anything about Second Life or have friends who are using it, you've probably heard some exciting stuff as well as some scary stuff. Safety is important to us, so you'll see lots of tips and tricks for staying safe and comfortable while you learn and explore. Have no worries. We're here to help.

If you're not convinced that SL is for you, what better way to find out than to jump in? And what better way to jump in than with a couple of Second Life old-timers by your side? We hope that with this book at your side, you won't be intimidated by seeing how to navigate Second Life, and that when you get into trouble (got a box on your head? If you don't get the joke now, you will later, promise!), you'll know you can flip open this book and find what you need.

Second Life For Dummies is written to do more than provide the basics, though. You'll find expert advice, seasoned insight, and handy tips and tricks to get you moving fast. Best of all, we (the authors) are residents of this crazy alternate world, too! When you find out how to make friends, you can look us up and actually talk to the authors of this book! You can't beat that kind of customer service. This book is just the beginning of a big experience, and we're happy to have you along for the ride.

What You Can Safely Ignore

Throughout the book, we include examples of code, steps for creating your own Second Life gear, and so on. If you're a consumer and don't want to be a producer, you can skip those sections. But you'll be back to them later. We know you.

Oh, and all those boxes mixed in throughout the pages? Those are sidebars. They provide nonessential information. You can skip them if you want, but you'll miss out on cool tips.

Foolish Assumptions

We'll be honest. We had to assume some things about you to write this book. So, here's what we assume about you:

- ✓ You already know a little something about the basics of using your own computer. You know how to install software, surf the Web, and other basics of living in the 20th century.

- ✓ You have at least a passing interest in Second Life. We're not here to convince you to want to use it: just to teach you how to use it better. If you're a skeptic, jump in and find out whether your assumptions are right. If you're a naysayer, well go sulk somewhere else. No grumps allowed at this party!

How This Book Is Organized

Every adventure needs a plan. We divided this book into six parts to help you easily find the information that you need.

Part I: Second Life Overview and Basics

If don't already have SL installed or don't have an account yet, this is where you'll want to start. We'll help you get set up and walk you through the Second Life tutorials so you can get in there and start having fun.

Part II: Living Your Second Life — Exploring and Socializing

In this section, we cover the basics of establishing who you are in SL. This includes moving around, customizing your avatar with cool clothes and accessories, learning to chat with other residents, and staying in your comfort zone.

Part III: Inventory, Cash, and Land

Second Life is full of stuff! Stuff you can make, stuff you can buy, and stuff you can do. It all adds up to a lot of stuff management. Whether you're a land baron, a money maker, or just a clothes horse, you'll want to read over these chapters to see how to get on top of all your stuff.

Part IV: Building and Customizing

Second only to all the great people you'll meet, the best part of SL is the ability to create awesome stuff. Build a house and live in it. Or better yet, build a house, sell it, and watch other people live in it and enjoy it. Maybe architecture isn't your thing. Maybe you're more into fashion? Well, SL has that, too. We show you how to make your first items of custom clothing (a t-shirt) and move on to making more complex items (skirts that sway and swish). We'll even dig into the most complex part of Second Life — scripting. Yes, you, too can be a programmer!

Part V: Real Life Opportunities in Second Life

Second Life might be a virtual world, but there is *real* money to be made. It's not easy to make a living in SL, but the tips we provide will give you a fighting chance and a leg up on the competition. We cover the basics of getting a job or starting a business, and then show you some examples of big business already in SL so you can learn from the masters. Finally, we'll explore the biggest growing area of SL — education. Yes, there are people getting degrees using Second Life. Will the amazement never end?

Part VI: The Parts of Tens

These chapters are one of the coolest parts of a *For Dummies* book. These lists feature cool places and even where to find the best shoes! We've toured the virtual world looking for the best places so you don't have to. Let us show you around.

Icons Used in This Book

Throughout the book are symbols in the margin. These symbols, or *icons,* mark important points.

This bull's-eye icon points to tips and tricks that will make you more Second Life savvy.

These warning icons alert you to something that could cause trouble. Be sure to pay attention to them to save yourself time and worry.

This icon will remind you of something we think it's important to keep in mind as you explore your new virtual life.

These technical tips might go over your head if you're not the geeky type. If you are the geeky type these tips will give you even greater insight into ways you can customize your Second Life experience.

Where to Go from Here

Just getting started with Second Life? Turn the page. Do you have a specific topic of interest? Use the index or the Table of Contents to find the topic and turn to that page. Go on. You know how to read a book. Time's a' wasting!

Part I
Second Life Overview and Basics

The 5th Wave   By Rich Tennant

NO SECOND LIFE

PLEASE

In this part . . .

*L*earning to use Second Life is kind of like riding a roller coaster. Going up that first hill is slow and steep, but after you get to the top, it's "Yeeeee-haaaaa!" all the way down. It's a fun, exciting place full of smart, engaging people, and you're going to be one of them. We show you how it's done.

Before you can really enjoy all the fun stuff that attracted you to Second Life in the first place, you need to know the basics. In Chapter 1, we tell you what all the fuss is about. Even though Second Life changes every day, a few standard elements of this virtual world keep drawing in folks. Chapter 2 will help you prepare to get started. You need the right tools for the job, and because hardware is one of the biggest barriers to using Second Life, we tell you how to get your computer up to snuff to enjoy Second Life at its best.

After you garner a bit of background and your computer is prepped, you're ready to jump in. In Chapter 3, you start getting your hands dirty by setting up an account. Finally, in Chapter 4, we show you how to log in and see how to get around. By the end of this part, you'll be flying, walking, and teleporting like a pro.

1

The Meaning of (Second) Life

In This Chapter

▶ Defining Second Life

▶ How Second Life is different from a game

▶ The origins of Second Life

▶ Who has a Second Life?

▶ Second Life is the Web of the future

*Y*ou keep hearing about it in the news. Reporters flying around a digital world talking about the strange things happening there. Politicians meeting their constituents in digital bodies. Music events with virtual bands playing for virtual audiences. Companies such as IBM, Reuters, American Apparel, and Nike have all staked their claim to open digital storefronts.

This is the world of Second Life (SL). A world of avatars and virtual landscapes where anything can happen and usually does. Whether you're a student taking online classes, a budding fashion designer looking for an opportunity to show off your latest threads, or just someone who likes to dance the night away without paying a cover charge, Second Life has something to offer. We'll show you how to get in there, get started, and get up to speed — so read on!

When One Life Isn't Enough: Explaining Second Life

Most of us have enough going in our First Lives (translation, our real lives) to wonder why anyone would need a second one. Running between meetings, trying to keep up with friends, and the occasional entertainment we might have time for seems to be enough to keep us busy morning to night. Rather than thinking about Second Life as just one more new technology to keep up with, though, think about it as a way to simplify much of what you already do. Instead of driving between meetings, you could fly.

Instead of making five phone calls to organize your friends for tonight's trip to the dance club, you could be sending them teleport requests to join you at the latest hip spot. Forget waiting in line to buy concert tickets; with Second Life, you can attend a live concert any time you'd like without paying ten bucks for a beverage.

So how does Second Life work? There are some basic elements to this cyber-world. After you understand how they work, you'll be able to dive right in and start having fun.

- **Account types:** Verified and unverified: If you associate a credit card or Paypal account with your account you'll be listed as verified, that is you proved who you were when you created your account. Basic and Premium: Basic accounts are free. If you own land you'll pay a monthly fee and be moved to a premium account. For more on account types, see Chapter 3.

- **Avatars:** An *avatar* is your virtual body in Second Life. You could be a bombshell, decked out in the latest Gucci knock-offs, or a dinosaur wagging your tail, as shown in Figure 1-1. In Second Life, the only limits to your appearance are the limits of your imagination, your time, and your wallet. If you can think it, you can be it. For info about customizing your avatar, jump to Chapter 5.

- **Moving:** Second Life allows you to get around in lots of ways. You can fly without without wings (see Figure 1-2), run, walk, drive a car, or teleport from place to place.

Figure 1-1: In Second Life you can lounge on the beach anytime you feel like getting a little sun.

✔ **Chatting:** Second Life offers lots of different ways to communicate with fellow residents. You can send Instant Messages, text chat with those around you (as shown in Figure 1-3), or even use your voice with a microphone. For more details about how to chat it up with your Second Life cronies, see Chapter 6.

✔ **L$ (virtual money):** Second Life has its own economy with a currency called the *Linden (L$)*. You can purchase Lindens to buy virtual schwag from other folks, buy a house, cruise in your dream car, and so on. But here's the best part: If you start a business or make money some other way in Second Life, you can exchange your L$ for cold hard cash. For more info about the Second Life economy, check out Chapter 10.

✔ **Building your world:** Everything in Second Life is built by Second Life residents. Every shopping mall (see Figure 1-4), every water slide, every awesome pair of sunglasses was made by someone just like you — and it's easy to discover how. To get started building objects in Second Life, head to Chapter 13.

Don't feel like you have to read this book in order from cover to cover. We organize this info to be used in chunks. For example, if you already know how to chat, jump to another chapter and see how to deck out your avatar. Keep the book handy as you explore Second Life and even after you become a pro. We'll be here to give you tips all along the way.

Figure 1-2: With or without wings, you can fly in Second Life.

Figure 1-3: Two newbie avatars' hands make typing motions as they chat on Welfare Island.

Figure 1-4: Malls in Second Life look much like the mall down the street.

Second Life: It's Not a Game

Want to make a bunch of Second Life users mad really quick? Call Second Life a *game*. Although it looks like a video game similar to *World of Warcraft* or *The*

Sims, Second Life isn't a game. In SL, you don't level-up, complete missions, or earn new armor. So exactly what do you do in Second Life? Well, you live a *second* life. Anything you can do in real life (from washing dishes and buying a house to getting a job and getting married), you can do in SL.

Because SL isn't a game, the folks who use it don't refer to themselves as *players.* Instead, the people who inhabit the SL world are *residents.*

There are games *in* SL, though. You can play poker, golf, baseball, pool, or any other real-life game you can imagine. There are also games unique to SL, such as *Slingo* (as shown in Figure 1-5), which is a bingo-like game first created by a SL resident and now available on many other platforms. You can also participate in role playing games as a vampire, werewolf, postapocalyptic scavenger, or whatever else your role-playing heart desires.

Figure 1-5: Folks waiting for a game of Slingo to begin on Dutchusa Island.

You can make your own games in SL by discovering how to program objects in Chapter 14.

Most people with an Internet connection have at least heard of social networking sites such as MySpace and Facebook. These Web sites let you connect with people with whom you have something in common and might enjoy talking to, and Second Life isn't much different. You'll be able to join groups centered around hobbies, affiliations, nationalities, and other interests. You'll also be able to make friends with people who are interested in similar things, thus building your own social circle in Second Life, which means you'll always have someone to hang out with.

A Bit of History

Linden Lab, creator of Second Life, created a virtual monster that now has a life of its own — only a few thousand users has grown to a few million in less than a year. From October, 2006 to September, 2007, the population of the SL environment increased 900 percent from 1 million accounts to 9 million accounts.

To read more about Second Life's history, check out the SL History Wiki (www.slhistory.org) and the official blog of Linden Lab (http://blog.secondlife.com).

Second Life is loosely based on a virtual reality featured in *Snow Crash,* a 1992 novel by Neal Stephenson. In the book, the main character "jacks" into a digital place called *the Metaverse* where people travel, socialize, and do business virtually. In the book, as in SL, the world is created by the people who populate it. Ten years later, Philip Rosedale and his company men created Linden World, which then became SL. The rest, as they say, is history.

In honor of SL's roots, we still refer to the environment as *the Metaverse.* Other SL lingo gets inspiration from other classic sci-fi sources. For example, when objects are created or taken out of your inventory, they're *rezzed,* which is a term that comes from the 1982 film *Tron* in which unstable digital objects that disappeared were said to "de-rez." But even though SL has roots in the geekiest of sci-fi, what it has become is far from, "Beam me up, Scotty."

To read up about some of the crazy firsts in Second Life history, visit the SL History Firsts page at www.slhistory.org/index.php/Firsts.

Who's in Second Life?

You've probably heard the news reports about companies like IBM and Dell claiming their territory in Second Life (as shown in Figure 1-6), but they wouldn't be there if tons of activity didn't already exist in the space. Big Business isn't alone in Second Life, so who else is in there with them?

Second Life residents are certainly early adopters. On the whole, they're the kind of people who feel the need to poke and prod at every new techy gizmo that comes along. Second Life statistics show that the average user is American and about 28 years of age. The population is split almost half between men and women.

Most people who use Second Life are interested in having fun. They use SL to connect with people who have common interests and generally hang out much as most of us do in real life. In addition, those of us who hang out in SL do a lot of shopping to deck out our avatars and our virtual homes so we can look good as we socialize and have a cool place to do it.

There are, of course, the residents of Second Life who create what the rest of us enjoy buying. SL is full of virtual store fronts selling everything from clothing and jewelry to homes, cars, and gadgets, as shown in Figure 1-7. With the building tools in SL and other software, such as Adobe Photoshop and Poser from e frontier, these creative people market and sell products so the rest of us can better enjoy SL. For more information about beginning your own business in Second Life, read Chapter 17.

Figure 1-6: IBM Island's business center has many meeting spots as well as product information.

Figure 1-7: The Muse jewelry shop has a beautiful display window to make you want to come inside.

Second Life is Web 2.0 in 3-D

A couple of years ago, Tim O'Reilly (www.oreilleynet.com) coined the term *Web 2.0* to describe the new boom of Web sites that invited users to interact in new ways. O'Reilly described the sites as

- ✔ A way to transform a Web site into a platform (Google documents, for example)
- ✔ A way of harnessing the powers of collective intelligence (such as Wikipedia)
- ✔ Allowing access to large specialized databases (such as Google maps)
- ✔ Providing services instead of products

In the past few years, we've become accustomed to Web 2.0 sites. Second Life might represent the next big thing in these kinds of Web services for the following reasons:

- ✔ **More than software:** The software that you download to access SL isn't SL itself: It's a way to connect to the servers that host the world. The software is just a viewer. The real value of SL is in the *grid* (the collection of islands that create the Second Life world) itself.

- ✔ **A collective effort:** The true beauty of SL is that all its wonders are created not by the company that made it (Linden Lab) but by the folks who use it.

- ✔ **A source of collaboration:** After you start exploring SL, you'll realize that the most powerful element of the environment is the people in it. They collaborate, cooperate, and create a fantastic experience for themselves and others. Sure, there are jerks, but jerks are everywhere. Overall, the population of SL is an amazing resource for all who choose to become part of it.

- ✔ **A service, not a product:** Linden Lab provides a service: access to the grid. The products that are sold in SL are sold by the residents. It's the people who live in SL who make money from their work, not Linden Lab.

The one and only way to get into Second Life is to create an account and log in. In the next few chapters, we walk you through the steps you need to get in there and start having fun — and a Second Life.

2

Tweaking Your System: Adjusting Your Computer to Best Run Second Life

In This Chapter

▶ The right equipment for the job

▶ What to do when Second Life seems to chug rather than glide

▶ What's making you lag?

▶ Adjusting the Second Life settings to work best

▶ Updating the software

*O*ne of the biggest obstacles to using Second Life is, well, using Second Life. Not just any computer can run it, and having the wrong hardware or Internet connection can make using Second Life as frustrating as herding cats.

If you've experienced any of the following, you probably need this chapter:

✔ You're walking or flying, and you can't stop.

✔ Walls, people, and landscapes are gray on your screen.

✔ Everything beyond your avatar's arms reach is invisible until you walk toward it.

✔ Your avatar looks gray or naked.

✔ You can't walk or walk very fast.

These problems and lots more can be remedied by using the right hardware, having the right Internet connection, and adjusting your Second Life settings.

In this chapter, we give you tips and tricks to make Second Life run best on your computer. You learn to troubleshoot the most common Second Life problems, update the software, and know what performance issues are your fault and what's just Second Life lag.

Hardware and Internet Requirements

You might have already checked the hardware and Internet suggestions on SecondLife.com before you downloaded the software. If you didn't, the following sections provide a quick reminder.

Please note that the requirements in the following sections are Linden Lab's *minimum* specs for hardware. The better your computer, the better Second Life will work. If you intend to run other applications in addition to Second Life, be sure to exceed the minimum specifications.

PC requirements

The following list covers the hardware and Internet requirements needed to get Second Life up and running on your PC:

✓ **Cable or DSL Internet connection:** Don't even think about using dial-up. Plugging in is much better than using a wireless connection.

- *Dial up:* If you hear a modem screeching when you connect to the Internet chances are you have dial-up. This kind of Internet connection simply isn't fast enough to connect to Second Life.

- *DSL:* DSL is an Internet connection that runs on your phone line but is always connected and works at a faster speed than dial-up. Most DSL connections will be fast enough to connect to SL.

- *Cable:* If your cable company provides Internet access you probably have a pretty fast connection. However, some cable systems split the signal between you and the other folks in your neighborhood. If you find that your connection seems slow we suggest you give your provider a call and ask whether the strength of your signal has been diminished by being shared. If it has, most companies will install a booster on your line that will fix the problem.

- *Wireless:* If you're using a laptop that isn't plugged into an Internet connection then you're relying on a wireless connection. On a home network wireless connection speeds may be high enough to run Second Life but sharing a wireless network on campus or at a coffee shop might diminish your signal enough that Second Life will lag.

Dealing with updates and other problems that aren't your fault

You'll be pleased to know that not all problems with Second Life are your fault. Known bugs do exist in Second Life. SL updates about twice monthly, and each new version has new features — as well as new bugs. When too many people are logged in to Second Life at once (typically over 40,000 avatars), you'll see some problems with teleporting, inventory management, and so on. When an emergency bug fix is released, you might see rolling updates that cause regions to reset and consequently kick you out of the program. Occasionally — and this is rare — you'll notice that your money (L$) is temporarily gone or that your inventory isn't accessible. These are pretty extreme bugs and really rare, but they do happen.

- **Windows XP:** Some folks are indeed running Second Life on Vista without problems. Others can be heard screaming obscenities across town. If you have Vista it's worth a shot to try to run Second Life if you have the current drivers for your video card installed.

- **An 800 MHz or better processor:** 800 MHz will get you in, but 1.66 MHz or better will give you better performance.

- **256MB RAM or better:** This must be a joke on Linden's part. Have at least 1 gigabyte (GB) of RAM.

- **Video cards:** This is the toughest requirement to meet. Second Life supports nVidia GeForce2; GeForce4 MX; and ATI Radeon 8500, 9250, or better cards. However, many officially unsupported cards work really well. Video cards that are referred to as being "on board" meaning that they aren't separate cards but are part of your motherboard will very seldom work. You need a card with at least 128 megs of onboard RAM and "on board" motherboards never have their own RAM. Make sure you have the latest drivers for your card by downloading them from your manufacturer's Web site.

Mac requirements

The following list covers the hardware and Internet requirements needed to get Second Life up and running on your Mac:

- **Cable or DLS Internet connection:** The connection restrictions with PCs are similar with Apple computers. AirPort: Using an Apple AirPort may cause lag due to diminished signal.

- **Mac OS X v. 10.3.9 (Panther) or better:** Update often to have the latest version.

✔ **1 GHz G4 processor or better:** Both PPC and Intel Apple computers are compatible.

✔ **512MB RAM or better:** Again, as with a PC, 1GB of RAM is far better.

✔ **Video cards:** Second Life supports nVidea GeForce 2; GeForce4 MX; and ATI Radeon 8500, 9250, or better cards. Most Macs come equipped with a fairly good video card.

Understanding Lag: Is It You or the Grid?

The more time you spend in Second Life, the more definitions of lag you'll hear. Anytime anyone is unhappy with the performance of Second Life, whether because of their own machine or from the Second Life servers, they complain about lag:

"Sorry, didn't mean to bump you. Lag."

"Boy, the lag is bad on this island. Too many people here."

"I didn't mean to show up naked to the party. I had on clothes but they didn't appear 'cuz of lag."

Lag is the slowing down of Second Life and may be caused by a number of things. Most references to lag may be caused by poor computer performance or a slow Internet connection. Here are a few symptoms of lag and how to diagnose where the blame falls.

Symptom: *I can look around, but I can't move.*

Diagnosis: You're disconnected from Second Life but haven't realized it yet. When you use Second Life, you're actually connected to lots of servers. Some provide the island you're on; others provide your inventory or your cash balance. Getting disconnected from any one of them will cause you to be sort of stuck in place. Chat might work, and you might even be able to open your inventory, but you can't walk. If you experience this "stuckness," close Second Life and restart it to reestablish the connection to the servers. Also, this is possibly the result of more than one person using Second Life on one network. If your co-workers or friends log on while you're on and you get locked up every time they do, you might need to contact your network administrator to allow multiple connections to Second Life.

Symptom: *I can move but when I try to walk I start walking and I can't stop.*

Diagnosis: You've got Internet connection problems. Either you're using a connection that's slow, you've tried to access SL using wireless, or that broadband you're paying for really isn't broadband. See the next section to find out the source of your lag.

Symptom: *My video is jerky. Things seem frozen.*

Diagnosis: Your computer isn't handling the video of Second Life well. This could be because of an incompatible video card, too little RAM, or your video settings in Second Life. See the next section.

Even with the best video card and connection, it takes time to load all the objects in SL. In very busy areas it will take some time to load everything so be patient.

Statistics: Finding Out the Source of Your Lag

No matter what kind of lag you're having, you should start your diagnosis by checking out your connection stats. To view the Statistics screen (as shown in Figure 2-1), choose View⇨Statistics Bar.

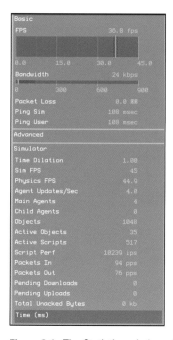

Figure 2-1: The Statistics window shows you valuable information.

The Statistics screen is full of cryptic information. Here's what it all means:

✓ **FPS:** Frames per second (fps). This rate tells you how often your computer is redrawing what you see onscreen. A frame rate between 15 and 30 fps is good. Higher is better, of course. If your rate is below 15, you might have a problem with your video card or your Internet connection.

✔ **Bandwidth:** This is the rate at which your computer is talking to the Second Life servers. This rate varies depending on how busy your location is and whether particle effects are there (sparkles, fireworks, or basically anything flying around). You'll see your bandwidth go up when you first arrive somewhere and drop after everything in the region has been rendered for you.

✔ **Packet Loss:** Your computer is constantly talking with the Second Life servers. Messages are passed back and forth between them like giggly girls in math class. When a message doesn't make it, the result is a *packet loss.* Lose too many packets, and the communication gets foggy and eventually shuts down. If your packet loss is above 10%, you're probably about to lose your connection either because the region you're in is having problems or your Internet connection is unstable.

✔ **Ping Sim:** This is the time it takes for packet of information to go from your computer to the Second Life servers. If it's slow, your Internet connection is slow.

✔ **Ping User:** This is how long it takes for a packet of information from the server to get to you. If your Ping Sim speed is low but Ping User is high, the problem is most likely with your Internet connection. If Ping User is low but Ping Sim is high, the region you're in is having problems.

The Advanced section of the Statistics Bar contains statistics that are not relevant to the regular user experience. Linden Lab support may ask you for the information contained there but a regular user doesn't need to know it.

Preference Settings for Optimal Performance

Your preferences allow you to customize your experience in Second Life. Changing some of the preferences can greatly improve your computer's performance. To access the Preferences dialog box, choose Edit⇨Preferences. The following sections discuss the options available to you through the Preferences screen.

General tab

Here's a breakdown of your options on the General tab, as shown in Figure 2-2.

✔ **Start Location:** This box allows you to specify where your avatar will start when you enter Second Life.

- *My Last Location:* This is the default option. Keeping this option places you at your last location when you log in.

- *My Home:* Selecting this option ensures that every time you log in, you start at your home. You can set your home location by choosing World⇨Set Home to Here.

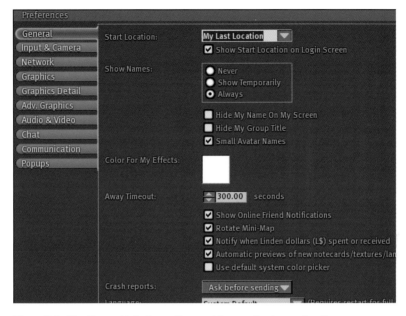

Figure 2-2: The General tab shows the most frequently changed settings.

- *<Type region name>:* Type a region name here to log in at that place each time you restart Second Life. For more on regions, see Chapter 4.

  Show Start Location on Login Screen: This option allows you to specify the location you want to start from on the login screen.

- **Show Names:** Names of avatars, by default, appear over their heads. Some people prefer to only show them briefly or not at all. People change how they look in SL so much it might be a good idea atleast at first to keep names set to always.

  - *Never:* This option hides the names of other avatars on your screen.

  - *Show Temporarily:* If you select this option, avatar names show up for a few seconds and then fade away.

  - *Always:* This is the default option. Avatar names appear over people's heads and will not go away.

- **Hide My Name on My Screen:** By default, this option is not selected. By selecting this option, other avatars will see your name, but it won't appear on your screen.

- **Hide My Group Title:** This option is not selected by default. Selecting this prevents your group title from appearing with your name. You won't see it, and neither will others. You can also accomplish this by choosing

None from the Groups menu on the right-click radial menu when you click on your avatar. For more information on groups, see Chapter 7. To find out more about the radial menu see Chapter 3.

- **Small Avatar Names:** This option is selected by default and displays avatar names in a much smaller font. If unchecked, avatar names appear in a slightly larger font. If you find the screen too busy you might want to keep small avatar names to "on".

- **Color for My Effects:** When you interact with objects, a beam of light shoots from your hand. With this setting, you can change the color of this beam from the default white color. This option, when changed, will change the beam color for any account on your computer. When you click on the white box, the color picker appears and allows you to pick a specific color.

- **Away Timeout:** Ever see people in Second Life slumped over like zombies? They're away from their keyboard, and Away will probably appear next to their name. Your setting (in seconds) for this option controls how long SL waits before it marks you as Away. The default value is 300 seconds (5 minutes), and the maximum value is 600 seconds (10 minutes).

- **Show Online Friend Notifications:** This option is selected by default. When your friends log in, you'll see a pop-up telling you that they're online. You'll also get a message when a friend logs out. To learn more about how to make friends see Chapter 7.

- **Rotate Mini-Map:** This option is selected by default. When selected, your Mini-Map rotates to match your change in direction. Deselect the option, and your Mini-Map always faces the same direction regardless of your movements. By default the map always has North on the top.

- **Notify When Linden Dollars (L$) Are Spent or Received:** This option is selected by default. Be sure to keep this option selected so you'll know when you're spending money or when other people are paying you.

- **Use Default System Color Picker:** By default, this option is not selected. SL allows you to tint objects by picking colors from a palette. The Color Picker in Second Life is nice, but if you prefer the Color Picker that is included in your operating system, select this check box.

- **Crash Reports:** When Second Life crashes, the program can send a crash report to Linden Lab to provide information about the crash. It takes a minute or so to send the report, but it helps Linden improve the stability of Second Life.

  - *Ask Before Sending:* Second Life asks you to confirm before it sends a crash report. This option is selected by default.

  - *Always Send:* Crash reports are always automatically sent.

  - *Never Send:* Crash reports are never sent.

✓ **Language:** Many translations of the Second Life interface are available. If your native language isn't English, give one of the other versions a shot. You systems default language is what is selected by Second Life as the default. Know, though, that these translations are constantly being improved, and some languages are supported better than others.

Input & Camera tab

Here's a breakdown of your options on the Input & General tab, as shown in Figure 2-3.

✓ **Mouselook Options:** Mouselook allows you to use the mouse to look around the world of Second Life. These settings help you fine tune your mouselook.

- *Mouse Sensitivity:* If you zoom your view all the way, to the point your avatar disappears, either by using your mouse wheel or the camera zoom control, you'll be in *Mouselook,* looking through the eyes of your avatar. Your movement in this mode is controlled by this setting. Increase the sensitivity by moving the bar to the left and you'll move farther with smaller mouse movements.

- *Invert Mouse:* With Invert Mouse control, moving the mouse up moves the view down, moving the mouse down moves the view up, and so on. Most folks find this setting counter-intuitive, but if it's what you're used to, select this check box.

✓ **Auto Fly Options:** In Second Life, you fly by pressing buttons or by click-ing the Fly button. This option turns the keyboard option on or off.

- *Fly/land on Holding Up/Down:* Selected by default, this option allows you to automatically start flying when you hold down the Jump/Fly Up key (E, Page Up, or the number pad 9), and stop flying if you touch the ground when holding down the Crouch/Fly Down key (C, Page Down, or number pad 3). If deselected, you'll start/stop flying only by pressing the Fly key (F, Home, or number pad 7).

✓ **Camera Options:** The view you have of Second Life is from a changeable point of view, called the camera. These options affect that view.

- *Camera Springiness:* This value affects how tight the camera follow-ing your avatar feels. Higher numbers result in the camera acting "looser" and more cinematic. Play with different settings to find something you like best.

- *Automatic Edit Camera Movement:* This option makes the camera automatically move to center on an object you're editing. This saves you time maneuvering your camera to get the best view but might inhibit you when you become a more advanced builder.

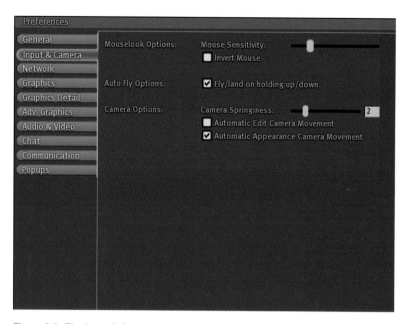

Figure 2-3: The Input & Camera tab allows you control how you see the world of Second Life.

- *Automatic Appearance Camera Movement:* Selected by default, this option makes your camera automatically zoom in on your avatar when you edit your appearance. It also automatically zooms as you select different Body Parts and Clothes tabs.

Network tab

Here's a breakdown of your options on the Network tab, as shown in Figure 2-4.

- **Maximum Bandwidth:** The higher your max bandwidth, the faster that objects, places, and people will load. However, set this too high, and you'll over-tax your computer and end up with lag. Experiment with different settings until you get the performance you want. The default value is 500 Kbps (kilobits per second).

- **Disk Cache Size (MB):** If you've been someplace before or you've already seen the graphics, your computer can call upon the cached graphics to make these object appear faster. The more disk cache space you set aside, the quicker these familiar things will appear. However, you'll also be putting a drain on your hard drive, which can slow things. By default, this is set to 500MB (megabytes). The clear cache button empties your cache. You may want to do this if you are in a graphic intensive area for a period of time.

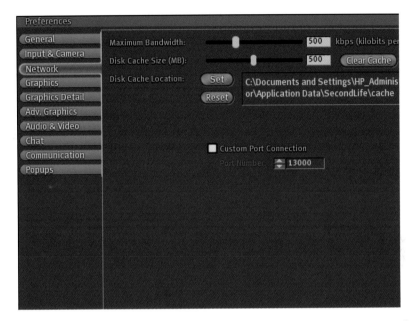

Figure 2-4: The Network tab shows settings that affect how to speed up your network connection.

✔ **Disk Cache Location:** This location should be on your local computer, not a networked drive. Be sure there is ample space, around a gig, on this hard drive.

Web tab

Here's a breakdown of your options on the Graphics tab, as shown in Figure 2-5.

This tab gives you options for viewing Web pages through Second Life.

✔ **Browser Cache:** This button clears the browser cache allowing you to reload pages to get the latest version.

✔ **Accept Cookies from Sites:** A cookie is a small file of information stored on your computer by a Web page. This option allows you to accept cookies from a Web site or pages you are viewing in Second Life.

✔ **Clear Now:** This button clears the cookies of Web pages you have viewed in Second Life.

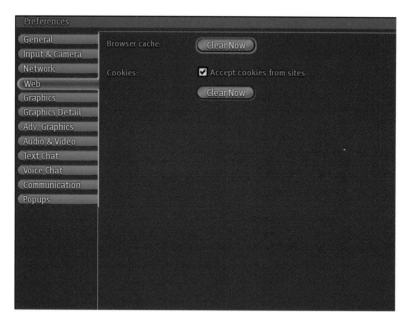

Figure 2-5: The Web tab contains the Web options for Second Life.

Graphics tab

Here's a breakdown of your options on the Graphics tab, as shown in Figure 2-6.

- **Display Resolution:** These options allow you to specify how you want Second Life to be displayed on your computer.

  - *Run in a Window:* If you're like us, you like to run several applications at once. I have Instant Message, a Web browser, and any number of other things running while I'm using Second Life. Running Second Life in a window allows me to see what's behind it and switch between applications easily. Running Second Life in a window will slow down your computer, but if you have good hardware, it might be worth it. You can also toggle between windowed and fullscreen mode by pressing Alt+Enter on a PC and option+Enter on a Mac.

  - *The resolution drop-down list:* Select the resolution to display Second Life.

- **Fullscreen Aspect Ratio (Width/Height):** Three options are available: 4:3, 5:8, and 16:9. Standard monitors have a 4:3 ratio (this is the default setting) or a 5:8 ratio (1280 x 1024 LCD), and widescreen monitors have a 16:9 aspect ratio. Selecting the Auto Detect check box is your best bet for getting the best setting.

Figure 2-6: The Graphics tab controls the resolution of your view of Second Life.

✓ **UI Size:** If you run Second Life at a high resolution, you might notice that the user interface is too small to read. You can move this slider to the right to enlarge windows, text, buttons, menus, and so on. The UI Size is set to 1.000 by default.

> • *Use Resolution Independent Scale:* This option, which is on by default, applies when you're running Second Life fullscreen (not in a window), and helps make sure that the user interface looks the same size at different resolutions.

✓ **Draw Distance:** The further you allow your computer to draw, the more resources you're using. The farther you can see, the more work your computer is doing to make more objects visible. If you're experiencing the kind of lag that makes your surrounding appear too slow, you should adjust this setting. This is most commonly set to 128 meters; lowering it to 64 meters is best to reduce lag. ***Remember:*** the lower the number, the faster.

✓ **Display Options:** This section is for mouselook graphic options.

> • *Show Avatar in Mouselook:* Select this option to make your avatar visible in Mouselook mode. You'll be able to look down and see yourself, just as you can in your First Life. Deselecting this option (which is the default setting) makes your avatar invisible to yourself while in Mouselook. Many Residents check this option for added immersion, particularly while holding objects or driving a vehicle.

Graphics Detail tab

Here's a breakdown of your options on the Graphics Detail tab, as shown in Figure 2-7.

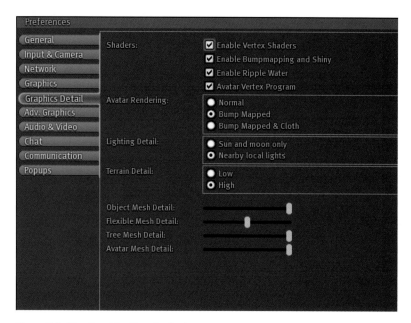

Figure 2-7: The Graphics Detail tab gives you greater power over your graphics settings.

✔ **Shaders:** Shaders rendered effects that offer graphic detail like reflections and shadows making Second Life more immersive. They can slow down your SL experience though.

- *Enable Vertex Shaders:* A vertex shader is a type of shader that increases the shape of polygons.

- *Enable Bumpmapping and Shiny:* This option allows you to see more detail on surface textures and shiny objects. This makes the world a prettier place but is a good option to turn off if you're experiencing local lag.

- *Enable Ripple Water:* Just like it says, this option enables rippling water textures. It's pretty, but it's one of the biggest drains on your computer's resources.

- *Avatar Vertex Program:* When this option is selected, avatars that you see are shaded naturally. If you have a recent graphics card with updated drivers, go ahead and select this check box. If you're running a Mac with OS 1.5.x, you won't be able to enable this option.

The availability of these options is dependant on video card and operating system.

✔ **Avatar Rendering:** These options control how well avatars, including your own are rendered.

- *Normal:* The default setting. Avatars display without additional details.

- *Bump Mapped:* Avatars display with clothing wrinkles.

- *Bump Mapped & Cloth:* Avatars display with clothing wrinkles and hair (not prim hair), and loose clothing will move in the wind. ***Note:*** This setting is really likely to cause Second Life to crash.

✔ **Lighting Detail:** These settings determine the lighting detail in Second Life. Again turning on all these settings may slow down Second Life.

- *Sun and Moon Only:* This is the default selection. The sky and light levels match Second Life day and night settings. Lighted objects won't cause actual light to appear on your screen. This is a good system resource-saving option.

- *Nearby Local Lights:* Lit objects cast light on the surrounding area, including the ground, other objects, and avatars. Lots of places are built with dramatic, beautiful lighting effects that are worth seeing. If you're experiencing lag, though, turn off this option.

✔ **Terrain Detail:** These settings are for setting graphic detail of the geography in Second Life.

- *Low:* Ground textures are blurry.

- *High:* Ground textures are noticeably sharper. This is one of the few higher graphics levels that won't have much effect on your system.

All the following settings have sliders. Play with settings until you have the best performance with an aesthetic that makes you happy.

✔ **Object Mesh Detail:** Sliding this changes how smoothly objects appear. Decreasing this (moving it to the left) makes curves look like a series of angles.

✔ **Flexible Mesh Detail:** Flexible prims can wave in the wind, fall, droop, and so on. When this setting is high (to the right), they will move smoothly. When it's set low (to the left), they'll move more jerky but demand less of your computer.

✔ **Tree Mesh Detail:** Special trees in Second Life — Linden Trees — look more natural and wave in the wind. If this setting is high, these trees are really beautiful. If you're experiencing lag, lower this setting by moving it to the left to spare yourself the lag.

✔ **Avatar Mesh Detail:** Some folks like their bling: shiny earrings, flexible clothes and hair, and so on. It's great for them to look so pretty, but it can drain your computer's resources to display it all.

Adv. Graphics tab

Here's a breakdown of your options on the Adv. (Advanced) Graphics tab, as shown in Figure 2-8.

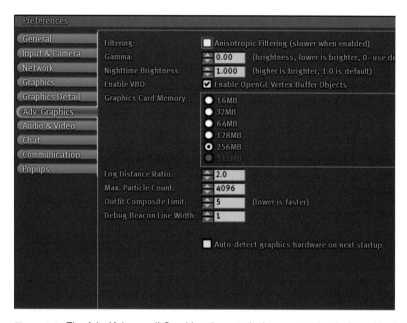

Figure 2-8: The Adv. (Advanced) Graphic tab controls the greatest level of graphical detail.

✓ **Filtering:** Filtering affects how you will see textures on objects.

• *Anisotropic Filtering:* This option allows textures to appear sharper, even when you're seeing them from an angle. This is a super drain on your computer, though.

✓ **Gamma:** Increasing this number makes your monitor brighter. Decreasing it makes your display darker.

✓ **Nighttime Brightness:** Increasing this number makes it easier to see in the dark. Lowering it results in increased contrast for lighted objects because glows stand out more.

✓ **Enable VBO:** Selecting this option improves your performance: It allows your computer hardware to use a faster OpenGL Vertex Buffer Objects mode for your graphics card. This isn't available for all systems.

✓ **Graphics Card Memory:** These options depend on your graphics card. Typically, you should set this as high as possible. Second Life is very texture intensive, and lowering these settings can result in blurry or blinking textures. Your options are 16, 32, 64, 128, 256, and 512 (all in MB).

- **Fog Distance Ratio:** Raising this number increases the cutoff clarity of your current Draw Distance, and it doesn't affect your performance at all. Most folks want to set it to the normal maximum of 4.0.

- **Max. Particle Count:** Fireworks, jewelry, and other objects put off *particle effects* (glows, sparks, shine, and so on). Leave this at 4096 unless you're experiencing lag. If you are experiencing lag, decrease this number.

- **Outfit Composite Limit:** Set this to 0 to not see the changes in those avatars who you can see when they change their appearance. Any other setting won't have much effect on what you see.

- **Debug Beacon Line Width:** This defines the width of beacons. Beacons are visual keys to help you understand what is going on with certain types of objects in SL. There is no reason to change this setting.

- **Auto-Detect Graphics Hardware on the Next Startup:** Check this to have Second Life configure itself for our hardware the next time it starts. Doing this will momentarily slow down the start up process.

Audio & Video tab

Here's a breakdown of your options on the Audio & Video tab, as shown in Figure 2-9.

- **Muting:** This mutes the sounds of Second Life.

  - *Mute Audio:* Select this option to disable all Second Life sound, including music and typing sounds. Each of these sliders gets louder the more you move it to the right.

  - *Master:* The is the master control slider of all the sounds from Second Life.

  - *Music:* This setting controls the volume of music being played in the world of Second Life.

  - *Media:* This setting controls the volume of media being played in Second Life like movies.

  - *Voice:* This setting controls the volume of other residence voice when they are talking to you.

  - *Sounds:* This setting controls the volume of all sounds in Second Life. This slider has no effect on the volume level of streaming music and video on land parcels, which allows you to silence background noises.

  - *Ambient*: This option controls the volume of ambient sounds.

  - *UI:* This option controls the volume of user interface sounds, such as the "ding" you hear when you receive an IM.

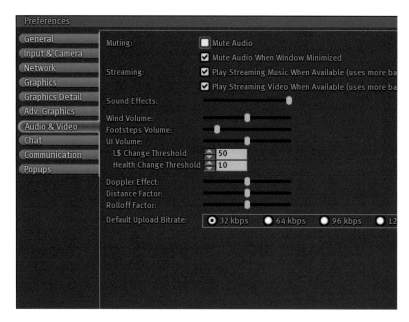

Figure 2-9: Use the Audio & Visual tab to set audio and video settings.

✓ **Streaming:** You can enable streaming media if you want to listen to music and watch movies in-world; disable it if your Internet connection isn't fast enough, or if you'd rather not make connections to a third-party server. Note that selecting either of the following options requires more bandwidth:

- *Play Streaming Music When Available:* Select this option to allow the Second Life client to play music streams.

- *Play Streaming Video When Available:* Select this option to allow the Second Life client to play movie streams.

- *Mute Audio When Window Minimized:* Select this to stop all in-world sound, including music, when the Second Life window is minimized.

✓ **Doppler Effect:** Moving this slider to the right increases Doppler effects, which makes sounds raise in pitch as they move faster toward you and lower in pitch as the object moves away. Sliding this to the left decreases this effect.

✓ **Distance Factor:** Changing this slider changes how close you have to be to an object to hear its sound effects.

✓ **Rolloff Factor:** Slide this to the right to make sounds fade away as you move away from the objects the sound comes from.

- *L$ Change Threshold:* You hear a cash register sound when you spend more than the amount put in this setting.

- *Health Change Threshold:* You can't die in Second Life, but you can play dead in areas that have health enabled. Use this setting to hear a grunt to let you know when you've lost health equal to what you've typed here.

✓ **Default Upload Bitrate:** When you choose File⇨Upload Sound (L$10), you can select the quality it will be encoded in. Your options are 32, 64, 96, and 128 Kbps. 32 Kbps is good for most sounds.

Text Chat tab

Here's a breakdown of your options on the Text Chat tab, as shown in Figure 2-10.

Figure 2-10: The Text Chat tab gives you options for how you communicate with other users.

✓ **Chat Font Size:** This option changes the size of the text that appears in the Chat Console (your area text chat, or "out loud" chat). It doesn't change how text appears in any window, including your Chat History. Your options are Small, Medium, and Large.

✓ **Chat Color:** Use these settings to change the colors of text in your Chat Console and Chat History:

- *System:* This option make server messages appear, such as inventory messages and online friend notifications.

- *Users:* This option changes the color of your chat and the chat of those around you.

- *Objects:* This option changes the color of messages that come from objects.

- *Owner:* This option changes the color of messages that come from owners of objects.

- *Bubble:* This option changes the color of messages in chat bubbles.

- *URLs:* This option changes the color of messages contain Web addresses.

✔ **Chat Console:** These options define how the chat console is displayed.

- *Fade Chat:* This option fades the chat console after a set number of seconds or lines.

- *Opacity:* This option defines how opaque the chat console appears. The greater the value the more opaque the chat console.

✔ **Chat Options:** These options are general chat options.

- *Chat uses full screen width:* This options makes the chat go the width of the screen if it needs to.

- *Close chat after hitting return:* This option closes the chat window after you press return.

- *Arrow keys always move the avatar while chatting:* This option allows you to move your avatar with the arrow keys.

- *Show timestamps in chat:* This option shows the time chat messages were received.

✔ **Bubble Chat:** These options are for bubble chat bubbles. Chat bubbles show the chat messages above people as they say them as if they were in a comic book.

- *Show Chat bubbles:* This option displays chat bubbles above people's heads as they talk.

- *Opacity:* This slider effects the opacity of chat bubbles. The farther to the left the more opaque the chat bubbles.

✔ **Script Errors:** These options are for errors that are produced by your scripts.

- *Show Script Errors:* This option is for displaying script errors in your chat console.

- *Color:* This selection is the color of script errors in your chat console.

Voice Chat tab

Here's a breakdown of your options on the Voice Chat tab, as shown in Figure 2-11. Voice chat allows you to use the Voice feature of Second Life like a digital telephone. You can speak to a group of people or privately with one person.

Figure 2-11: The new Voice Chat options.

- ✔ **Enable Voice Chat:** This option turns voice chat on or off.

- ✔ **Hear Voice Chat from Camera Position:** This option allows you to hear public chat from where your camera is positioned.

- ✔ **Hear Voice Chat from Avatar Position:** This option allows you to hear public chat from where your avatar is positioned.

- ✔ **Push to Talk:** Push to talk mode allows you to control when your voice is heard and when it is not picked up by your microphone. The mode is determined by pressing a trigger.

  - *Start Viewer in Push to Talk Mode:* This option starts Second Life in the Push-to-Talk mode.

  - *Use Push-to-Talk in Toggle Mode:* This option puts Push-to-Talk on in toggle mode. Toggle mode allows you to turn the microphone on and off with the trigger. When not in toggle mode, you have to hold down the trigger to talk.

- *Push-to-Talk Trigger:* This option sets the trigger for Push-to-Talk mode. Press the Set Key button to set a key or MiddleMouse button to return it to the middle mouse button, which is the default.

✔ **Privacy Options:** The privacy option allows you to only be able to accept voice calls from people on your friends list.

✔ **Device Settings:** This opens the device setting window that allows you to assign the input and output devices. There is also an input level meter to make sure you are speaking at the correct level.

✔ **Run Voice Setup Wizard:** This wizard steps you through setting up your voice system to work with Second Life. Read the documentation on the screen as you move through the wizard.

Communication tab

Here's a breakdown of your options on the Communications tab, as shown in Figure 2-12.

✔ **Profile Online Status:** This option allows you to make your status visible to anyone who is your friend from the Second Life Web site. They would have to log in but if checked your status would be displayed privately to them.

✔ **IM Options:** These options are settings for your personal IM messages between you and others in Second Life.

- *Send IM to Email:* This option allows you to have IM messages sent to you while you are offline forwarded to your e-mail.

- *Include IM in Chat History:* This option includes your IM's in your chat history logs.

- *Show timestamps in IM*: This option shows timestamps in IM messages.

✔ **Busy Mode Response:** These text field contains the message sent to people who message you when you are busy mode. There is a default text that works well. Try not to leave this blank.

✔ **Logging Options:** These options are for your logging functions in Second Life.

- *Log Instant Messages:* This option allows you to log instant messages.

- *Show Timestamp in IM Log:* This option includes a timestamp for each entry in the IM log.

- *Show End of Last IM Conversation:* This option is only available if you are logging chat. The option allows you to show the end of the last IM conversation in the Chat log.

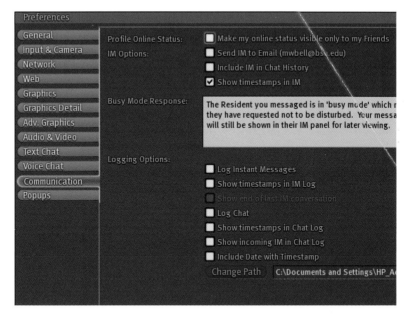

Figure 2-12: The Communications tab covers IM, busy, and logging options.

- *Log Chat*: This option allows you to log chat to the path listed beside the Change Path button.

- *Show Timestamps in Chat Log:* This option allows you to show time-stamps for each entry in the chat log.

- *Show Incoming IM in Chat Log:* This option allows you to show incoming IM messages in your chat log.

- *Include Date with Timestamp:* This option includes the current date on each timestamp in the chat log.

- *Change Path:* This option allows you to change the path where your chat log files are stored.

Popups tab

Here's a breakdown of your options on the Popups tab, as shown in Figure 2-13. A popup is any message window that shows up to let you know some-thing has happened in Second Life.

✔ **Do Not Show Popups:** This window lists popups that won't be shown.

✔ **Show Popups:** This window lists popups that will be shown.

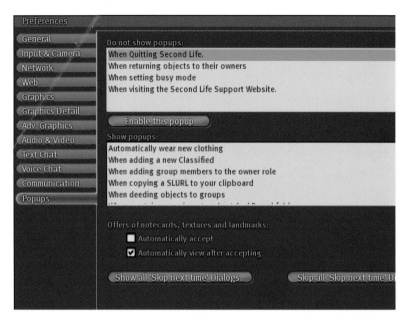

Figure 2-13: The Popups tab.

✔ **Offers:** These options are for Notecards, textures, and landmarks given to you by other people.

- *Automatically accept:* This option automatically accepts those objects. I would not turn this on because you never know what someone will send you.

- *Automatically view after accepting:* This option automatically views those types of objects when you have accepted them. This is on by default.

✔ **Show All "Skip Next Time" Dialogs:** This shows all skip next time dialogs in the popup list.

✔ **Skip All "Skip Next Time" Dialogs:** This skips all skip next time dialogs in the popup list.

Starting Your Second Life

In This Chapter

▶ Setting up your account

▶ Completing Orientation Island

▶ Going to Help Island

*Y*ou made up your mind to jump into the exciting world of Second Life (SL). You're sitting at your computer, raring to go, but where to start? In this chapter, we walk you through how to get started, from creating an account to logging in and making it through the orientation tutorials. Get ready! Get set! Go!

Creating Your Account

When starting out in Second Life you'll need to decide what kind of account you want to create. Most people will be fine with a basic free account but you should know your options before you decide. Here's what you need to know about your choices:

- ✔ **First Basic:** If this is your first Second Life account (if you already have an account and you've decided to have a second one you can't use this account type) and you don't intend to buy land right away you should be fine choosing a First Basic account. This is a free account.

- ✔ **Additional Basic:** If you already have an account but you want a second avatar you should choose this type of account. You'll be charged for this second account ($9.99 at the time of this writing). This is a one time charge. Basic accounts (whether first or additional) are not landholding accounts and will have to be upgraded to Premium if you choose to buy land later.

- ✔ **Premium:** If you know you'll be purchasing land right away you might want to select a Premium account. You'll be charged a monthly fee based on how much land you choose to own.

Now that you have the low-down on the account types, are you ready to get started in SL? For this book, we show you how to create a First Basic account. Here's how:

1. **Go to `www.secondlife.com` and click the orange Sign Up Now button, as shown in Figure 3-1. This will take you to the account creation page.**

   You can find lots of useful links on the Second Life home page, but this big orange button is all you need to worry about right now.

Click this button to get started.

Figure 3-1: The Second Life home page.

2. **Choose your avatar name.**

   a. *Choose a last name from the drop-down list and then type in a first name.*

   b. *Click the Check this Name for Availability link to see whether the name you chose is available.*

   You might need a few tries to find a name that no one has picked yet.

Choose a name that's easy to spell. It might be fun to spell your name funny — like K8y for Katie — but if others can't spell it, they probably won't be able to find you and become friends. If you're a woman and worried about being hit on, you might want to choose a gender-neutral name.

3. **Fill in the rest of the information (as in Figure 3-2), including a valid e-mail address and click Continue.**

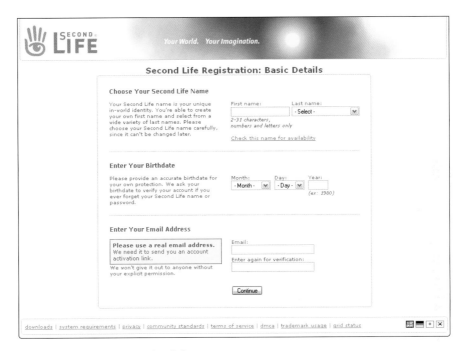

Figure 3-2: Enter your basic details here.

4. **Select your beginning avatar, as shown in Figure 3-3.**

   As soon as you log in the first time, you can make changes, so just pick any avatar you like. Choosing male or female doesn't even matter because you can change gender any time you like. For more on customizing your avatar, see Chapter 5. Click Choose this Avatar to move on to the next screen.

5. **Fill out your Real Life (RL) information, as shown in Figure 3-4.**

   Be sure to jot down your password so you don't forget it. To create a more secure password, use a mix of numbers and letters.

Figure 3-3: Choose your beginning avatar from some basic models.

6. **Choose the free First Basic account type.**

   You can always change this later. For most, the free First Basic account will work fine.

   (Optional) You need a Premium account only if you plan to own land right away. Otherwise, you can upgrade later to Premium. If you do select Premium, you need to enter your payment preference, as shown in Figure 3-5.

   A welcome screen pops up, showing you what e-mail address was used to send an account confirmation.

7. **When you receive the confirmation e-mail, click the link to confirm your account.**

   Another browser window opens. It's time to download the software.

8. **Click the orange DOWNLOAD button next to the platform you use, as shown in Figure 3-6.**

   Second Life is available for Windows, Mac, and Linux.

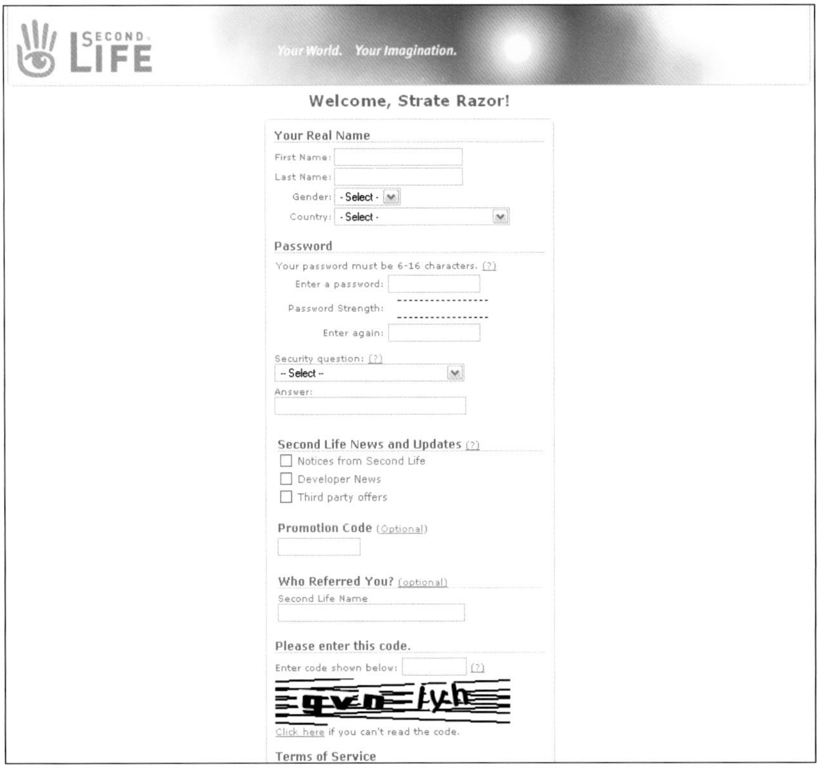

Figure 3-4: Enter your personal information.

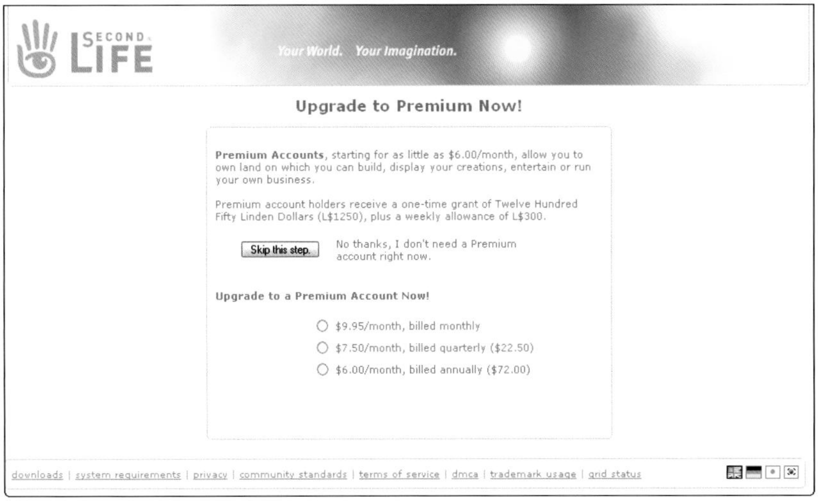

Figure 3-5: Select your payment preference if you pick a Premium account.

Figure 3-6: Download the Second Life software.

You can also refer your friends to SL from this screen by clicking the Take Me to the Referral Form link.

A pop-up appears onscreen asking where you want to save the Second Life application. The default will choose your program folder on your main hard drive. This is a good place but you can change the save location if you'd rather have the software installed in a different folder.

9. **Choose your download location; double-click the program to install it.**

10. **Click the Save File button to begin the download. When the download is finished you will be prompted to install the software. Click yes and the software will begin to install. When installation is finished you'll be asked if you want to start the program, click Yes and you're on your way.**

If you use a Mac, the steps for downloading the software are basically the same except you need to drag the program icon into your Applications folder to install the software.

Getting through Orientation Island

After you create your account, download the software, and access SL for the first time, you see the log-in screen, as shown in Figure 3-7.

Figure 3-7: Log in to your Second Life.

To log in to SL, follow these steps:

1. **Type your avatar's first and last name and your password into the fields on the bottom-left of the screen and then click Connect.**

   The top right of the log-in screen provides useful information about the status of the SL world. Be sure to check it out.

   If you select the Remember Password check box, you won't have to type your password in the next time you log in. *Don't use this option if you share a computer or log in on a public computer.*

2. **The first time you log in, you'll be asked to agree to the Second Life Terms of Service (TOS), as shown in Figure 3-8.**

   Be sure to read it thoroughly because agreeing to it acts as a legally binding agreement for your behavior in SL. Scroll down through the TOS and read it over, select the I Agree to the Terms of Service radio button, and then click the blue Continue button at the bottom right.

   You're asked to read over a statement of Community Standards. These are important guidelines about behavior in SL.

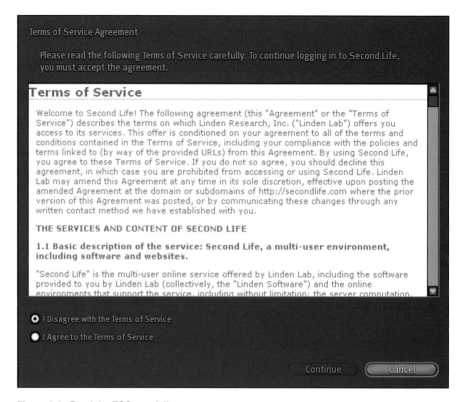

Figure 3-8: Read the TOS carefully.

3. **Read the rules (shown in Figure 3-9), select the I Agree radio button, and then click the blue Continue button.**

Be sure to read these Community Standards. You might not plan to break any rules, but if you know what the rules are, you'll know whether others are breaking them and should be reported.

After agreeing to the TOS and Community Standards, you will be logged in to the Second Life world and find yourself on Orientation Island in the central plaza, ready to start your Second Life. Orientation Island is a really helpful place. This is where you'll discover all the basics of getting around in SL. Some folks have a little trouble finishing the Orientation Island tutorial, so keep reading as we walk you through it, step by step.

The four required tutorials for all SL residents are

- Your First Steps
- Your Inventory
- Chat
- Open the Map

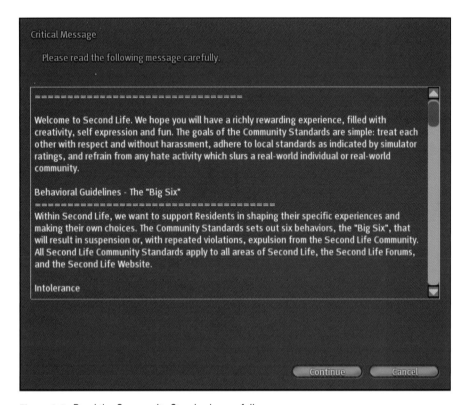

Figure 3-9: Read the Community Standards carefully.

We walk you through only the four required tutorials located in the central plaza of Orientation Island (where you first appear on the island). You can pick up other optional skills on Orientation Island by crossing the bridges leading away from the central plaza.

As soon as your avatar appears in the Second Life world, you're asked what language you speak, as shown in Figure 3-10. Time to start!

1. **Click the button that corresponds to your language of choice. To continue, click the flashing arrow that appears.**

   As you make your way through Orientation Island, you can use the graphic shown in Figure 3-11 to track your progress in the tutorial.

2. **Your first task is to learn to walk.**

   a. *Use your arrow keys to rotate your camera until you see the Move sign.*

   b. *Use your forward arrow to walk to the red flashing dot below the sign, as shown in Figure 3-12.*

Select your language here.

Figure 3-10: Choose your language.

Track your progress here.

Figure 3-11: This graphic shows your progress in the tutorial.

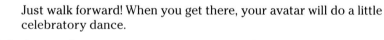

Figure 3-12: Can you hit the bull's-eye?

Just walk forward! When you get there, your avatar will do a little celebratory dance.

To find more about moving your avatar, cross the bridge by the Move sign or flip to Chapter 4.

3. **Your second task is using your Inventory.**

   a. *Turn and walk into the orange circle in front of the Appearance sign.*

      You need to access your Inventory, find a torch stored there, and put it on.

   b. *Click the Inventory button at the bottom-right of your screen.*

   c. *Click the little arrow next to the Library folder in your Inventory, and then click the Objects folder.*

   d. *Scroll down until you find the Torch listing in your Inventory, as shown in Figure 3-13.*

   e. *Click and hold the Torch in your Inventory; then drag it onto your avatar, as shown in Figure 3-14.*

If your avatar is hidden behind your Inventory window, just click and drag the Inventory window to move it to the side.

After you succeed in wearing the torch, you'll see it in your hand, and your avatar will do a little dance.

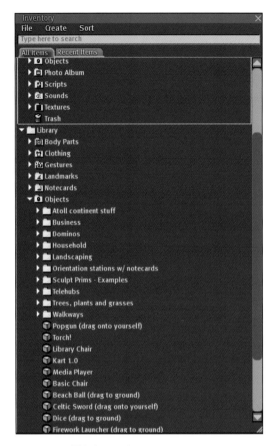

Figure 3-13: This is your Inventory.

TIP

If you want to learn more about editing your appearance, you can cross the bridge by the Appearance sign to get to the castle where there are other tutorials, or you can flip to Chapter 5. You can also read more about managing your inventory by flipping to Chapter 9.

f. *To take off the torch, right-click it and then choose Detach from the radial menu that opens.*

The progress menu shows that you completed two of four tasks. Just two more to go!

4. **Use your arrow keys to walk your avatar over to the purple circle in front of the Communication sign, where you complete your third task, learning to chat.**

a. *Click the Chat button on the bottom-left of your screen.*

b. *When you see the little Chat window open at the bottom of your screen, click the flashing arrow on the tutorial window.*

Figure 3-14: Now you have light to guide your way.

Your Chat window might already be open. If it is, clicking the Chat button will close it. Just click it again to open it up.

c. *Type anything you want in the Chat box and then click the Say or Shout button (or just press Enter). You'll see your chat appear at the bottom of the screen to show that you've said something that others could hear.*

You completed the Chat part of the tutorial.

To find out more about communication, you can cross the bridge by the Communication sign or flip to Chapter 6.

5. **Walk over to the blue circle by the Search sign to finish the tutorials, learning about search.**

a. *Click the Map button on the bottom-right of your screen to open you map.*

b. *Click the flashing arrow to go on to the next step.*

The map often takes a few minutes to resolve. Don't be alarmed if at first, you see only a big blue box where the map ought to be.

c. *When the map resolves, click the flashing arrow.*

You see a gold circle symbolizing your location on the map.

d. *Click the button that corresponds with that symbol to finish the tutorial.*

You can see the symbol legend anytime at the top-right of the Map window, as shown in Figure 3-15.

The map symbol legend.

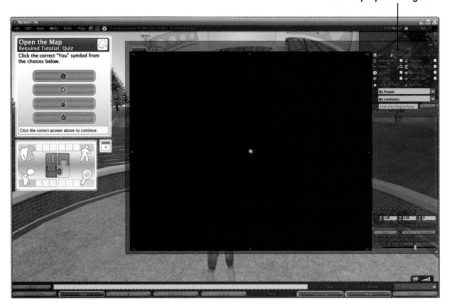

Figure 3-15: The map symbol legend.

> e. (Optional) Cross the bridge by the Map sign to learn more about search, or flip to Chapter 4.

If you want to retry any of the tutorials, just look for the sign shown in Figure 3-16 while standing in the colored circle for each tutorial.

After you finished all four required tutorials, you'd probably expect Second Life to tell you where to begin exploring the world — but it doesn't quite work that way. You're also probably wondering how to make the Tutorial menu go away. Have no fear. We'll show you what to do next!

To make the Tutorial menu go away, you can use one of two methods.

✓ **From the Tutorial**

1. Right-click the Tutorial itself (or ⌘-click on a Mac).

2. Choose Detach from the radial menu.

✓ **From your Inventory**

Figure 3-16: You can try the tutorial again.

1. Open your Inventory and type **worn** into the Search box at the top.

2. In the result list, right-click Orientation Guide and then choose Detach from Yourself.

After the Tutorial menu is no longer on the screen, you need to decide where to go. Need help? Check out the next section for our recommendation on your first post-Orientation Island stop.

Making Your Way to Help Island

After you complete Orientation Island, where should you go now? Your best bet is Help Island, which it is a great place for beginners to visit. To go to Help Island, follow these steps:

1. **To go to Help Island from the central Orientation Island plaza, click the billboard for Help Island (see Figure 3-17)**

2. **When the pop-up window appears, click the Teleport button shown in Figure 3-18.**

   Voilá! You're at Help Island.

Second Life asks you whether you want to keep the landmark for Help Island. Landmarks are handy for finding your way back to locations in Second Life but this one won't be of much help because once you leave Help Island you can't return. For more on landmarks, see Chapter 4.

Figure 3-17: Your ticket to Help Island!

Figure 3-18: Click the Teleport button, and you're on your way to Help Island.

Exploring Help Island

After you're on Help Island, why not help yourself to some freebies? Check your Mini-Map at the top-right of your screen and head southeast, following the Help Island Freebie Store signs. Take a look around the store to see whether there's anything you like. The store offers clothes, animations (to make you groove!), furniture, cars, and other fun items. If you can't read what a sign says, just wait a minute while the texture resolves.

Grab some basics. In this example, we grab a copy of Sparkly Dress with Shoes (shown in Figure 3-19), but you can grab anything you'd like. Here's how to grab an item.

1. **Right-click the sign and choose Touch from the radial menu.**

   You see a blue pop-up that asks whether you'd like to keep the folder. If you'd like to keep the folder, it will be put in your Inventory.

Figure 3-19: You can pick from a variety of freebies.

   2. To keep the folder, click the Keep button.

Here's how to make sure you got your freebie:

   1. **Open your Inventory by clicking the Inventory button at the bottom of the screen.**

   2. **Click the Recent Items tab at the top to see a folder named after the freebie you just grabbed.**

      For this example, find the Gwen's Sparkly Dress folder.

   3. **To wear what's in it, drag the folder onto your avatar, as shown in Figure 3-20.**

For more information about customizing your avatar with items you pick up along the way, flip to Chapter 5.

You'll notice some free textures in the Freebie Store as well. These can be used in buildings and to make clothes. Grab any that you might like. We'll show you how to use them later in the book.

Explore the rest of Help Island to your heart's content. When you're ready to leave and head out, here's the drill.

After you leave Help Island, you can't come back, so be sure that you've explored as much as you want before leaving.

Figure 3-20: Wearing a new, free dress.

1. **Look for a big green Exit sign, as shown in Figure 3-21.**

   When you click the sign, you'll be asked to keep a notecard (a little text document that will appear like a pop up on your screen but can be stored in your inventory so you can read it again later), which will open automatically. At the bottom is a link to a place called Hanja, a central welcome location where all newbies land when they leave Help Island.

2. **Click the link and then click the Teleport button, as shown in Figure 3-22.**

   You arrive in the Welcome Area. This is where it all begins. You're free to fly away, search for places that interest you, socialize with others in the Welcome Area, or start shopping. The whole Second Life world is at your fingertips! Have fun!

If at any time you get stuck, confused, or otherwise kerfluffled, don't be afraid to ask folks around you for help. People in Second Life tend to be very friendly.

Figure 3-21: Click this sign to escape Help Island.

Click this link.

Figure 3-22: Click the link at the bottom of the notecard to teleport away from Help Island.

Navigating the Second Life Interface and World

*T*he world of Second Life is big. No, we mean really big! Over 16,000 square acres of land are added every month. That's a whole lot of parties, clubs, shopping, and fun to be found. So how do you know where the fun is let alone how you get there after you find it? Sit back, relax, and let the world come to you. We'll show you how.

In this chapter, we help you learn how to get around so you can enjoy all that Second Life has to offer. We include the basics of moving your avatar (walking, flying, driving, and so on), as well as how to travel longer distances by teleporting. In addition to navigating in the world, we show you how to navigate the interface so you know which menus can help you do what.

Exploring the Basic Menus

Second Life offers lots of menus with lots of different ways to access them. The best way to master the tools in Second Life is to learn them as you need them. We start here with a few menus that you'll want to know right away. Because SL has so many menus, we can't cover them all in this chapter. Be sure to use the book's index to find others or refer to the Cheat Sheet (at the beginning of the book) to quickly reference other menus.

Menus for Second Life are found in two places: at the top left of your screen as well as across the bottom (look for the buttons), as shown in Figure 4-1. Time to start exploring!

Menus locations

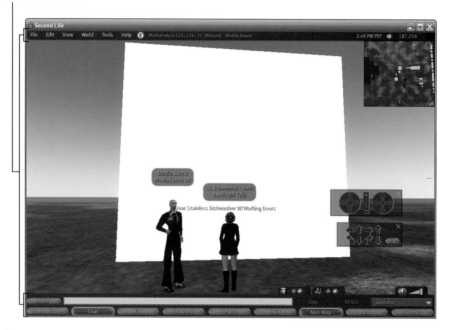

Figure 4-1: Menus can be found at the top left of the screen and through the buttons along the bottom of your screen.

The File menu

The File Menu is used to manage your files. This menu allows you to upload files, work with snap shots, or manage your windows.

- **Upload Image:** Use this command to upload an image file.
- **Upload Sound:** Use this command to upload a sound file.
- **Upload Animation:** Use this command to upload an animation created in a third-party software.
- **Bulk Upload:** Use this command to upload multiple files at once.
- **Close Window:** Use this command to close the currently selected window like Search.
- **Close All Windows:** Use this command to close all open windows.
- **Save Texture As:** Use this command to save an open selected texture to your hard disk.
- **Take Snapshot:** Use this command to take a snapshot in Second Life that you can save, send as a postcard, or upload.

- ✔ **Shapshot to Disk:** Use this command to take a snapshot and save it to a location on your hard disk.

- ✔ **Star/Stop Movie to Disk:** Use this command to start or stop recording a movie to disk.

- ✔ **Set Window Size:** Use this command to set your window size based on what is available form your video card.

- ✔ **Quit:** Use this command to quit Second Life and log out.

The Edit menu

This menu allows you to control editing of files, search, attach and detach objects and clothes, and access your profile and appearance editor.

- ✔ **Undo:** Use this command to undo the last command. This may or may not work depending on the situation.

- ✔ **Redo:** Use this command to redo the last command. This may or may not work depending on the situation.

- ✔ **Cut:** Use this command to copy an object or text to the clipboard and then delete it. This may or may not work depending on the situation.

- ✔ **Copy:** Use this command to copy an object or text to the clipboard. This may or may not work depending on the situation.

- ✔ **Paste:** Use this command to paste a copied object or text from the clipboard. This may or may not work depending on the situation.

- ✔ **Search:** Use this command to open the search window.

- ✔ **Select All:** Use this command to select all objects or text.

- ✔ **Deselect:** Use this command to deselect any object or text.

- ✔ **Duplicate:** Use this command to duplicate any selected object or text.

- ✔ **Attach Object:** Use this command to attach a selected object to a particular body part.

- ✔ **Detach Object:** Use this command to detach a selected object to a particular body part.

- ✔ **Take Off Clothing:** Use this command to take off a particular piece or all your clothes.

- ✔ **Gesture:** Use this command to open the gestures window.

- ✔ **Profile:** Use this command to open your profile window.

- ✔ **Appearance:** Use this command to open the appearance editor.

- ✔ **Friends:** Use this command to open your friends list.

- ✔ **Groups:** Use this command to open your groups list.

- ✔ **Preferences:** Use this command to open the preferences window.

The View menu

This menu covers how and what you see in the world of Second Life. If you want to change how things look or find tools to help, I would start here.

- ✓ **Mouselook:** Use this command to enter the mouselook view.

- ✓ **Build:** Use this command to open the build tool.

- ✓ **Reset View:** Use this command to reset your view to the default view that you start Second Life with.

- ✓ **Look at Last Chatter:** Use this command to turn your avatar in the direction of the last chatter.

- ✓ **Toolbar:** Use this command to display the toolbar at the bottom of the screen.

- ✓ **Chat History:** Use this command to open the Chat History window.

- ✓ **Instant Messages:** Use this command to open the Chat Messages window.

- ✓ **Inventory:** Use this command to open your Inventory window.

- ✓ **Active Speakers:** Use this command to open the Active Speakers window.

- ✓ **Mute List:** Use this command to open the Mute List window.

- ✓ **Camera Controls:** Use this command to open the camera controls window.

- ✓ **Movement Controls:** Use this command to open the Movement Control window.

- ✓ **World Map:** Use this command to open the World Map window.

- ✓ **Mini-Map:** Use this command to open the Mini Map window.

- ✓ **Statistics Bar:** Use this command to open the Statistics Bar.

- ✓ **Property Lines:** Use this command to display property lines.

- ✓ **Land Owners:** Use this command to display land owners on land you can see.

- ✓ **Hover Tips:** Use this command to display hover tips to help you in Second Life.

- ✓ **Beacons Always On:** Use this command to always display beacons.

- ✓ **Highlight Transparent:** Use this command to make the highlights transparent to the user.

- ✓ **Beacons:** Use this command to display certain types of beacons.

- ✓ **Show HUD Attachments:** Use this command to display Heads Up Display (HUD) attachments.

✓ **Zoom In:** Use this command to zoom your camera view in.

✓ **Zoom Default:** Use this command to return to the default zoom level.

✓ **Zoom Out:** Use this command to zoom your camera view out.

✓ **Toggle Fullscreen:** Use this command to toggle to fullscreen mode.

✓ **Set UI Size to Default:** Use this command to return the UI to the default view size.

The World menu

This menu involves activates and actions in Second Life.

✓ **Chat:** Use this command to open the Chat window.

✓ **Start Gesture:** Use this command to open the Gestures window.

✓ **Always Run:** Use this command to always run and never walk while traveling on the ground.

✓ **Fly:** Use this command to begin to fly.

✓ **Create Landmark Here:** Use this command to create a landmark at your current location.

✓ **Set Home to Here:** Use this command to set your current location to Home.

✓ **Teleport Home:** Use this command to teleport to your home location.

✓ **Set Away:** Use this command to set your avatar's status to Away.

✓ **Set Busy:** Use this command to set your avatar's status to Busy.

✓ **Account History:** Use this command to open your account history on the Second Life Web site.

✓ **Manage My Account:** Use this command to open the about management page on the Second Life Web site.

✓ **Buy L$:** Use this command to buy Linden dollars.

✓ **My Land:** Use this command to open the My Land window, which displays all your current land holdings.

✓ **About Land:** Use this command to open the land window for the land you are currently on.

✓ **Buy Land:** Use this command to open the Buy Land window.

✓ **Region/Estate:** Use this command to open the Regions Estate Control window.

✓ **Force Sun:** Use this command to force the sun to a certain location. This includes noon, dusk, dawn, and midnight.

The Tools menu

This menu allows you to access tools to do things like building in Second Life.

- ✔ **Select Tool:** Use this command to select a building tool.
- ✔ **Select Only My Objects:** Use this command to just select yours when you have multiple objects selected.
- ✔ **Select Only Movable Objects:** Use this command to select objects that can be moved when multiple objects are selected.
- ✔ **Select By Surrounding:** Use this command to select multiple objects by surrounding.
- ✔ **Show Hidden Selection:** Use this command to show hidden objects when selecting multiple objects.
- ✔ **Show Light Radius for Selection:** Use this command to show the light radius (as a cone) of lighted objects.
- ✔ **Show Selection Beam:** Use this command to show a dotted line from your avatar's hand to an object when building.
- ✔ **Snap To Grid:** Use this command to snap your objects to a grid when you edit them.
- ✔ **Snap Object to XY to Grid:** Use this command to snap a moving object to an XY grid.
- ✔ **Use Selection for Grid:** Use this command to use the current selection to define the grid to snap to.
- ✔ **Grid Options:** Use this command to open the Grid Options window.
- ✔ **Edit Linked Parts:** Use this command to selectively edit linked parts of an object without unlinking them.
- ✔ **Link:** Use this command to link the selected objects together.
- ✔ **Unlink:** Use this command to unlink the objects in a multi-object linked object.
- ✔ **Stop All Animations:** Use this command to stop all animations being performed by your avatar.
- ✔ **Focus on Selection:** Use this command to focus your view on your current selection.
- ✔ **Zoom to Selection:** Use this command to zoom in on your current selection.
- ✔ **Take:** Use this command to take the currently selected object and store it in your inventory.
- ✔ **Take Copy:** Use this command to take a copy of the currently selected object.

  ✔ **Save Object Back to My Inventory:** Use this command to save the currently selected object back to your own inventory.

  ✔ **Save Object Back to Object Contents:** Use this command to save the selected object back to the objet that originally contained it.

  ✔ **Show Script Warning/Error Window:** Use this command to show the Script Warning/Error window.

  ✔ **Recompile Scripts in Selection:** Use this command to recompile the scripts in an object to restart them.

  ✔ **Reset Scripts in Selection:** Use this command to reset the scripts in an object to their original settings.

  ✔ **Set Scripts to Running in Selection:** Use this command to set all the scripts in a selected object to the running state.

  ✔ **Set Scripts to Not Running in Selection:** Use this command to stop all scripts in a selected object.

  ✔ **Bug Reporting:** Use this command to report a bug in Second Life.

The Help menu

When you need some help in Second Life this menu points you in the right direction to get what you need.

  ✔ **Second Life Help:** Use this command to visit the Second Life Support Web site.

  ✔ **In-World Help:** Use this command to open the in-world Help menu.

  ✔ **Additional Help:** Use this command to open the additional Help window.

  ✔ **Official Linden Blog:** Use this command to open the official Linden Lab blog Web page.

  ✔ **Scripting Guide:** Use this command to open the scripting guide Web page.

  ✔ **Scripting Portal:** Use this command to open the LSL portal Web site.

  ✔ **Message of the Day:** Use this command to display the message of the day

  ✔ **Report Abuse:** Use this command to open the Report Abuse window when someone is causing you problems.

  ✔ **Bumps, Pushes & Hits:** Use this command to open the Bumps, Pushes and Hits window to see who has bumped or hit you.

  ✔ **Release Notes:** Use this command to open the release notes of the current version of the Second Life viewer you are running.

  ✔ **About Second Life:** Use this command to open the About Second Life window.

Controlling the sun

When you log in to SL for the first time, it might be nighttime in the SL world. The Sun in SL goes through a 4-hour cycle. And although the stars in the sky might indeed be pretty, you probably want to be able to see your way around. In SL, *you* control your very own sun.

To set the sun to your liking, follow these steps:

1. **Choose World⇨Force Sun.**

   The Force Sun window opens.

2. **Select the sun setting you'd like:**

   - *Sunrise:* This setting shows the sun rising.
   - *Noon:* This setting puts the sun at the highest point in the sky. Noon is the brightest.
   - *Sunset:* This puts the sun setting on the horizon.
   - *Midnight:* This is total darkness.
   - *Revert to Region Default:* This reverts to the regions default sun location.

3. **Once you make a selection the change goes into effect immediately.**

Changing the position of the sun affects only your screen. For example, if you're in a dark place and you set your sun to Noon, your screen becomes bright and sunny, but those around you still see things as they were before you changed them. It's like having your own personal sun!

 You can also set your sun to noon by pressing Crtl+Shift+Y. Although the Noon setting makes your surroundings easiest to see, experiment with other Force Sun settings to enjoy more dramatic views in specially designed places. Some locations are made to be best enjoyed in the dark, such as Midian City and some vampire regions.

Controlling your views

The SL default view is a three-quarter view above and behind your avatar. This is the best position to see where you're going. Some times, however, you'll probably want to zoom in, see around a corner, or even see how you look from the front. Using Camera Controls allows you to change from the default view to see whatever you'd like.

To open Camera Controls, choose View⇨Camera Controls. The Camera Controls appear, as shown in Figure 4-2.

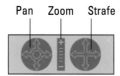

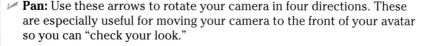

Figure 4-2: The SL Camera Controls.

The three basic areas of the Camera Controls are

- **Pan:** Use these arrows to rotate your camera in four directions. These are especially useful for moving your camera to the front of your avatar so you can "check your look."

  Want to see around a wall or a locked door? Satisfy your voyeuristic desires by clicking on the arrows of your Camera Controls to peer around into hidden spaces.

- **Zoom:** Use the plus and minus button in this middle section to zoom your camera in and out, respectively.

  If you have a scroll wheel on your mouse, you can use it to zoom in and out, too.

- **Strafe:** Use these arrows to slide your camera in four directions without rotating it. This movement is useful for seeing things above you on walls and upper and lower floors in buildings.

Your camera will move back to the default position as soon as you move your avatar.

Here are the keyboard shortcuts for each of these camera controls:

- **Pan:** To pan around an object, hold down the Alt key and click an object or avatar; then use the left and right arrows to pan around.
- **Zoom:** Use the Page Up and Page Down buttons on your keyboard to zoom in and out.
- **Strafe:** Hold down Ctrl+Alt+Shift and click an object or avatar; then use the arrow keys to strafe left, right, up, or down.

If you lose your Camera Controls behind Instant Messages, click and hold on the corner of the Camera Controls and drag them to the right side of your screen where they will be easier to find.

Getting Around in Second Life

In Second Life, you can get around by walking, running, flying, teleporting, or even driving a vehicle. Doing these things gracefully, though, isn't always easy. And who wants to look like a newbie by crashing into walls all the time? Here's the lowdown on getting around SL like a pro.

Using your keyboard

Perhaps the easiest way to control your avatar's movement is by simply using the direction keys on your keyboard. Pressing the up-arrow key (↑) and the down-arrow (↓) moves you forward and back, respectively. Pressing the left-arrow key (←) and the right-arrow key (→) *strafes* (slides) you in either direction. You can also press W (move forward), A (move backward), S (strafe left), and D (strafe right) buttons on your keyboard to do the same. Pressing F when you're not in chat mode (the chat box is not displayed at the bottom of your screen) makes you fly. Pressing F again halts flying. Pressing Ctrl+R toggles running instead of walking.

To see how to teleport (move instantly between two locations), read the "Creating and Using Landmarks" section later in this chapter.

Using Movement Controls

Movement Controls look very similar to Camera Controls. Instead of moving your camera, though, these controls move your avatar.

To open your Movement Controls, choose View⇨Movement Controls. The Movement Controls appear, as shown in Figure 4-3.

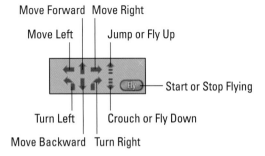

Figure 4-3: These controls help you get around in Second Life.

You can use Movement Controls to move forward or backward, move left or right, turn left or right, jump, crouch, or fly by simply clicking the appropriate action.

Douglas Adams once said that flying is like falling except you forget to hit the ground. Well, what goes up must come down, even in SL, and landing is the toughest part. Use Fly Down on the Movement Controls to come to a controlled landing instead of crashing down like a newbie.

Controlling vehicles, such as motorcycles and cars, is the same as walking or running. You just do it with a vehicle wrapped around you. Use the same controls as you would to move without the vehicle.

The Second Life World

One of the best things about Second Life is that it constantly changes. New islands, clubs, and stores are added everyday. But how do you find them? With the handy dandy World Map, of course! After you know where you'd like to go, you can teleport there — but first you must know how to find these great spots to visit.

To open the World Map, click the Map button at the bottom right of your screen.

There's a lot happening on the World Map, as shown in Figure 4-4. We'll take it one area at a time.

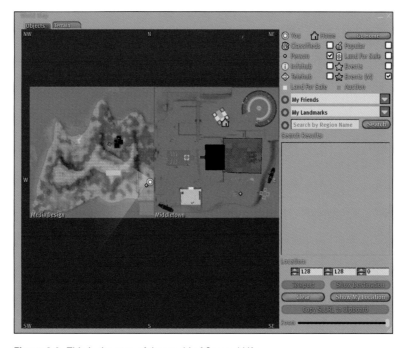

Figure 4-4: This is the map of the world of Second Life.

✐ **The map:** The map might take a while to appear onscreen. You should see lots of islands and a couple of larger continents. You can move around the map by clicking and dragging. You can either view the terrain of the land or the objects on that terrain based on the tab you select at the top.

✐ **Filters:** At the top right of the World Map screen, you're presented with lots of filters to control what you want displayed on the map. Selecting/clearing each option toggles these options on and off your map display.

✐ **My Friends:** If you've made friends and they give you permission to see their locations, click the arrow to the right of the My Friends field to display a drop-down list of your friends. Clicking a name displays where this friend, who has allowed you to see them, is on the map. You can then teleport to that location by clicking the Teleport button at the bottom right of the map screen. For more information on making friends, see Chapter 6.

✐ **My Landmarks:** If you set landmarks to your favorite places, you can click the arrow to the right of this field to display them on a drop-down list. Click the one you want to visit and then click the Teleport button at the bottom right of your map screen. For more on setting landmarks, see the next section in this chapter.

✐ **Search by Region Name:** If you know the name of the region you'd like to visit, type it in this box and then click the Search button to the right. If you find the spot you're looking for, you can teleport there right away by clicking the Teleport button at the bottom right of your map screen.

✐ **Location:** These coordinates pinpoint where you are in a region by latitude, longitude, and elevation — in that order.

✐ **Teleport button:** Click this button to teleport to your selected location on the map.

✐ **Show Destination button:** Click this button to zoom in on the location you searched for using the My Friends, My Landmarks, or Search by Region Name fields.

✐ **Clear button:** Clicking this button turns off the red destination marker on your map. This is displayed once you arrive in a location.

✐ **Show My Location button:** Click this button to move the map to your current location. This is handy for seeing where you are compared with where you want to be.

✐ **Copy SLURL to Clipboard button:** Use this button to copy a Second Life location shortcut URL to your Clipboard. You can then paste this into another program, such as e-mail or IM chat, to send someone right to that location even if he isn't logged in to SL.

✐ **Zoom:** This slider zooms in and out on the world map.

Teleporting right next to someone without IM-ing them first is considered bad SL etiquette.

Creating and Using Landmarks

When you find a great site online, you probably make a bookmark of the page so you can find it again easily. Second Life's version of bookmarks is a *landmark*. You create and save landmarks so you can use them later to find places that you want to return to.

If you find a place in SL that you really enjoy, follow these steps to create a landmark for it:

1. **From the World menu, choose Create Landmark Here.**

   The Add Landmark screen appears.

2. **Type in the desired description in the text field.**

   This text is the name of the landmark in your inventory, so name it something you'll remember.

To access and use one of your landmarks, follow these steps:

1. **Click the Inventory button on the bottom of the screen.**

   The Inventory window opens.

2. **Click the arrow to the left of the Landmarks folder.**

   A list of your landmarks appears with an icon that looks like a thumb-tack next to them.

3. **Double-click the landmark you want.**

   A window opens, with the name of the landmark and the options of tele-porting there or viewing the landmark's location on the map.

4. **Make your selection by clicking the appropriate button.**

   You can also open a list of your landmarks on the Map. Click the Map button on the bottom right, use the My Landmarks drop-down list to select a landmark from your inventory, and then teleport there.

Part II
Living Your Second Life – Exploring and Socializing

The 5th Wave   By Rich Tennant

"Phil is so excited. He was passed over again as a full partner at the law firm, but was accepted into the Necromancer group in Second Life."

In this part . . .

I don't care to belong to any club that will have me as a member.

—Groucho Marx

What's the use of being in a world of amazing people if you don't know how to talk to them, or you're so goofy-looking that they won't talk back? It's time to get suave and get social. In Chapter 5, you discover the basics of customizing your avatar to express your personality and look your best. In Chapter 6, we show you how to jump into the conversation so you can chat and instant message in Second Life.

With all your newly learned social skills, you'll no doubt be eager to connect with some cool people, so Chapter 7 covers refining your profile to express yourself. You can also read here all the ways to find people you have something in common with, to form groups, and to find events. Of course, after you become social, you risk getting into some "sticky" situations. Never fear because reading Chapter 8 will help you avoid trouble and always feel in control.

Creating Your Second Life Persona

In This Chapter

▶ Parts of your virtual body

▶ Editing your appearance

▶ Putting on clothes and objects

▶ Virtual grooming

*W*e don't know about you, but many mornings, we stand in front of the mirror wishing we could just take off 20 pounds, grow out a bad hair cut faster, or make the pants that are suddenly just a little snug fit a little better. One of the best parts of Second Life is the fun you can have with your avatar. Your *avatar* is your digital body in Second Life, and there's no end to how you can customize it. With just a simple click, you can change from male to female, fat to thin, tall to short — and those are just some of the possibilities!

In this chapter, we walk you through making changes to your avatar so you can shed that newbie look we created in Chapter 3 and get a custom body that suits your personal style.

Avatar Anatomy

Before you can start editing your avatar, you need to get familiar with your avatar's anatomy (see Figure 5-1). Much of what you'll see here is similar to your real life body, but you'll note some important differences. Just like your real life body you have arms, legs, feet, torso, hands, and a head (see Figure 5-2). What you don't have in your virtual body are sex organs and imperfections (unless you add them).

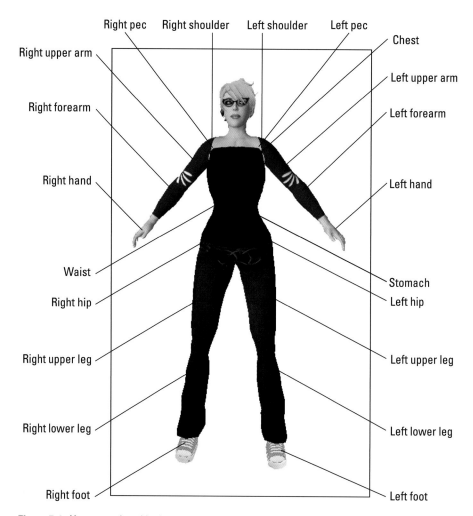

Right pec   Right shoulder   Left shoulder   Left pec

Chest

Right upper arm

Left upper arm

Right forearm

Left forearm

Right hand

Left hand

Waist

Stomach

Right hip

Left hip

Right upper leg

Left upper leg

Right lower leg

Left lower leg

Right foot

Left foot

Figure 5-1: Your new virtual body.

Understanding the layers of clothing on your avatar can help you imagine new possibilities for fetching combinations. For example, on your upper body, you can wear an undershirt, a shirt, a jacket, and gloves. On your lower body, you can wear underpants, pants, shoes, socks, and a skirt. These are the clothing objects you can wear but you can wear almost any object on your body, though wearing a house on your head doesn't make sense.

If you have a male avatar, don't assume that you'll never use the skirt layer on your avatar. Jackets and shirts stop at the waist, so if you want a longer jacket — like a lab coat or a duster — chances are that the bottom of the jacket will actually be a skirt that is open in the front to match the top half of the jacket.

Chin Mouth Nose Skull Left eyeball Left ear

Figure 5-2: The parts of an avatar's face.

In addition to your clothing layers, you also have lots of attachment points on your body, such as *right pec* or *left hip.* These are locations where you can attach an object, such as glasses, a belt, or a hat. In Second Life, an *object* is anything that is not land or an avatar. It can be a box, a car, or a building.

You need to understand these attachment points because they limit how many objects can be attached to your avatar, where the object gets placed, and how the object will behave. For instance, attaching a glass of wine to your right hand makes the glass move whenever your right hand moves. This will also help you understand why putting on a hat, for instance, might make your hairdo disappear. If your hair is an attachment, it's probably attached to your skull — which is where the hat attaches as well — so one will replace the other. We cover attaching objects in the upcoming section, "Attaching and Detaching Objects."

Editing Your Avatar's Appearance

Most of the basic changes that you can make to your avatar can be done via the Appearance screen, as shown in Figure 5-3. It's easy to use and fun to experiment with. To open the Appearance screen, just right-click your avatar and choose Appearance from the radial menu (or choose Edit⇨Appearance).

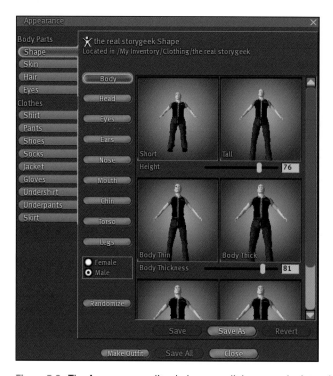

Figure 5-3: The Appearance editor helps you edit how your look to other residents.

From the Appearance screen, you can edit body parts (shape, skin, hair, and eyes) and clothes (shirt, pants, shoes, socks, jacket, gloves, undershirt, underpants, and skirt).

Body parts

This section of the appearance editor changes the physical parts of your body in Second Life. This includes the shape your body, skin, hair, and eyes.

Shape

On this tab, you can alter the general shape of your body. The Shape tab contains the following options:

- **Body:** This option sets the dimensions of your whole body such as height and weight.

- **Head:** This option sets the dimensions for your head including size and shape.

- **Eyes:** This option sets the size and shape of your avatar's eyes.

- **Nose:** This option sets the size and shape of your nose.

- **Mouth:** This option sets the size and shape of your mouth.

- **Chin:** This option sets the size and shape of your chin and lower face.

- **Torso:** This option sets the dimensions for the upper part of your body including musculature, thickness, and width.

- **Legs:** This option sets the dimensions for your avatar's legs including length, width, and butt size.

- **Gender selection:** This section allows you to select either Male or Female for the gender of your avatar.

- **Randomize:** Getting frustrated with all of the previous choices? Click the Randomize button to let Second Life make the choices for you. You get some pretty crazy combinations.

Skin

On this tab (see Figure 5-4) you can define your skin color and how your face looks. This includes your face details and make up. You can also add further body details. Such as freckles and body definition.

- **Skin Color:** Your avatar comes with skin that can be tinted (use the Pigment slider) and made flush (with the Ruddiness slider). The last slider on the Skin Color tab allows you to change your skin to "nonnatural" colors, such as green or purple.

- **Face Detail:** Use this set of controls to give yourself wrinkles or rosy cheeks.

- **Makeup:** Everything from lipstick to nail polish can be customized using these settings.

- **Body Detail:** Add shadows for definition or freckles with this tool.

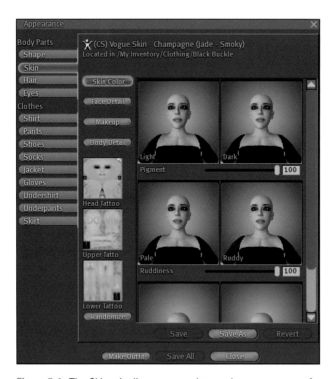

Figure 5-4: The Skin tab allows you to change the appearance of your avatar's skin.

Below these buttons are three tattoo spots on the menu: Head, Upper, and Lower. Adding an image to these spaces on the tool applies a tattoo to your skin — just not necessarily how you think. Second Life uses JPEG and Targa files (image files that can be created in Photoshop and other image editing software) along with templates (which can be found at www.secondlife.com) to wrap images around your avatar. We talk more about these and how to create and wear them in Chapter 15.

Hair

Hair in Second Life comes in two basic flavors: system hair and prim hair. The sliders on this tab (see Figure 5-5) create *system hair:* that is, hair that is part of your avatar rather than being attached. We talk more about *prim hair* (worn like a wig) in the upcoming section, "Hair." The options on the Hair tab are as follows:

- **Color:** You can create custom colors from white to purple to red by using a combination of the color choices on this menu. Mix them to change the color until you like it, as shown in Figure 5-6.

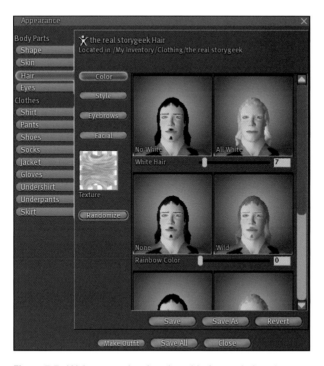

Figure 5-5: Welcome to the virtual world of crazy hair styles.

Figure 5-6: Sometimes you can come up with wild hair designs.

- **Style:** Use these sliders to actually make your hair. This includes the length, style, and color. Again, experiment until you like your look.

System hair is usually fine for men with short hair. However, for women, prim hair offers much more sophisticated styles. To avoid the newbie look, replace your system hair with prim hair as soon as you can. For more information on how to do this go to the "Hair" section later in this chapter.

- **Eyebrows:** This is pretty self explanatory. Use these tools to customize your eyebrows. Note that the color of your eyebrows will always match the color you choose for your hair.

- **Facial:** This button appears only if you pick the Male gender on the Shape tab. These options include things like moustache, beard, Van Dyck, or soul patch. For more subtle facial hair that doesn't change the shape of your face, you might want to opt for wearing a custom skin with painted-on facial hair. You can read more on this later in the upcoming section, "Skin."

- **Texture box:** The texture on this menu dictates the image that is applied to your hair, making it curly or straight, fine or frizzy. You can even choose plaid or polka dots if you want to get really wild. You have several textures for hair in your inventory under Library⇨Textures⇨Hair Textures. To quickly get to the hair textures in your Inventory, click in the Texture box.

You don't have to limit yourself to the Hair Textures. Experiment by choosing other texture types in your inventory — such as grass or stripes — and see what happens.

- **Randomize:** Getting frustrated with all of the previous choices? Click the Randomize button to let Second Life make the choices for you. You get some pretty crazy combinations.

Eyes

On this tab (shown in Figure 5-7), you can change the color and texture of your eyes. For example, you can replace the default eye image with, say, a cat's eye.

Try all black or all white for a really creepy look. You can also find really beautiful eye textures in stores that even have a bit of lifelike reflection on them.

- **Iris:** This is the texture applied to the iris of the eye. Unless you want some freaky eyes leave it as is.

- **Eye Color:** This option sets the color of the eye.

- **Eye Lightness:** This option sets the brightness of your avatar's eyes.

- **Randomize:** Getting frustrated with all of the previous choices? Click the Randomize button to let Second Life make the choices for you. You get some pretty crazy combinations.

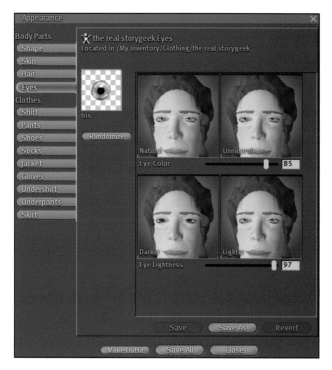

Figure 5-7: Look into my eyes as they change color.

Clothes

These options are for the clothes you wear on your body. They come in a few set varieties (Shirt, Pants, Shoes, and so on). They do not change the shape of your avatar's body but like your clothes cover it in layers.

Shirt

This is a piece of clothing on your torso and arms. It stops at your neck, wrists, and waist.

 ✔ **Fabric:** This is the texture applied to the fabric of the shirt.

 ✔ **Color/Tint:** This is the color that is laid on top of the texture of your shirt.

Pants

This piece of clothing covers your legs from your waist to your ankles.

 ✔ **Fabric:** This is the texture applied to the fabric of the pants.

 ✔ **Color/Tint:** This is the color that is laid on top of the texture of your pants.

Shoes

These pieces of clothing cover your feet to the lower ankles.

- **Fabric:** This is the texture applied to the fabric of the shoes.
- **Color/Tint:** This is the color that is laid on top of the texture of your shoes.

Socks

These pieces of clothing cover your upper ankles and lower legs. There are underpants and shoes.

- **Create New Socks:** This button lets you create new socks. Including setting the fabric, color, tint, and length.

Jacket

This piece of clothing is worn on the torso and is on top of the shirt.

- **Create New Jacket:** This button lets you create a new jacket. Including setting the fabric, color, tint, and length.

Gloves

This piece of clothing covers the hands and lower arms.

- **Create New Gloves:** This button lets you create new gloves. Including setting the fabric, color, tint, and length.

Undershirt

This piece of clothing is worn on the torso under the shirt.

- **Fabric:** This is the texture applied to the fabric of the undershirt.
- **Color/Tint:** This is the color that is laid on top of the texture of your undershirt.

Underpants

This piece of clothing covers the area below the waist to the knees under pants.

- **Fabric:** This is the texture applied to the fabric of the underpants.
- **Color/Tint:** This is the color that is laid on top of the texture of your underpants.

Skirt

This piece of clothing covers your waist and is worn on top of pants or underpants.

✓ **Create New Skirt:** This button lets you create a new skirt. Including setting the fabric, color, tint, and length.

Customizing Your Avatar's Appearance

Sometimes the options on the Appearance screen (refer to Figure 5-3) just aren't enough to get you just what you want. This is when you need to start shopping. Vendors all over Second Life use their skills in third-party software (such as image editors) to create physical options far beyond what the SL software settings will allow you to create. The following sections discuss some of the ways you can customize your avatar's appearance.

Buying an avatar shape

If you've played with the body shape sliders in the Appearance screen, you know that they're limited. For example, if you'd like to be chubby, you'll find that your avatar ends up being rather out of proportion if you rely on the sliders. If you're meticulous, you might be able to create that buff body that you want with the Appearance screen, but why not let someone else do the work for you?

You probably already have a shape or two in your inventory. To access your inventory and check for existing shapes, follow these steps:

1. **Click the Inventory button on the bottom of the screen.**

2. **In the Search field type** shape.

   A list of Inventory items with the word shape in them appear. Shapes have unique icons (shown in Figure 5-8).

Figure 5-8: A shape listed in the Inventory.

To find shapes in the rest of the world use the Search feature to look for places that have the word " shape" associated with them. This will give you shape stores, places for free shoes, and shape making help locations.

Once you have a shape, simply right-clicking a shape in your inventory and choosing Wear will apply the shape to your body, keeping all your clothes, hair, skin, and so on intact. You can easily go from chubby to muscle-bound with a few clicks, as shown in Figure 5-9.

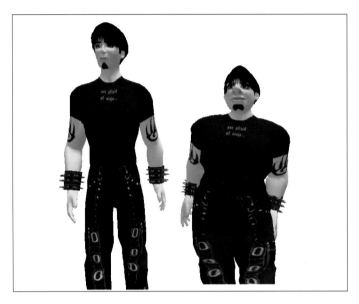

Figure 5-9: Your shape can really change how you look.

Skins

Your avatar comes with *system skin,* which is an exterior that you can tint and change from the Appearance screen. Also, a layer of your body can take a texture to be used as a skin. Think of this like a spray-on tan. The skin layer is like having your whole body painted complete with ripped abs, dimples in all the right places, makeup, or facial and body hair. Some skins completely cover your body, and others are mostly transparent and just feature small tattoos that cover only certain parts of your system skin.

Some of the best skins in Second Life can be found at The Body Politik (Eventide South 66,228, 35). This is the island name and location on that island.

These skins (shown in Figure 5-10) are made in Photoshop (see Figure 5-11) and use the body templates that are available on the download page of the Second Life Web site.

As you can see here, this head skin has makeup painted on it that aligns itself with the parts of the avatar's face. Finally, makeup that will never smear or wear off!

For more info on exactly how to create skins, see Chapter 15.

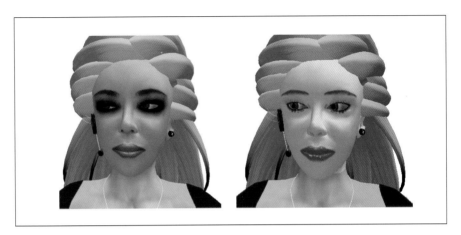

Figure 5-10: The difference between purchased skin and system-created skin is huge.

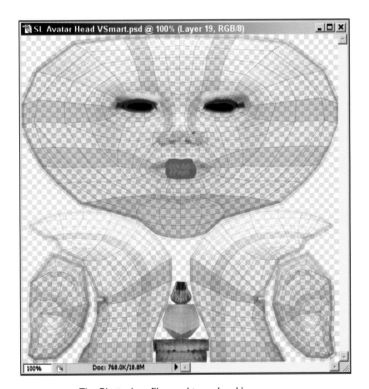

Figure 5-11: The Photoshop file used to make skins.

"Other" body parts

Basic avatars are built like Barbie and Ken dolls. Um, that is, they're missing some, um, equipment. (Have we winked and nudged enough yet for you to get the point?) You can buy these parts to attach to your avatar when you need them. Some are basic, and some are quite fancy with programs and animations built into them. The choice is up to you whether you think you need to be anatomically correct. Just be sure not to buy a part that "shouts" things in public spaces. (You can read about shouting in Chapter 6.) Some controversy was stirred in Second Life when the Excite script became popular in adult venues. It broadcast the level of arousal of the person wearing it and got quite annoying to those around who just felt like this was too much information.

Getting Dressed

Putting on clothes is simple. Just find them in your inventory, right-click an item, and then choose Wear. Putting them on is just the beginning, though, because you can make adjustments to make them look a little better and express more of your personality. Time to go back to the Appearance screen. Right-click your avatar and choose Appearance from the radial menu, or choose Edit⇨Appearance.

The bottom section of buttons on the Appearance screen all deal with clothes — that's why they're under the Clothes section. From here, you can create your own clothes from scratch or adjust the clothes you're already wearing. We cover making clothes in Chapter 15. For now, explore how to adjust the clothing you have on.

Turning pants into shorts

Long pants are easy to turn into shorts (see Figure 5-12). To do so, follow these steps:

1. **Right-click your avatar and choose Appearance from the radial menu.**

   The Appearance Editor appears.

2. **Click the Pants tab in the Clothes section.**

3. **Move the Pants Length slider to around 30.**

   Your pants become shorts.

   Moving the slider to the left (closer to 0) shortens your pants even more; moving the slider to the right will increase the length of your pants. Go figure.

4. **Click Save.**

Figure 5-12: Pants can be full length or shorts.

Be sure to minimize the Cuff Flare after you shorten your jeans, or you'll end up with bare, fat ankles. Cuff Flare is also found on the Pants tab.

Changing a shirt into a bikini

You can change your shirt, jacket, or undershirt into a bikini or tank top with these easy steps:

1. **Right-click your avatar and choose Appearance from the radial menu.**

   The Appearance Editor appears.

2. **Click the Shirt tab in the Clothes section.**

3. **Move the Sleeve Length slider to 0 (all the way to the left).**

4. **Move the Shirt Bottom slider to 0 (all the way to the left).**

5. **Click Save.**

Arm warmers

Turn gloves into nifty arm warmers by following these steps:

1. **Right-click your avatar and choose Appearance from the radial menu.**

   The Appearance Editor appears.

2. **Click the Gloves tab in the Clothes section. If you have never created gloves click the Create gloves button.**

3. **Move the Glove Length slider to 100 (all the way to the right). This means they go to the upper arms.**

4. **Move the Glove Fingers slider to 0 (all the way to the left). So only the hands are covered.**

5. **Click Save.**

Attaching and Detaching Objects

In addition to clothing and skin, you can also attach objects to your avatar. Of course, you can attach a glass to your hand and glasses to your face, but you can also attach objects that look like part of your clothes. Collars, capes, skirts, jewelry, and belts can all be attachments. Earlier in this chapter, we describe the many parts of your avatar that can receive an attachment. Your avatar comes with a few free things you can attach but most attachments need to be found in freebie areas or purchased.

For the most part, well-made attachments that you purchase will "know" which part of your body they should attach to, but sometimes they need a little adjustment. As an example, here's how to put on a skirt. The steps to adjust a cape, collar, or other item are the same.

Before you begin, you need to buy a prim skirt or some other prim attachment. Searching for *prim* in addition to the type of clothing will find these special kinds of items. You might also want to search for flexi skirts. These are skirts made out of flexible object so they move more like real clothing.

To wear a skirt that you purchased, follow these directions:

1. **Click the Inventory button.**

2. **Use the Search box to find a skirt.**

3. **Right-click the skirt and choose Wear.**

To move the skirt's placement on your avatar, follow these steps:

1. **Right-click the skirt and choose Edit from the radial menu.**

2. **On the Edit tool, click Stretch.**

3. **Move the handles to stretch the object and move it from the wrong place (see Figure 5-13) to the correct place (see Figure 5-14) on the avatar.**

Try these steps to put a hat in your hand instead of on your head, to slide your sunglasses up on your head instead of wearing them on your face, or to make a short skirt into the flouncy part of a longer, mermaid-style skirt.

Figure 5-13: A skirt positioned to the wrong place.

Figure 5-14: The skirt is positioned to the right place.

Hair

After you play with *system hair* (the hair you can make from the Appearance screen), you'll no doubt realize that you're surrounded by people with much cooler hair. Pony tails that swing, cool spikes, and other fancy dos can make your default hair look rather lame. The hair these folks are wearing is *attachment hair.* It's made of *prims,* which are the objects you can build in Second Life to create a house, car, belt, (and, yes) hair. Prim hair is a little strange because you wear it like a wig. Underneath it, you must be totally bald, so most prim hair comes with a *bald cap* that makes all your system hair disappear without you having to edit your appearance. Most attachment hair ranges in price from L$50 to L$300 (usually under $1 USD). You can buy hair in a ton of places in Second Life, so just do a search for *hair* and any special specifications you want (like *pony tail* or *men's*), and you're bound to find dozens of places to shop.

Most hair makers will allow you to grab a free demo version of a style to try on before you buy the real thing. These demos are usually rainbow colored or might even have demo written all over them. If a style is really expensive or far from what you think you might like, grab the demo first. You'll look silly in the store as you try it on but it's better than wasting L$300 on a hairdo you don't like.

Wearing prim hair is no different than wearing any other object. After you purchase prim hair, follow these steps to put it on:

1. **Click the Inventory button on the bottom of the screen.**

2. **Use the Search box to find the hair.**

3. **Right-click the hair and choose Wear, as shown in Figure 5-15.**

Most hair will be the right size, but if you have a head that is unusually small or large, you might have to resize it.

1. **Right-click the hair and choose Edit from the radial menu.**

2. **On the Edit tool, click Stretch.**

3. **Move the handles to stretch the object.**

Some hair is *flexi.* This hair is made from some flexible prims and looks more realistic. If you want bouncy pony tails or a bouffant that waves in the wind, search for *flexi hair.*

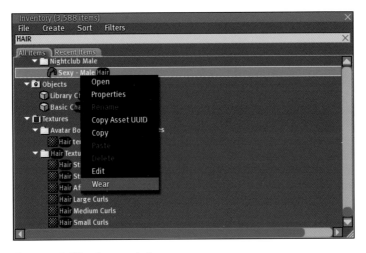

Figure 5-15: Wearing your hair.

Accessories

In Second Life, you can accessorize until your heart's content. You can literally attach an object to every point on your body if you want. From necklaces and earrings to little dogs in a bag to knitting needles complete with a scarf that grows off of them the longer you hold them, the sky is the limit! Most well-made attachments already "know" which part of your body they should be worn on, so all you need to do is follow the instructions in the previous section; just choose the accessory to wear.

Not all jewelry is made the same. Some necklaces, for example, are attachments, and others are actually worn as an undershirt with only a necklace on it. Be sure to inspect what you're about to buy to see what kind of object it is. You don't want to buy that great ring to wear over your gloves to later find out that the ring is actually made *as* a glove.

Too much can be too much. Some jewelry and other accessories are programmed with special effects, such as glows or flashes (referred to as *bling* in Second Life) or other interactions. If you have on too many programmed accessories, you can actually cause lag for those around you. Be cautious with your accessories if you intend to hang out in busy places. You might look good, but you might find yourself on the street (be kicked out a region) if your bling is slowing everyone down.

Quick Changes: Saving Your Appearance as an Outfit

This might very well be the most time-saving advice in this chapter. No, seriously! Say you spend hours getting your avatar to look ultimately cool and then decide to try on some goofy dinosaur outfit or spaceman gear only to find out that you can't simply revert to your normally cool self. We know a quick solution to this problem, and trust us — after you messed up your avatar, you'll never forget it. Here's the down-low: Save your appearance as an outfit.

After you save how you look, you can do super-quick changes between outfits, and this doesn't just include clothes. You can quick-change between totally different forms: dinosaur to dog, male to female, and so on.

Here's how to save your appearance as an outfit:

1. **Right-click your avatar and choose Appearance from the radial menu.**

2. **After changing your appearance, click the Make Outfit button.**

   The Make Outfit screen appears.

3. **In the Folder Name box, enter the name of the outfit.**

4. **Select which items you want to include in the folder.**

   Be sure to select *every* check box on the Save As an Outfit menu and let it rename the objects in a folder. This makes your outfits easy to find. I've even created a folder in my inventory called Outfits so I can find mine easily. For more information on Inventory management, check out Chapter 9.

5. **Select Rename Clothing to Folder Name to ensure that the clothing in the folder has the same name as the folder.**

6. **Click Save.**

Wearing an Avatar on Your Avatar

No, this section isn't about piggy back rides. Your body in Second Life is your *avatar,* but something else in SL is also referred to as an avatar. When you put on an outfit made of attached objects that totally changes how your body looks, it's also called an avatar. Confusing, huh? The confusion is worth it, though. These are some of the wildest looks you can get in Second Life. Here's how they work.

Find free avatars to play with at a junk yard in Second Life. The Kool-Aid man, aliens, and samurai are just a few of the free ones you'll find.

When you buy or find an avatar, they're in a box. Inside the box is a collection of objects that are worn all over your body. For example, you'll see upper and lower arms, a head, a body, and leg parts. You'll probably also find a shape that will shrink your actual body down to the right size to fit inside the attached parts. Right-click each part in your inventory and wear it. You'll see your avatar change one bit at a time until your human form is gone and replaced by the form of the avatar you're putting on. After you have it, on be sure to save it as an outfit (see the previous section) so you can just drag the folder on to your body from your inventory to put the whole outfit on again later.

Most "furry" (cartoonish animal) avatars are entirely made of objects that are attached to your body.

A well-made avatar will be perfect the first time you wear it, but you might need to make a tweak here or there if it's not quite right. To edit the position of a body part, follow the earlier instructions.

For some crazy fun, put on an avatar and then adjust each piece so they sit a meter or so away from your body but in the same position to each other as they'd be if they were attached to you. This creates an avatar puppet that moves along with you, like a robot. It's very strange to see but really fun to do.

Some avatars also come with specially programmed toolbars called *HUDs* (Heads Up Displays). HUDs can change the color of the avatar or give you control over special animations. For example, I have a dog avatar that can scratch, beg, and even roll over using HUD controls that came along with it. Avatars with HUDs are more expensive, but they can be well worth the money for the controls they give you.

Jumping into the Conversation: Express Yourself

In This Chapter

▶ Finding people to meet

▶ How to chat

▶ Exploring your chat options

▶ Using Instant Messaging to talk to friends and groups

▶ Will you be my friend?

▶ Making use of notecards

▶ Using Voice Chat in Second Life

▶ Actions speak louder than words

▶ Body language

Second Life is, after all, a social space — a world of people eager to get to know each other, chat, and share a brave new world. However, like with any other new society, there are some rules to learn and some behaviors to avoid. Besides, who wants to look like a newbie by making a social *faux pas?*

In this chapter, we show you how to get in touch with other folks in Second Life. After all, what's the point in being in a virtual world if you can't make virtual friends? We cover several ways to communicate as well as how to gesture and invite people to be your friends so you can get in touch with them again easily.

Where My Peeps At?

You logged in to Second Life, learned how to get around without crashing, and even found a few places you like and created landmarks so you can get back to them easily. (For more on creating landmarks, see Chapter 4.) Now it's time to add some folks to your friends list.

Meeting people in Second Life isn't all that different from mixing and mingling in real life. You can join groups of people with common interests, attend events that pique your attention, or just hang out in a dance club or mall until you find people you want to talk to. People are generally friendly to folks who respect their space and don't intrude on conversation.

The best places to meet people are at high-traffic locations. You can find these spots by looking at the Popular Places tab on your Search menu. Traffic in a location is tracked. The more people, the more traffic. And the more popular places will appear on the Popular Places tab. These are hot spots that are usually teeming with folks. Try out a few that look interesting to see whether you can meet some folks.

To visit a location on the Popular Places list, follow these steps:

1. **Click Search.**

   This opens the search window.

2. **Click the Popular Places tab.**

   This displays the most popular places in Second Life.

3. **To show only popular places that have pictures associated with them, select the Only Show Places with Pictures check box.**

4. **If you want mature parcels or islands displayed, select the Include Parcels with Mature Content check box.**

Chatting with Other Residents

There are lots of ways to talk to people in Second Life. You can chat *out loud* so that those within 20 meters of you can "hear" you, or you can chat through instant messaging (IM, which works sort of like telepathy).

To chat out loud, follow these steps:

1. **Click the Chat button at the bottom of the screen, as shown in Figure 6-1.**

2. **Type your message in the text box.**

Chat button

Figure 6-1: The Chat button.

3. Click the Say button to the right of the text box, or press Enter.

You message is displayed in the bottom-left corner of the screen, as shown in Figure 6-2.

You shout: Happy Birthday!

Figure 6-2: Your message shows up on screen.

When you're typing a message in Chat, your avatar's hands likewise move in a typing motion. This lets others know that you're about to say something. Without this animation, it would be hard to know whether someone is still chatting with you, has spaced out, is away from their keyboard, or is just ignoring you.

Sometimes the typing animation is a bit behind your actual chat. You'll see folks type and type and type just to say, "I agree" or something else short. It's all a lag thing, so don't worry.

Folks who are more than 20 meters away might be able to see your hands moving, but they won't be able to "hear" what you're saying unless you shout.

To shout a message, follow the steps:

1. Click the Chat button at the bottom of the screen (refer to Figure 6-2).

2. Type in your message in the text box at the bottom of your screen, just as you do when chatting.

3. Click the Shout button to make your voice heard region-wide.

When you shout, you'll see your avatar's hands go to his or her mouth as if to yell. When you shout, avatars within a parcel of land will hear you.

It's generally considered rude to shout too often because it "spams" other resident's screens with your text. Shout only when necessary. You may shout to tell people about a party that is starting or if a game on the parcel is beginning. And, just like your mom told you when you were little — "Look at me when I'm talking to you!" — try facing your avatar to look at folks you're chatting with. It lets them know that you're talking to them and not someone nearby.

Chat Options, History, and Logs

Sometimes chat just goes by too fast, especially when you're in a large group and everyone is typing away. Here are some handy ways to keep track of chat.

Chat options

See Chapter 2 for chat options.

History

If your chat is blipping off your screen faster than you can read it, you can pull up your chat history to go back into the conversation and catch what you missed. Chat history goes back to the time you logged in.

To open the Chat History window, follow these steps:

1. **Click the Chat button at the bottom of the screen (refer to Figure 6-2).**

2. **Click the History button located to the left of the text box where you enter your chat text.**

   The Chat History window appears.

3. **Use the scroll bar on the right side of the window to move back and forth in the conversation.**

4. **To resume live chat, click the Chat button in the Chat History window.**

5. **To exit Chat History, close the Chat History window.**

Logging chat

If worst comes to worst and you can't keep up with a chat (even by using the Chat History), you can log all your chat — even IMs — so you can read them later.

To log a chat, follow these steps:

1. **Choose Edit⇨Preferences.**

   The Preferences window appears.

2. **Click the Communication tab.**

3. **Select the Log Chat check box in the IM Options section.**

4. **To mark the end of the last IM in the log so that you can easily differentiate between conversations, click the Show End of Last IM Conversation box.**

5. **To change the location of the saved chat log, click the Change Path button, enter a different path, and then click OK.**

6. **Click OK.**

To open logged chats

1. **Open a file explorer on your computer.**

2. **Navigate to the log location you specified.**

   The default is C:\Users\<username>\AppData\Roaming\SecondLife.

3. **The logs are stored in this location in .txt files, so all you need to do is double-click them.**

Publishing chat logs online without the expressed permission of all residents participating in the chat goes against the Second Life Terms of Service. Before you publish chat logs in your blog (or elsewhere), be sure that everyone involved in the chat knows your intentions and agrees to be published.

Making a Resident a Friend

Maybe you had trouble making friends on the playground as a kid, but it's easy as pie in Second Life. After you find residents and chat with them, you might find yourself wanting to become friends with them.

To offer friendship to a fellow resident, follow these steps:

1. **Right-click the resident whom you would like to add as a friend.**

2. **On the radial menu that appears, choose Add Friend.**

   A warning appears that you have offered friendship.

3. **If your offer is accepted, a window appears to alert you.**

   Consequently, if your offer is rejected you will receive a message telling you that your proposal was rejected. In a non-invasive manner you might want to ask them why they rejected you but don't be a pest.

Being someone's friend means that you can give her permission to see when you're logged in to Second Life or even to edit your objects. To control these permissions, click the toggles on the Friends list.

It's generally considered bad manners to offer friendship to someone without obvious reasons or without asking them first. You can offer your calling card to anyone, though, without stepping on toes. A *calling card* is like a digital business card. It is an object signifying a person.

To give a calling card to someone, follow these steps:

1. **Right-click the resident to whom you would like to give a calling card.**

2. **From the radial menu that appears, choose More and then choose Give Card.**

Instant Messaging: Individual and Group

You've probably used instant messaging in other applications. Maybe you chat with friends via AIM or Yahoo!. This easy, quick way to send short messages back and forth with a friend is no different when used in Second Life.

You can IM with anyone, but it's easiest to IM with friends.

To IM friends, follow these steps:

1. **Click the Friends button at the bottom of the screen.**

   The Friends window appears, as shown in Figure 6-3.

Figure 6-3: This is a list of your friends.

  2. Select the friend you want to IM and then click the IM button.

    The Instant Message screen appears.

  3. Enter your message in the text box and then press Enter.

  4. To end a chat session just close the IM window.

To IM someone who is not your friend, follow these steps:

  1. Click the Search button at the bottom of the screen.

    The Search window appears.

  2. Click the People tab.

  3. Enter the name of the resident you're searching for and then click the Search button.

  4. Select the resident you want to IM and then click the Instant Message button.

    The Instant Message screen appears.

  5. Enter your message in the text box and then press Enter.

  6. To end the session close the IM window.

IM-ing all the members of a group to which you belong is as easy as IM-ing a friend. To IM a group, follow these steps:

  1. Click the IM button at the bottom of the screen.

    The Instant Message window appears (refer to Figure 6-3).

  2. Select the name of the group you want to IM and then click Start.

    The Instant Message screen appears.

  3. Enter your message in the text box and then press Enter.

  4. To end an IM session, close the IM window.

You can IM people who are not logged in. If that's the case, you receive a message telling you that they will receive the message the next time they log in.

The difference between chat and IM

In SL chat is public discussion and IM is private. A chat message is said out loud and can be seen by anyone up to 20 meters from you. An IM is between two people and cannot be overheard by others. IM's are not geographically dependant. I can IM you from anywhere in the world.

Notecards

Sometimes chatting just isn't enough, and you need to share a picture, a land-mark, or written text that others can read later. *Notecards* are the simple text documents that you can create and share in Second Life. They're great for storing information, such as instructions on how to use an object or for shar-ing a list of your favorite Second Life locations.

To make a new notecard, follow these steps:

1. **Click the Inventory button at the bottom of the screen.**

   The Inventory screen appears, as shown in Figure 6-4.

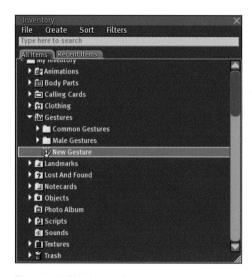

Figure 6-4: This is your Inventory screen.

2. **From the Create menu, choose New Note.**

   A new notecard appears.

3. **Enter a description and the text you want to save.**

4. **Click Keep.**

5. **To access the note card again you just need to find it in your Inventory and double-click it.**

Note cards can be very useful for storing images and lists of landmarks. For instance you might have a notecard for the prettiest places in Second Life that could have pictures and landmarks built in.

To add landmarks or images to a notecard, follow these steps:

1. **Click the Inventory button at the bottom of the page.**

   The Inventory screen appears (refer to Figure 6-4).

2. **Open the Notecards folder.**

3. **Double-click a notecard.**

   The notecard opens.

4. **To add a landmark, open the Landmark folder in your inventory, select a landmark, and drag it onto the open notecard.**

   A link to the landmark appears.

5. **To add an image, open the Textures folder in your inventory, select a texture, and drag it onto the open notecard.**

   You can have few types of pictures in SL. They can be textures or snapshots.

   A link to the image appears. Clicking on the link will open the file.

6. **Click Keep.**

7. **To access the card again, find it in your inventory and double-click it to display the contents.**

If you want to create a series of notecards that are linked together like a hypertext book or help file, you can have notecards linked to each other.

To link two notecards, follow these steps:

1. **Click the Inventory button at the bottom of the screen.**

   The Inventory screen appears (refer to Figure 6-4).

2. **Open the Notecards folder.**

3. **Double-click a notecard.**

   The notecard opens.

4. **To add a link to another notecard, select another notecard and drag it onto the open notecard.**

   A link to the notecard appears.

5. **Click Keep.**

All notecards are named New Note in your inventory. To give a notecard a specific name, right-click the note in your inventory, choose Rename, and type in a new name. You're set.

Gestures and Animations

What good is having an awesome avatar if you can't make it do your bidding? In Second Life, you can make your avatar dance, tumble, and even stick out its tongue. *Animations* are the physical and facial motions that your avatar can perform to communicate with others. When you string animations together or add sound and other effects, they're called *gestures*. Here's how to use them.

In your inventory, you have an Animations folder. It's probably empty if you haven't purchased any new animations or picked up some free ones. This doesn't mean you can't perform some smooth moves, though.

 You can pick up lots of free animations at Yadni's Junk Yard. Use your Search screen to find his place and grab a few boxes of free animations from the freebie wall.

You'll also see a Gestures folder. In this folder are two subfolders:

- **Common Gestures:** *Common Gestures* contain gestures that everyone can use, including motions such as clapping, bowing, dancing, playing rock paper scissors, and falling down.

- **Female Gestures or Male Gestures:** Male or Female Gestures contains gestures specific to your avatar's gender. For instance a male avatar and a female avatar have different movement when they blow a kiss. Just imagine switching it.

Expand either folder by clicking the small triangle next to the folder. Then double-click the gesture in your folder.

To use a gesture, follow these steps:

1. **Click Chat.**

2. **Click the Gestures list.**

3. **Click the gesture you want.**

   You can also use the gesture trigger in your chat box.

To create your own gesture, follow these steps:

1. **Click Inventory.**

   The Inventory screen appears.

2. **Open the Gestures folder.**

3. **Double-click New Gesture.**

   The New Gesture screen opens.

4. **In the Description box, enter what the gesture does.**

5. **In the Trigger box, enter what trigger to use for the gesture. A trigger is a text shortcut that runs the gesture. For instance something like /lol for a big belly laugh gesture.**

6. **Select the shortcut keys you want to use for the gesture.**

7. **Select the type of item you want to use from the library.**

8. **Click Add.**

9. **Select the specific item.**

10. **Click Start or Stop that item.**

11. **Click Move Up or Move Down to order the items.**

12. **To preview the gesture, click Preview.**

13. **Click Save.**

Have fun combining new animations, uploaded sounds, and so on to create custom gestures that are truly yours!

You can create your own animations by using Poser or other 3-D modeling software, but free solutions are available, too. Posemaker by Caladan (http://caladan.nanosoft.ca/c4/software/posemaker.php) and Avimator by Vinay Pulim (www.avimator.com) are both easy to use and allow you to create your own animations for free (or for a small donation).

Pose balls

You might have seen balls sitting in the seats of furniture, floating over beds, or even on a dance floor in Second Life and wondered what they are. Some are labeled with text like Sit or Kiss Him. These balls are *pose balls*. If you right-click one and then choose Pose or Sit Here, they'll pose your avatar into the pose that is included by the person who created the pose ball.

Not all pose balls are PG rated. Be sure to read the text over the poseball before you click it to avoid embarrassing positions.

You can also purchase sets of pose balls to place on furniture you make yourself. Most purchased furniture will come equipped with a pose programmed into it or with an attached pose ball.

Getting a Social Second Life

In This Chapter

▷ Setting avatar profiles

▷ Understanding groups

▷ Engaging events

*F*inding residents in Second Life is always an interesting topic. You can run into folks by just wandering around or perhaps meet them at events. You can also use the Search tool (covered in depth in Chapter 4) to find them. Just remember, like in your First Life, not everyone wants to be found.

After you find someone, it's time to get social. In this chapter, we discuss allowing yourself to be found, joining groups, and attending events where you can meet even more people or share common activities.

Your Second Life Profile

Who you are in Second Life (SL) is really a combination of a number of things, including what you do, what you say to other people, how you look, and the things you put in your profile. Imagine this: Across the room at a crowded party, you can peer into someone's wallet to see their birth date, what clubs they belong to, and even a list of their likes and dislikes. In SL, you can — simply by viewing someone's profile. Here are the basics about your profile:

 ▸ **Viewing:** People can view your profile at any time (whether you are logged in to Second Life or not), and you will never know. Your profile is always viewable — what are you willing to let them know?

 ▸ **Auto profile:** A portion of your profile is automatically generated. This information about you — such as birth date in Second Life — is generated by the system and is unchangeable.

 ▸ **Notes:** Like mental notes you might make about people you meet, profiles offer you a place to make notes in someone's profile that only you can see.

To view a Second Life profile, right-click your avatar (or someone else's avatar) and choose Profile from the radial menu, as shown in Figure 7-1. Doing this allows you to see your profile or any other avatar's profile in SL. However, you can edit only your own profile, not the profiles of others. After an avatar's profile is displayed (see Figure 7-2), you can see several pieces of information about the avatar on the 2nd Life tab:

- **Name:** This is your avatar name as it appears to other people. After your name is chosen (when you set up your account), you can't change it.

- **Born:** This is the date when your account was created, not your actual birth date or the date when you actually logged in to SL. This is one of the first things people will look at when they view your profile. Your birthday helps identify you as a newb (someone new) or an experienced SL resident.

- **Account:** This area shows the status of your account. This tells whether you are a resident and whether you have payment information on file. The payment information means that you have assigned a valid credit card to your account.

- **Partner:** If you are *partnered* (married) in SL, the name of your avatar partner appears here. Adding a partner is done through the Second Life Web site.

  A partner is like a spouse but purely in title only. Being a partner does not give the other user any abilities or privileges she/he doesn't already have. You can "propose" to someone to become your partner using the account controls on the Second Life Web site.

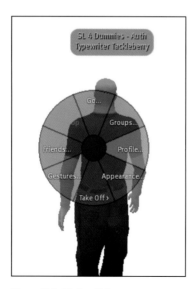

Figure 7-1: Right-click on your avatar and select Profile from the radial menu.

Figure 7-2: My profile in Second Life.

✒ **Photo:** This is a photo you choose. It can be any graphic file you have in your inventory, such as a screen shot of your avatar. Try to choose a photo that represents how you want to be seen in Second Life. To add a photo here click on the empty image spot and use the image selection tool that opens to navigate to the image file you'd like to display in your profile. Click the select button to make your choice appear in your profile. You can change this image any time you'd like.

✒ **Groups:** This is an alphabetic list of the groups to which you belong. Anyone viewing your profile can see these groups. We'll talk more about groups later in this chapter.

✒ **About:** The text here is about you, by you. You have up to 500 characters to make a statement about who you are or what you like. This is something that defines who you are in SL, so keep it up to date.

✒ **Give Item:** Via someone else's profile, you can give him an inventory item: Just drag it into this area of the profile. When you do, the recipient is notified that a new item was given. The item must be transferable for this to happen.

✒ **Web Profiles:** You may choose to list your profile on `www.second life.com`. This allows residents to view your profile without logging in to Second Life. Click the "Publish on the Web" box to allow your profile to be searchable via the Second Life Web site.

In addition to the 2nd Life tab, several other tabs are available on the Profile screen that provide you with even more information about an avatar:

- ⮑ **Web:** This tab allows you to display and link to an external Web page. Some people use it to link to their MySpace or Facebook accounts, as shown in Figure 7-3. Others use it to promote their business' Web site. You can either view the Web page in the profile or open it in your browser. To add a Web page, all you need to do is add the URL to the list.

- ⮑ **Interests:** This tab displays things you are interested in within Second Life, such as:

  - *I Want To:* This area allows you to note activities that you're interested in doing in SL. Select any of the check boxes you're interested in; for example, if you're interested in being hired, select the Be Hired check box. If something you fancy isn't there, enter it into the text field.

  - *Skills:* Select those skills you have that you want others to know about. If a skill you have isn't listed, add it in the text box. Scripting and Event Planning are probably the most sought after skills in this list but very few people who are interested in hiring will search profiles to find potential employees.

  - *Languages:* Here, list what languages you can read or write.

Figure 7-3: A profile displaying a link to a Facebook page.

✐ **Picks:** Everyone likes recognition. If you find something or someone in SL you like, tell people about it here on this tab, as shown in Figure 7-4. If you have a business, make sure you list its name, coordinates, and what it sells in your picks. To add a new Pick, click New. The place you are currently at appears in the list.

✐ **Classified:** This tab allows you to place classified ads. These ads appear both in your profile and when someone uses the Search menu to find classifieds. You determine how much you want to spend on an ad. Spend more money, and it is given a higher ranking and seen by more people. We discuss classified ads in greater detail in Chapter 17.

✐ **1st Life:** This tab is about your First Life (FL): your life outside SL. You can add a picture and text here, just like on the 2nd Life tab we discuss earlier in this section. See Figure 7-5. In the Info text field enter text about your FL that you want to share. You have up to 250 characters at your disposal, including letters and spaces.

You are under no obligation to add this information or put a picture here.

✐ **My Notes:** This tab allows you to write notes about people for your own use. For instance, if you find a vendor you like, you can write in the notes section that you liked them and their products, as well as what you bought. No one but you can see these note.

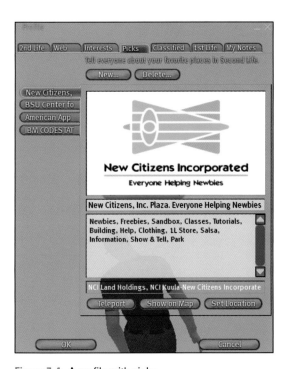

Figure 7-4: A profile with picks.

Telling others about your First Life

Residents of Second Life have varying opinions about sharing information about their First Life. For instance, some people share who they are in the non-digital world by including pictures of who they are in their First Life. Other residents keep their First Life very private and put nothing on their 1st Life tab or post warnings not to ask them about their First Life. As a rule, always read someone's complete profile, including both the 2nd and 1st Life tabs, before asking them about their First Life.

You also need to decide how much you are going to share about your First Life. Again, there is no requirement to share anything, but some people like to know more about the First Life of the people they're interacting with in SL. So decide what you are comfortable sharing, and then add it to your 1st Life tab. Remember: You can always change this.

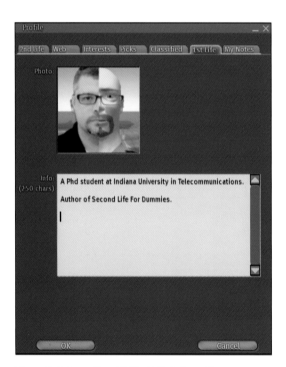

Figure 7-5: A profile with First Life information.

Second Life Groups

Some people in SL have words — *tags* — that appear above their Second Life avatar's name. These words come from the groups they belong to. A *group* in Second Life is like a club of three or more people, linked by the purpose of the group. Groups can be for serious things (such as cancer survivors) or for silly things (such as people who like to dress like cartoon characters). Although there is no limit to the group purpose, you can only belong to a max of 25 groups.

Your current active group — the group that provides the tag above your avatar name — appears bold in the list. If you want to be identified with a certain group, display that group's tag. To activate a group, select the group in the group list (which you'll find on the right-click radial menu when you click on your avatar) and click the Activate button. To remove all tags from your avatar, activate the None group.

Groups have a creator and members. The *creator* is the person who starts the group. It currently costs L$100 to create a group. Group membership can be free or cost per membership, based on what the creator decides. In addition to fees, group creators also have to right to grant or refuse membership to anyone who requests to join a group. Groups can also have *officers* with privileges other members don't have. These privileges are based on roles created by the group owner.

Groups are great for connecting socially with other residents. You can find other people who share interests with you. Groups can be also used to control privileges on land, including who can interact with certain objects, leave items on land areas, and control access to land. You can search out groups to join, have membership offered to you, or start your own group. To display the list of groups you belong to, right-click your avatar and choose Groups from the radial menu; see Figure 7-6.

A creator of a group can designate it as Mature. As you can likely guess, this means that the content or subject of the group is of a mature nature. This does not mean you will be overwhelmed with porn spam if you join a Mature-classified group. The Mature designation is just a helpful guide provided by the group owner. If you're not interested in mature material in groups, just don't search for or join them. Examples of mature groups might be fans of a fashion designer whose merchandise is revealing, fans of an adult club, or a group which discusses topics considered adult like gender issues or relationships.

Finding groups

When you start in SL, you aren't a member of any group. To find groups you might be interested in, use the Search tool. This tool helps you find groups, read information about them, and allows you to join them. To find a group via the Search tool, follow these steps:

Figure 7-6: View your list of groups.

1. **Choose Edit⇨Search and then click the Groups tab.**

   This tool allows you to do a text search for groups.

2. **(Optional) If you're willing to include Mature groups, select the Include Mature Groups check box.**

3. **In the Find text box, enter a search term; then click the Search button.**

   A list of groups meeting your criteria is returned with the group selected appearing in the right pane, as shown in Figure 7-7. The profile of the selected group is displayed in the left pane.

   It might take a few seconds for the group's profile to appear in the right pane.

Group profiles

Like every SL resident, each group has a profile. When you do a search for a group or double-click it on another person's profile, the group profile appears. Like an avatar's profile, a group's profile has the following tabs that contain information about the group:

   ✔ **General:** This tab (see Figure 7-8) shows general information about the group, including the name of the group, the owner, members, and the group charter. This is the central source of information about the group. This tab also contains the button that allows you to join the group. If the group has a membership price, it appears here as well.

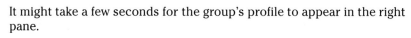

   If you don't see a Join button below the group's image on the General tab then the group is by invitation only and you'll need to contact the group's owner to ask to join.

Figure 7-7: The Search window with a list of groups displayed.

Figure 7-8: The Group profile with the General tab shown.

- **Members & Roles:** This tab shows the members of a group as well as who has what roles and abilities. This is not visible unless you are a member of the group.

- **Notices:** This tab shows all available *group notices,* which are notes that the entire group can read. Notices can also include copyable and transferable items from your inventory. However, folders can't be attached to notices. Notices are only visible to group members.

- **Proposals:** *Proposals* are items that group members can vote on. You might want to propose certain group policies to the group members. To do this, you use a proposal. After a proposal is created on this tab, a message is sent to each group member, and each can vote on the proposal. Voting history is also displayed on this tab. This is not visible unless you are a member of the group.

- **Land & L$:** This tab displays all the land and Linden dollars held by the group. This is used when buying or selling land based on people in a group. For more on land management, consult Chapter 12. This is not visible unless you are a member of the group.

Joining groups

To join a group in Second Life, follow these steps:

1. **On a group's Profile, click the Join button.**

   A Join window appears. This window double-checks to make sure that you want to join this group, and it restates how much it costs to join.

2. **Click the Join button again.**

   Second Life confirms that you joined the group and then makes it your active group. Sometimes, an owner or officer has to confirm or deny your request to join.

Most groups in SL are free. Be very wary of any group that charges you L$l to join because it might just be a ruse for someone to make easy money. Confirm with the group owner if you're unsure about any costs.

Second Life allows you to join only 25 groups. If you try to join a 26th group, the system asks you to quit one of your current groups before joining the new one. And think about it: Do you really need to belong to that many groups? You might want to look at groups that are stagnant or annoying and cull them from your list if you're reaching membership in nearly 25 groups.

Creating a group

If you're interested in connecting with people and can't find the right group, feel free to create your own group. Creating your own group means that you have to pay the fee to create the group and then be responsible for managing the group. Groups are as much work as you choose to make them. Say you set up a new clothing store in SL, and you have a few fans of your designs. By creating a group and getting customers to join it, you can send members messages when you're having a sale or when new products are available. After you pay the start-up fee of L$100, no other fee is required to run a group or send messages to its members.

Before creating your own group, you should do two things.

- ✔ **Join and learn.** Join a few groups like the one you're thinking of creating and see what you like or dislike about them. This research will help you make a better group of your own.

- ✔ **Research.** Do a search for any group that might be like the group you're thinking of creating. For example, creating a Cancer Survivor's group is a waste of money if one already exists.

To create a group, follow these steps:

1. **Choose Edit⇨Groups.**

   This opens your group list.

2. **Click the Create button. If the Choose button is gray then you already have too many groups and you'll need to leave one before you can create a new one.**

3. **Enter the name of your group in the top text field. Remember that others will be using their Search to find your group so make the name descriptive.**

   For example, if you collect antique typewriters, you might want to call this group something like Antique Typewriter Collectors.

4. **Add any texture or image in your inventory to the Group Insignia box, just like when adding a profile picture. See Chapter 6 for more info about adding images to profiles and group profiles.**

5. **In the Group Charter Box, enter the charter of the group you're creating.**

   A *charter* tells the world what your group is about.

   If you have a Web site related to the group, you should put a link to it here by pasting in the page's URL address.

6. **In the Group Preferences area, enter what settings you would like the group to have.**

   For example, you might want the list of members shown in the groups list and on the Web so people can find it when they search for keywords such as *typewriter*. If you want to charge people to join the group, you set the Enrollment Fee here. If you want your group to be free, just leave it at L$0.000.

Consider charging for group membership to make your membership more exclusive. If you're running a private club, for example, you might want to charge people for joining. If someone has to pay for membership, they're more likely not to join in passing but to really want to be active in the group.

7. Click the Apply button.

You see a message that creating a group will cost L$100.

8. Click Yes to accept the cost of creating a group.

You new group is created, and you can begin finding other members.

You group needs to have three or more members, or it will be closed by SL after 24 hours, and your money is not refunded. This stops people from creating joke groups that clog the search. Be sure you have a few friends who will join your group right away so it won't be deleted due to lack of membership.

Members' roles and abilities

Groups are made of members, and those members have roles and abilities. For example, let's say you run a clothing store and you have employees who help you run the store. As the owner of the group you have the ability to add new members, delete members and send members of the group messages about changes in the business. Your employees would be assigned "employee" roles and might be able to send messages to everyone in the group but wouldn't be given permission to add or delete members.

A *role* is just a collection of abilities assigned to a member. You can have up to ten different roles per group, and each member can belong to multiple roles. Every member of a group must be at least in the system-generated role called Everyone. This is the base role to which every member belongs. The system also creates Owner and Officer roles. You configure the membership and roles for your group on the Members & Roles tab of the Group profile, as shown in Figure 7-9. Roles allow you to grant certain abilities that share some of the responsibilities of running the group among its members. You can assign a role to a member when you invite her to join the group or after she joins the group.

To assign a role when inviting someone to become a new member, follow these steps:

1. From the Edit menu, choose Groups and, click the group to which you want to add members and then click the Info button.

2. Click the Members & Roles tab.

Here, you can edit membership, roles, and abilities in your group.

3. Click the Invite New Person button.

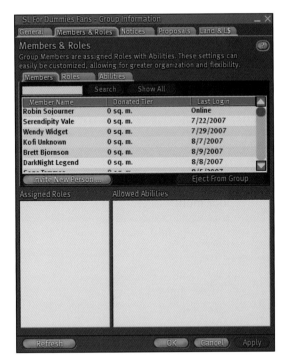

Figure 7-9: The Group profile with the Members & Roles tab shown.

This opens the group invitation window, which you use for inviting people to your group and assigning them a role.

4. **Click the Open People Chooser button to display the Choose Resident dialog box.**

This allows you to search for people to invite to your group. Or, you can select them from the calling cards in your inventory. For more information about calling cards in your Inventory check into Chapter 9.

5. **After you find who you want to invite to your group, click the Select button.**

This adds those folks' names to the list of invitees on the Group Invitation window.

6. **Click the Close button when your invitee list is complete.**

7. **Choose a role from the drop-down list for each person you're inviting to your group.**

This is the role each person will have if he accepts your invitation.

8. **Click the Send Invitations button.**

Everyone on your Group Invitation list is sent an invitation to join your new group.

Just like a dinner party, you can invite as many people as you want — but that doesn't mean all invitees will join your group. Try not to send blanket invites to your Whole Friends list unless you think a majority of the people on it would be interested in joining your new group.

To assign a role to already-existing members of a group, follow these steps:

1. **From the Edit menu, choose Groups and, click the group to which you want to assign roles and then click the info button.**

2. **Click the Members & Roles tab.**

3. **On the Members sub-tab, select the member to whom you wish to assign a new role.**

4. **In the Assigned Roles box field, check the appropriate roles for that member and click OK.**

You might want to expand the number of roles in your group. After all, a role is just a group of abilities. These abilities can allow the role to control abilities, such as membership, role creation, group identity, and land management.

To add new roles to a group, follow these steps:

1. **From the Edit menu, choose Groups –and, click the group to which you want to add roles and then click the info button.**

2. **Click the Members & Roles tab, and then click the Roles sub-tab.**

   This displays the Role Management property sheet.

3. **Click the Create New Role button.**

   This allows you to create a new role; give it a name, title, and description; and assign abilities.

4. **Enter the name and title of your role.**

   The role name appears in the Role section of the profile; the title name appears above the avatar who has that role in the group.

5. **In the Description text box, enter a description of the new role.**

6. **In the Allowed Abilities text box, select any abilities you want to assign to this role.**

   Some of the abilities are very powerful, so choose very carefully what abilities to assign to new roles. As the creator and owner of the group, you have all these abilities.

7. **Click Apply.**

   If you want to know more about a particular ability, click the Abilities sub-tab. Selecting the ability in the list gives you a description and what roles and members have that ability.

Group Notices

If you have some information or an object you want to share with the entire group, you can send a Group Notice (as shown in Figure 7-10). These are similar to group messages but stay around longer. You create a notice like an e-mail. It has a subject and a message body, and you can add attachments to it. To learn more about group messages flip to Chapter 6.

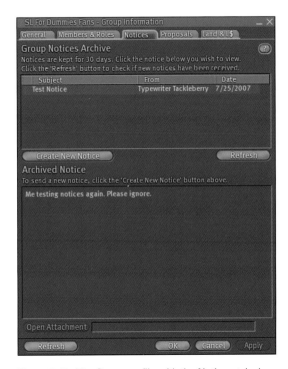

Figure 7-10: The Group profile with the Notices tab shown.

You can attach only those objects that are copyable and transferable.

To create a Group Notice, follow these steps:

1. **Open the Group Profile by clicking the Edit menu and selecting groups. Click the group from your list that you want to send a message to and then click Info.**

2. **Click the Notices tab.**

   This is the tab you use to send new and read archived group notices.

3. **Click the Create New Notice button.**

4. **Enter a subject for your notice.**

If you want to send a notice to your group about an upcoming event, put the title of the event and the date in the Subject line.

5. In the Message text box, enter the body of your message.

In your message, identify the event and what people should know about it.

6. Click the Send Notice button.

The Notice is sent to all group members.

To reread a notice, you can find them archived on the Notices tab. After 30 days, these notices are removed.

Group Notices might get e-mailed to members who are offline. Sending too many notices can be irritating to members. When you join a group you can choose whether you want to receive group notices by unchecking the box at the bottom right of the membership screen. You can go uncheck this box anytime.

Group proposals

Sometimes you might want to know what other group members think on a certain topic, such as whether you should charge to join the group or make a certain member an officer. *Proposals* are non-binding Yes- or No-answered questions you can ask all the group members. You essentially are voting for or against a proposal. You can create proposals as well as define the question, *quorum* (how many must vote), the majority required to pass the proposal, and the time limit for discussing the proposal.

To create a proposal, follow these steps:

1. Click the Proposals tab (as shown in Figure 7-11) at the top of the group menu.

In addition to creating a proposal here, you can also view proposals and see results.

2. Click the Create Proposal button.

This displays the proposal creation area where you enter new proposals.

3. Enter a Proposal Description.

This is the proposal you want to make. Remember that the members will be given a Yes or No choice, so don't ask open-ended questions (such as, "What is your favorite color?").

Try leading off your proposal with, "I propose . . ." so that your members know what they're voting on.

4. Select a Majority that will pass the proposal.

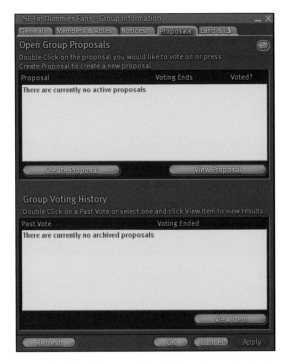

Figure 7-11: The Group profile with the Proposals tab shown.

Your proposal can pass or fail, dependent upon this Majority setting. According to your choice, a proposal can pass with 51% (Simple Majority) or two-thirds of the vote, or set to pass only with a unanimous vote. Different proposals might require different Majority settings.

5. Select the Quorum needed to have a vote.

This is the number of group members who must vote for the proposal to be considered binding. If you have a proposal that only three people of 400 group members vote on, the result probably should not be binding. Also, if the proposal requires members to agree to help with a project or commit time in another way you'll want enough yes votes as people you need to help on the project. In addition, having a majority vote on a proposal that affects everyone in the group might cause dissenters to leave the group (which may or may not be what you want to result).

6. Select a Duration.

Give your members time to respond to your proposal. The Duration setting allows you to set the number of days before the proposal is terminated. On time-sensitive things, you want to have your proposal given enough time to react to it. You might want some proposals to last longer, allowing your membership time to think about the proposal.

7. **Click the Submit Proposal button.**

   Your proposal is submitted, and all the group members are sent a message saying new proposals are available to vote on. If a member is logged on, a small window appears alerting them. If a member is offline, the system alerts him the next time he logs on.

To vote on the proposal, follow these steps:

1. **When you receive the alert, choose to Vote Now or Later.**

   You don't have to vote right away on a group proposal. If you do choose to vote right away, go ahead and vote when the Group Profile opens. If you choose to vote later, just open the Group Profile when you're ready.

2. **View the proposal by selecting it from the list of active proposals and then clicking the View Proposal button.**

   This opens a details window about the proposal.

3. **Vote Yes, No, or Abstain by clicking the appropriate button.**

Land and Linden dollar (L$) management

Much like a corporation, a group can own land. Members can deed land to a group, and that group can then sell the land and collect the money. This is covered in greater detail in Chapter 12.

Building with groups

No one likes to work alone. You can use a group to collect the people you want to work with collaboratively on a building project. Maybe you want to have one friend help you with a small part of your new hairdo, or you have a team of builders working on multiple buildings on a parcel of land. Either way, a group allows you to grant privileges to people and allow them to create, edit, or delete objects that the group has control over. This is covered in more detail in Chapter 14.

Messaging groups

Messaging a number of people at one time can be both a great tool and an awful pain. You can solicit a group *en masse,* however, to get a recommendation where to buy cool boots or help for a script you're working on. Messaging a group is covered in Chapter 6.

Remember that Group Instant Messaging is different than sending out a group notice. Group IM is simply a conversation with all group members who are currently online. Group Notices should only be used for important matters that must reach all members, even those who are not logged in.

Second Life Events

Like in folks' First Life, people in Second Life get together for events. An *event* is really when any group of avatars get together for a reason, from sitting around a campfire telling stories to attending a huge concert. You're limited only by your imagination. Events are excellent ways to see what's going on in Second Life and meet new people. Events are happening all the time, so enjoy exploring.

Finding events

To find events, use the Search tool. The Search tool is covered in detail in Chapter 4. You can search for in-progress events or ones on an upcoming date. You can also search for events in a category, or with a particular name or description. You can also include Mature events in your search; read how earlier in this chapter.

If you include Mature events in your search, you might get events that appear to be innocent but are actually of a more adult nature.

To find events, follow these steps:

1. **Click the Search button and then click the Events tab.**

   This tab shows you all the events that match your search criteria. This example shows a search for music events happening today.

2. **Select In-Progress and Upcoming, or enter a specific date.**

   For example, to find musical events happening today, choose Date.

3. **Select a category or enter a name or description.**

   What the hey? Try the live music category.

4. **Click the Search button (or the Today button if searching for events happening today).**

   The list of events that meet your search criteria is displayed, as shown in Figure 7-12.

Attending events

After you have an event selected, you can teleport there, show the event location on the map, or be notified when the event is about to start. However you get there, go and have fun.

Look closely when the event you want to go to is being held. You don't want to teleport there hours before the event. The planners might not be there or might still be setting it up.

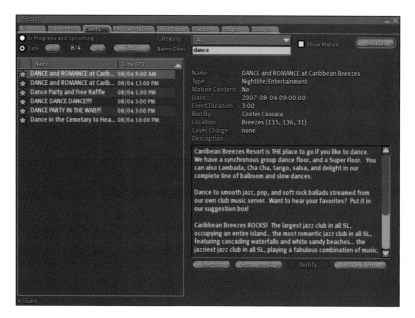

Figure 7-12: The Search window with a list of events displayed.

Adding events

When you create or add events, you are directed by Second Life to the Community: Events Web page on www.secondlife.com. This page allows you to search events and add new events. To create an event, follow these steps:

1. **Open your internet browser and navigate to http://secondlife.com/events/.**

2. **Click the add Event link.**

   You might need to log in to the Second Life Web site. If so, use your Second Life login and password.

4. **Read and agree to the event guidelines.**

5. **Enter your event information.**

   This screen lets you enter all the relevant information about your event and then submit it. Remember that your event listing is your ad for the event so you should make it sound exciting, fun, and worth while.

   This Web page is subject to change without notice. Always consult the Second Life Web site if the event-posting process is different than we describe here.

Staying in Your Second Life Comfort Zone

We've all seen the *Dateline* "To Catch a Predator" episodes. Watch enough of them, and you begin to feel like the Internet is jam-packed with folks whose prime motivation is to be creepy and end up in handcuffs in someone's driveway. Although you'd be naïve to think that no risks are involved in online living, you don't have to think that everyone online is a pervert. The best way to be safe online is to be informed. You just need to know how to avoid attracting trouble and what tools you have to defend yourself with should someone target you with creepy behavior.

In this chapter, we dismiss many of the scary stories you've heard about Second Life and online communities in general. We help you identify potential trouble, prevent invasions of privacy, stick to places where you'll be comfy, and tell you how to deal with trouble should it arise.

Understanding the Risks in Second Life

People join Second Life (SL) for a wide variety of reasons. Some log in to check out a cool technology, some want to meet up with friends who are too far away to see face to face, and others have dreams of finding that special virtual someone. Not everyone falls into these harmless categories, though.

Some folks — like in just about any community — make trouble for innocent people. You know the types: those who can be a little too forward, a little too pushy, or just downright scary. Whether they're making sexual comments, following you, Instant-Messaging you when you'd rather they not, or *griefing* you (a new kind of behavior only exhibited in online worlds in which people seem to enjoy just generally being persistently annoying), you have recourse in Second Life that you might not have in real life (RL).

A friend of ours is a researcher who studies griefers and their communities. She's infiltrated their gangs in Second Life and tells us of horrible things they do for fun, including following people around, shouting defamatory and untrue things about them in public places, or even taking pictures of their avatar and hanging them around the SL world. Our friend also told us, however, that these griefer groups seem to target people who are sort of asking for it — that is, people who make themselves a target by being annoying themselves.

More commonly, we have to deal with people in SL who don't seem to respect privacy or don't heed social cues like, "Get away from me!" The first step is prevention. The second step is ignoring them. The third step is calling in the higher powers. Read along to see how to take it step by step.

Drawing a Line between Your First and Second Life

Becoming fast friends with someone in Second Life is easy. You spend the night dancing next to a wonderful guy/gal, and pretty soon, you're chatting it up over a virtual martini and adding each other as friends. (For more about becoming friends in SL, see Chapter 6.) But, wait — is it you or your avatar who is making friends? This might seem like a silly question, but consider these pretty profound ramifications.

Second Life allows us to take on a *persona* — an alternate personality. By day, you might be a mild-mannered banker; but at night, you're a virtual DJ in the hottest SL club. Do you tell people you meet about your day job? Your kids? Where you live? It all depends on whom you're talking to and who you are. There's value in both being someone else and being someone completely different.

On one hand, taking on a fantastic persona and exploring a facet of yourself you don't usually get to express is fun. There's certainly no harm in it. Go ahead — spend your day dressed up as a ninja granny in Second Life swinging from tree branches and howling at the moon. It's okay to be someone different. However, if you choose this fantasy persona path, you lose the opportunity to make a more genuine kind of friend in Second Life, one with whom you have real life (RL) things in common and with whom you might become friends outside Second Life.

On the other hand, you can be yourself in Second Life. My avatar looks just like me (see Figure 8-1) except that her makeup is always perfect, and she fits into that cute dress that is still in the back of my real life closet waiting for the last ten pounds to drop. Check out Figure 8-1 to see just how similar we are. There's very little difference between my SL self and my RL self, and that's okay with me. The downside is that I don't get to experiment with different personas, and I run the risk of telling people things about me that might reveal more about my personal life than I should.

Figure 8-1: Some folks, like Sarah, choose to create avatars that look similar to their real life selves.

On your profile (which you can access by right-clicking on your avatar and choosing Profile) are both Second Life and First Life information tabs (2nd Life and 1st Life, respectively). You're not required to fill either one out, and certainly no Truth Police will make sure that what you type there is true.

Giving away too much information about yourself can open you up to stalkers and other potential creeps. Don't provide your e-mail or Web address unless you're in Second Life to do business and you want people to be able to reach you. Include a RL picture only if you're comfortable with it. If you're not, simply follow the examples of lots of other folks and keep your first life to yourself as you see in Figure 8-2.

To read more about your profile, check out Chapter 6.

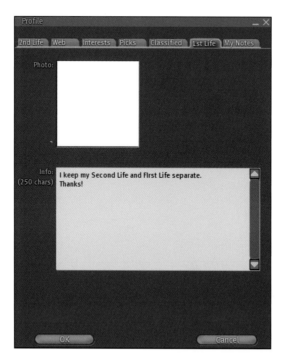

Figure 8-2: If you want to keep your real life private, you might want to say so by writing something like this on your 1st tab.

Ratings: PG and Mature Regions

Regions (usually in the form of islands) are rated for their content. When you buy an island, you get to choose whether you want it to be rated PG or Mature. PG lands are encouraged to be friendly to all kinds of folks and shouldn't contain any adult material. Mature regions can contain PG material but don't guarantee an absence of adult content within their borders. Even if a region has been split into individual parcels, all of the parcels of an island will be rated the same. To learn more about land management see Chapter 12.

Island owners are the only ones who enforce content standards on their space. And what might be PG to one person might be Mature to another.

You can filter out Mature regions when you search for places to visit by following these steps. If you do, though, you might also filter out lots of great content located in regions that are rated Mature.

1. Click the Search button at the bottom of your screen.

2. Type in search terms such as "Amusement park," "women's clothing," or whatever you're interested in finding.

3. Deselect the Include Mature Content check box, as shown in Figure 8-3.

Include Mature Content check box

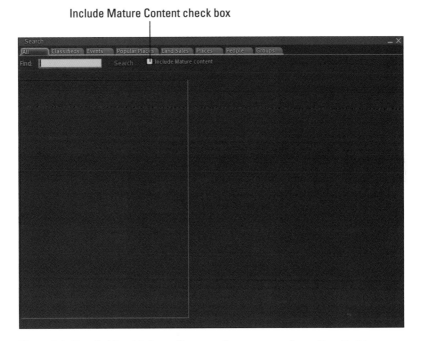

Figure 8-3: Deselecting this box will ensure that your search results will all be locations in PG rated areas.

The main grid of Second Life is intended for adults 18 years of age and older. There are no parental controls available in the main grid because the assumption is that all residents are adults. There is a teen grid intended for 14-17 year olds where there are rules in place to limit mature content. To learn more about the teen grid, see Chapter 19.

Handling Problem Residents: Muting and Reporting Trouble

We've all seen it. That guy in the crowd who just won't take "no" for an answer. Or perhaps your friend has a home in Second Life with a noisy neighbor whose home is so close by that his chat appears on your screen while you're trying to have a conversation with your friend. How do you cut the intrusive neighbor out of your conversation?

It happens in RL, and it happens in Second Life. So what do you do to stop it? It's easy. Just mute the resident. (If only we could do this in real life . . .)

To mute an avatar, follow these simple steps:

1. **Right-click the avatar of the resident you'd like to mute.**
2. **From the radial menu that appears, choose Mute.**

So you muted that guy who was pestering you. But now, even though you can't hear him any more, he's still not going away. Harassment is taken seriously in Second Life, and reporting someone for being abusive is easy. To report abuse, follow these steps:

1. **From the Help menu, choose Report Abuse as shown in Figure 8-4.**

   The Report Abuse screen appears.

Figure 8-4: The Report Abuse option appears from the Help pull-down menu.

2. **Click the Object picker (see Figure 8-5) and then click the object or avatar you want to report is abusing you.**

   It might seem strange that an object could be abusive, but it's true. If you encounter an object, for example, that keeps sending text across your screen or is blanketing the area with offensive images flying through the air you might want to report the object (thereby reporting the object's owner) for abuse.

3. **To include a screenshot of the abuse, select Include Screenshot.**

Object picker

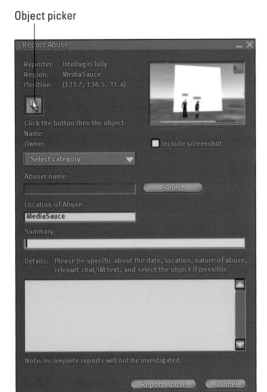

Figure 8-5: The Abuse Report menu allows you to use the Object picker to select an avatar or an object, which you would like to report for abusive behavior.

4. **Click Select Category to select an abuse category. The categories are as follows:**

- **Intolerance:** Use this category to report hate speech, racist behavior, or other blatant intolerance.

- **Harassment:** Use this category to report stalking or other repeated behavior that is making your feel uncomfortable or unsafe.

- **Assault:** If another resident repeatedly shoves you, shoots you with a weapon, puts you in a cage or other actions are taken toward your avatar that make it impossible for you to enjoy your Second Life experience you should use this category.

- **Disclosure:** Should another resident reveal personal details about you that aren't readily available in your profile you can report them for abuse using this category. You may also use this category to alert Linden Lab about the publication of chat logs without permission.

- **Indecency:** Nakedness or other lewd behavior in a public event or in a PG region should be reported using this category.

- **Age:** If a resident admits to being under 18 you should report them right away including a chat transcript.

- **Parcel:** If your neighbor infringes on your land and doesn't respond when you ask them to move objects or interlopers leave objects on your land you can report them using this category.

- **Other:** Have a problem that doesn't quite fit into one of the other categories? Then use Other.

Remember that if someone or something is bothering you that you can simply teleport somewhere else to get away. Folks can't follow you unless you're friends with them.

5. **Click Select to confirm that the person you clicked on with the Object Picker is the person you wish to report. Or, type the avatar's name in the box and then click Select to confirm that the name is correct.**

6. **Enter a summary of the abuse in the Summary field.**

7. **Enter a complete, detailed account of the abuse in the Details field.**

8. **Click Report Abuse.**

Depending on the severity of the complaint, you will be contacted by a Linden Lab liaison (usually through a Second Life instant message) who will ask you to clarify the event if necessary. In most cases the abuse report will be verified by confronting the offender if possible. Offenders will be given opportunities to change their ways but if they prove to be repeat offenders they will be suspended or their account terminated. Having your account terminated is pretty serious because your inventory and land holdings will be deleted as well. Abuse reports should be taken very seriously and not filed without a good reason. Your first resort should always be to rectify the problem yourself either by muting the resident or confronting them to let them now that they're bothering you or offending you.

If you're feeling voyeuristic and want to see the latest in abuse reports, you can check out the police blotter on the Second Life Web site at http:// secondlife.com/community/blotter.php.

Part III
Inventory, Cash, and Land

The 5th Wave   By Rich Tennant

"The yen is up, the dollar is down, the franc is all over the place. The only currency I'm comfortable with are my Linden-Dollars in Second Life."

In this part . . .

Money. Money. Money.

Even in the virtual world, you can't get away from money. It's what makes even a virtual world go 'round. The Second Life economy has made a few millionaires, but far more folks are making a few bucks here and there. We help you find your place in the virtual global economy.

In Chapter 9, we show you how to manage your Inventory so you can organize all the virtual stuff you might be buying or selling. After all, what good is that awesome pair of shoes if you can't find them to wear? (Gee, isn't the virtual world a little too much like the real world? At least in Second Life, you can't lose your house keys.)

In Chapter 10, you get a primer on the Second Life economy: where money comes from, where it goes, how to buy it, how to sell it, and how to begin earning some of your own. When the virtual cash in your virtual pocket starts to burn in a hole in your virtual jeans, we show you the wisest ways to spend it in Chapter 11.

Finally, in Chapter 12, we talk about the best investment in Second Life — land. It's *Monopoly* on a grand scale — and you, too, can become a land baron.

Becoming Materialistic with Your Second Life Inventory

. . . .

In This Chapter

▷ Discovering an object's attributes

▷ Utilizing your Inventory

▷ Working with objects

▷ Opening boxes

. . . .

*S*ay you're at the office and spill something on your shirt. Wouldn't it be great if you could instantly change your clothes, no matter where you were? Even better, wouldn't it be nice to have everything you owned right at your fingertips? In Second Life (SL) you can, courtesy of your Inventory.

Your Inventory is like a bottomless pocket you carry around with you, storing all the objects you have in SL. Everything but avatars, land, and water in SL is an *object*. This includes everything you see, including things such as notecards and textures. We have known people to carry things like houses, boats, and cars in their Inventory.

Some virtual worlds impose a limit on the size of your Inventory, but not so in SL — there is no limit to your Inventory size. Some people have terabytes (TB) of data in their inventories.

In this chapter, we cover the parts of your Inventory and how to use them. We also explain what an object is and what you can do with it.

Using Your Inventory

Your Inventory is where you store all the objects you acquire in SL, as shown in Figure 9-1. You can create objects, share them, delete them, and rename them. You can also sort them into folders, which is a survival technique you'll want to master. If you spend any time in SL, your Inventory fills up quickly and gets hard to manage unless you keep it organized. In this section, we help you keep your infinite virtual closet straight.

Things in your Inventory don't have to have a unique name. Theoretically, you can have 40 boxes called Box01. Confusing, isn't it? To keep it all straight, make sure to name objects well — clearly — when you're creating them.

The Inventory window

The Inventory window is how you access your Inventory. It contains all the objects that belong to you and allows you to work with them.

You're not limited to one Inventory window at a time. By creating a new Inventory window, you can sort your inventory a lot better.

Figure 9-1: An avatar with his Inventory showing.

To create a new Inventory window, follow these steps:

1. **Click the Inventory button to open your Inventory.**

2. **From the File menu choose New Window.**

   A new Inventory window is opened.

To open your Inventory window, click the Inventory button on the bottom-right of the screen. The Inventory window is made up of two parts:

- ✔ **Menus** allow you access commands that affect your Inventory.

- ✔ **Contents** show what's in your Inventory.

The File menu

The File menu, as shown in Figure 9-2, allows you to work with existing objects and your Inventory as a whole. The File menu options are as follows:

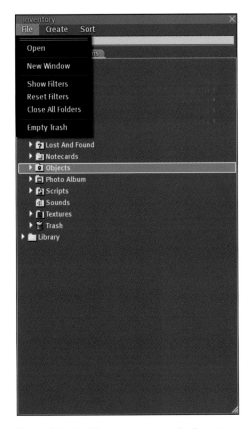

Figure 9-2: The File menu open on the Inventory window.

✔ **Open:** This command opens the properties of a selected object only — it doesn't show properties for folders.

✔ **New Window:** This opens another Inventory window for you. You can open several Inventory windows at once, which helps you with Inventory clean-up. Whatever happens in one window happens in them all instantly.

✔ **Show Filters:** This shows you the Filters dialog box, from which you can filter what you see in your Inventory. Read more about this in the section, "Sorting and filtering objects in your Inventory," later in this chapter.

✔ **Reset Filters:** This turns off all your current filters off so you can see all the objects in your Inventory. Read more about this in the upcoming section, "Sorting and filtering objects in your Inventory."

✔ **Close All Folders:** Sometimes when you're working in your Inventory, you end up with so many folders open that you lose your place. This menu item closes all open folders.

✔ **Empty Trash:** This empties the Trash can for your Inventory: All deleted items are really deleted. For more information, see the section, "Deleting objects in your Inventory," later in this chapter.

Don't empty your Trash without making sure that everything in the special Trash folder is something you never want again. *Always double-check before emptying your Trash.* Because your Inventory has no size limit, there really is no reason to empty your Trash folder.

The Create menu

Use Create menu items to create new objects. Each object is created in your Inventory with a generic name. You can change the name later by right-clicking on the file and choosing rename. The Create menu options are as follows:

✔ **New Folder:** This creates a folder in your Inventory called New Folder. The New Folder is placed by default on the list in alphabetical order, following the system folders of your Inventory. You should rename this folder as soon as you create it. For more on the system folders, see the section, "The My Inventory folder," later in this chapter.

✔ **New Script:** This creates an empty script file and places it in the Scripts folder. To find out more about scripts, check out Chapter 14.

✔ **New Note:** This creates an empty notecard file and places it in the Notecards folder. Second Life also opens the notecard so you can start typing your content right away. To read more about notecards, check out Chapter 13.

✔ **New Gesture:** This creates an empty gesture file and places it in the Gestures folder. For the scoop on gestures, flip to Chapter 16.

- **New Clothes:** Use this to create new clothes. Clothes come in many different forms, so check out the submenu for the specific piece of clothing you want to create. For more on creating clothing, read Chapter 15.

- **New Body Parts:** This allows you to create new body parts. Like clothes, parts come in many different forms. Look for the submenu for the specific body part you want to create. For more on creating body parts, see Chapter 15.

The Sort menu

The Sort menu allows you to control how your Inventory items are listed. The Sort menu options are as follows:

- **By Name:** This sorts objects in your Inventory alphabetically by the name of the objects within each folder.

- **By Date:** This sorts objects in your Inventory based on the date they were created.

- **Folders Always by Name:** This option always sorts the folders by their name.

- **System Folders to Top:** This option ensures that system folders display higher than all other folders in your Inventory. For more on the system folders, see the upcoming section, "The My Inventory folder."

Contents view

As we mention earlier, the Inventory window is made up of two parts: the menus and the contents. The contents section has two tabs: All Items and Recent Items. The All Items tab contains everything in your Inventory, including Recent Items. The Recent Items tab contains only those objects that you received since you logged in for the current SL session. When you log out of SL, the Recent Items tab empties, but the objects are still located in your Inventory and can be seen on the All Items tab.

When you buy something new, don't go searching through your whole Inventory to find it. Start searching in your Recent Items tabs to find it quicker.

Regardless of whether you're on the All Items or Recent Items tab, all folders are contained in one of two main folders — My Inventory or Library.

The My Inventory folder

This is the very first folder listed in your Inventory. It contains every object you have stored. Underneath it are the system folders (special folders created by SL for specific purposes) and then all the folders you create.

There are 12 system folders. (See Figure 9-3; the figure also shows the system folders for the Library folder, discussed in the next section.) These folders are there the very first time you open your Inventory. System folders can't be deleted, but you can put your own items in them. When you create items of these types they will automatically appear in the appropriate system folders. The 12 system folders are as follows:

- **Animations:** This folder contains all animations you import. For more about importing animations, see Chapter 16.

- **Body Parts:** When you create a body part, this is where it ends up. Different icons for different types of body parts (skin, eyes, hair, and so on) help you easily identify them.

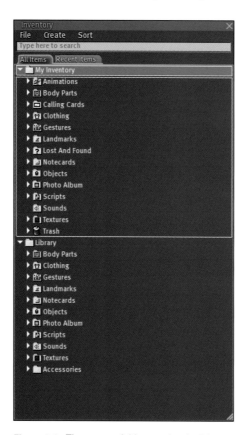

Figure 9-3: The system folders under the My Inventory and Library folders.

- **Calling Cards:** This folder contains all the notecards of your friends and people who have given you a notecard. A notecard is like a shortcut to their profile. You don't have to be friends with a person to have their notecard. To read more about notecards, check out Chapter 13.

- **Clothing:** This is your unlimited walk-in closet. It houses all the clothes you create and buy/get for free. In the beginning, you will just have a female and male shape and outfit. If you are brand-new to SL, this will likely be what you're wearing.

- **Gestures:** Gestures are collections of animations, sounds, chat messages, and wait times (periods of inaction between gestures). These act together to create more life-like avatars. To start, you have a set of common gestures and a folder of gestures related to your gender.

- **Landmarks:** These are like bookmarks for locations. They contain all the information you need to find a place again, including the island name and coordinates. When someone gives you a landmark (or you create one), this is the folder it ends up in. For more on landmarks, see Chapter 4.

- **Lost and Found:** When someone returns one of your objects that you accidentally left behind, this is the folder where the object is placed. While building things in a sandbox, you should be cleaning up any objects you leave lying around, but sometimes you forget. You will get a note when an object is returned to you.

- **Notecards:** When you create a new notecard, it shows up in this folder. When someone gives you a notecard, it is also stored in this folder.

- **Objects:** When you "take" any object in SL, it's automatically stored in this folder. This is a space meant for generic objects that don't fit in any of the other system folders.

- **Photo Album:** When you upload a snapshot, it appears in this folder. For more on taking pictures, see Chapter 7.

- **Scripts:** Any script you create appears in this folder. For more on scripting, check out Chapter 14.

- **Sounds:** This folder contains all the sounds you import. For more about importing sounds, see Chapter 13.

- **Textures:** This folder contains all textures you import. For more about textures, see Chapter 13.

- **Trash:** Like with your computer, when you delete something from your Inventory, it goes in the Trash. This is like the Recycle Bin in Windows or the Trash on a Mac. After an item is in the Trash folder, an item is off your list but not gone forever. You can move it back to your Inventory or empty the trash folder from the File menu.

Because your Inventory has no size limit, there's really no reason to empty the Trash folder.

The Library folder

When you start SL you really have nothing of your own. Second Life does, however, give you a bunch of things, and these things are stored in your Library folder. Essentially, the My Inventory folder contains items you have created or acquired on your own, and the Library folders contains items that SL gave you when you first created you account. The system folders in the Library folder have the same names as the system folders in the My Inventory folder (see the previous section). Take some time and explore these folders. You'll find lots of interesting stuff, such as cars, textures, and useful scripts.

Searching Your Inventory

So Linden Lab gives you this unlimited pocket to hold all your things in and what do you do? Fill it with as much stuff as you can, of course, and then you can't find anything. Well, sort of. You can use the search function to filter your Inventory to show objects that match your search word.

To search your Inventory for an object, follow these steps:

1. **Click the Inventory button on the bottom-right of your screen.**

   This opens your Inventory window. The folders are displayed, just like you left them the last time you were using your Inventory.

2. **In the search box under the Inventory menus, type your search term** (shoes, **for example**).

   The Inventory finds all the objects with this term in the name and displays them, as shown in Figure 9-4. To return the view to normal, just delete the search term.

   You can search both the All Items tab and the Recent Items tab. Just click the tab you want to search before entering the search term.

Working with Objects

After you start to put objects into your Inventory, you'll likely want to start working more directly with them. This section covers some very basic actions you can do with objects in your Inventory that are essential to getting the most out of SL.

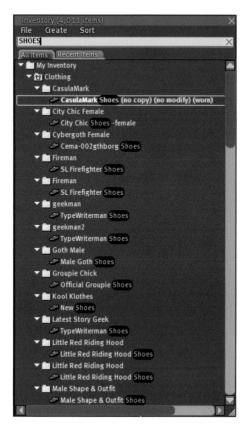

Figure 9-4: An Inventory after a search for shoes.

Understanding object attributes

An *object* is the basic building block in SL. They come in an almost-infinite variety of shapes and sizes. Each object has permissions associated with it that allow you to share, copy/transfer, or modify them. Before you start working with objects, you need to understand the permissions that can be associated with them. To view an object's permissions, right-click on the object and choose edit.

Here's a breakdown of the three object permission types:

✔ **Sharing:** Objects can be shared between residents. This means that you give the actual object to another resident, and you no longer have it. You can also define the permissions that the next owner of the object will have. For instance, if you upload a texture and want to share it with only one friend, you can set permission so that no one can modify, copy, or resell that texture.

✔ **Copying:** Copying objects means creating a version of the object for yourself and leaving the original version. So, the original owner has one version of the object, and you have your very own copy. For example, while doing collaborative building, you might want to share a copyable version of an object with a friend of yours. Make sure that if you're selling the object, you don't allow the next owner to copy it. To set permissions go to Chapter 14.

✔ **Modifying:** This attribute means that you can change the properties of the object. Say you find a near-perfect hair object, but you just want to change this one little part of it. For you to be able to make the change, the object must be modifiable.

Giving and receiving objects

Sometimes you want to share an object with someone in Second Life. First, you have to make sure you can share the object, or you won't be allowed to transfer the object. If the object is share-able, follow these steps to give it to another SL resident:

1. **Find the object in your Inventory.**

2. **Right-click the object and choose Properties.**

   This displays the properties of the object.

3. **Under the Next Owner Can section, make sure that the Resell/Give Away check box is selected.**

   This means you can give someone this object.

4. **Open the profile of the avatar you wish to give the object to by dropping it on the "Place Inventory Items Here" area.**

   This resident does not need to be near you or even online to receive an object.

5. **Drag the object from your Inventory onto the Drop Inventory Item Here area on their profile, as shown in Figure 9-5.**

   A copy of that object is given to that resident. Simple!

You can transfer only one object at a time in this manner. However, if you have the right permissions on all the objects in a folder, you can transfer a folder and all its contents. You are given a notification in SL when the resident accepts or rejects your object.

When someone has been nice enough to give you something, SL tells you what the object was and who gave it to you. You're given the choice to keep it (the object is added to your Inventory) or discard it.

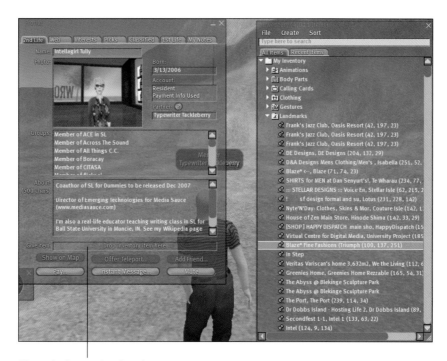

Place the item to be given here.

Figure 9-5: Typewriter is giving Intellagirl a landmark from his Inventory.

If you don't want to know when every single person gives you every single object, you can chose to mute the notifications. We recommend that you keep the notifications on so you know who is giving you what unless you are always getting a huge amount of items.

Deleting objects in your Inventory

Ever find you have multiple copies of the same thing? How many socks can one person own? There may come a time when you want to delete things from your Inventory. Remember that there are no limits to space in your Inventory, so you might not want do this.

When the object is deleted, it is merely moved to the Trash folder in your Inventory. That gets it out of your way, but you can restore it from there or permanently delete it — but why would you when there is no need to do this?

If you absolutely want to delete an item in your Inventory, follow these steps:

1. **In your Inventory, find the object you want to delete.**

2. Right-click the object and choose Delete, as shown in Figure 9-6.

The object is moved to your Trash folder.

The only way to empty your Trash folder is to do it yourself. It's not automatically cleared.

Renaming objects in your Inventory

As we mention earlier, you can end up an Inventory that has a bunch of same-named items. This will hamper your organization and make you crazy when you're trying to find something fast. A good rule is to change the names of any two objects with the same name as soon as you can. You'll be thankful in the long run that you did.

To rename an object in your Inventory, follow these steps:

1. In your Inventory, find the object you want to rename.

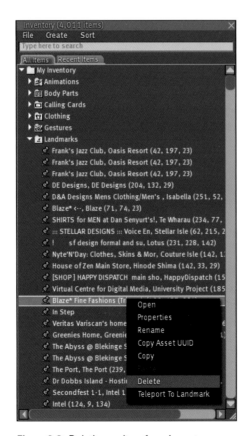

Figure 9-6: Deleting an item from Inventory.

2. **Right-click the object and choose Rename.**

   The name of the object in your inventory becomes editable, as shown in Figure 9-7.

3. **Type in a new name for the object.**

4. **Press Enter.**

   The object now has the new name and is sorted according to what ever sort criteria you have set.

Sorting and filtering objects in your Inventory

The simplest tool you have to organize your SL Inventory is a folder. By putting like items into folders and naming them correctly (known as *sorting*), you can greatly reduce the chaos your Inventory can quickly descend into. Choose Create➪Folder to create a folder, and then give it a useful name. Fill it full of good stuff, and you should see a cleaner Inventory.

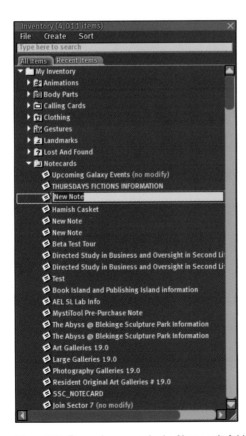

Figure 9-7: Renaming a note in the Notecards folder.

Filters allow you to display only certain types of objects in your Inventory. Say you're looking for a particular texture, but it's not in your Textures folder. You can use the filters to display only the textures in your Inventory. You can also use the filters to show objects based on hours and days old (meaning how much time has passed since you acquired the object).

To use filters to locate an object, follow these steps:

1. **Click the Inventory button on the bottom-right of the screen to open your Inventory.**

2. **Choose File⇨Show Filters.**

   This opens the Filters window beside your Inventory window, as shown in Figure 9-8.

Figure 9-8: The filters appear on the side of your Inventory window.

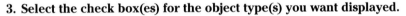
3. **Select the check box(es) for the object type(s) you want displayed.**

   For example, if you want to see only textures, clear all the check boxes but the one beside Textures.

   To select all or none of the check boxes at one time, click the appropriate same-named button.

4. **(Optional) If you want to see the folders while you filter, select the Always Show Folders check box.**

5. **(Optional) If you want to see items that you received since you last logged off, select the Since Logoff check box.**

6. **(Optional) To set the time-sensitive filters for hours and days, use the increase/decrease spinners or enter a specific number for the Hours Ago and Days Ago fields.**

   As you change the filters, your Inventory is automatically filtered according to your criteria.

   If you can't find something in your Inventory, you might have an existing filter applied to the list. Just choose File⇨Reset Filter to make sure that no filters are applied.

Unpacking boxes to acquire objects

Some stores don't sell their items one at a time, but in a box. These boxes might actually look like boxes, or they might look like shopping bags. You need to open these boxes, put the contents in you Inventory, and then store the box.

Don't wear these boxes, or you will look like an avatar with a box on your head — because you will, in fact, be wearing the box on your head.

To open a box and retrieve its contents, follow these steps:

1. **Drop the box on the ground by right-clicking it and clicking Drop.**

   This allows you to open the box.

2. **Right-click the box and choose Open from the radial menu.**

   This shows you the contents of the box and allows you to copy them, as shown in Figure 9-9.

3. **If you're unpacking clothes you want to wear right away, click the Copy and Wear button. If you're unpacking anything other than clothes, click the Copy to Inventory button.**

   You successfully unpacked the box and saved the contents.

Figure 9-9: Unpacking a box of textures.

Understanding the Second Life Economy

In This Chapter

▶ Understanding Linden dollars and the LindeX

▶ Trading on the LindeX

▶ Spending your virtual cash

▶ Bringing home virtual bacon

▶ Getting your weekly stipend

*Y*ou walk by a window of a large department store. Inside, you see the shoes you've been looking for. They look both stylish and comfortable, but then you see the price. You can just afford them if you make a little more money. Sound familiar? When it comes to money, Second Life and your First Life are very similar. There is a currency (called Lindens) and a thriving economy. How you make money is a little different, but it is still fun to spend money, even if it is virtual.

Money, Money, Money! — Linden Dollars and the LindeX

Second Life has a currency, jobs, and lots of products to buy. And just like in your First Life, you need to budget your money, spend it wisely, and try to find ways to earn more.

The Second Life currency is *Linden dollars*. Some people call them *Lindens* or use the *L$* abbreviation. Your L$ balance is located in the top-right of your screen, as shown in Figure 10-1.

Your L$ balance

Figure 10-1: Find your L$ balance here.

You can use this currency in SL to

- Buy resident-created items, such as clothes or buildings.
- Pay other residents for services (scripters, builders, and other careers).
- Upload files, such as graphics or textures to be used in building clothes, buildings, or other objects.
- Upload snapshots you can view outside of SL or send as a postcard.

We talk about how you literally buy things in SL in Chapter 11.

This currency's value exists only in SL. Where it differs from other virtual world currency is that you can trade it on a currency exchange — the *LindeX* — and convert it to currency outside Second Life. Yes, if you make money in Second Life, you can cash it out and pay for real-life stuff! Collect the rent for your virtual real estate, cash it out, and pay your real rent.

Some folks refer to Lindens as play money or Monopoly money. This is and is not true: Currently, the Linden dollar is worth about 30 cents (US). Think of Lindens as coins on your dresser. You start with just a handful of loose change, but before too long, you have a pile of coins and then a bowl full. When you convert that bowl of coins to bills, you're likely stunned how much you actually have there. This is important to keep in mind as you accumulate L$ and then spend them.

Buying and Selling Linden Dollars

Second Life has money in it. Virtual currency that you can, if you wish, trade for real currency. You can buy Second Life dollars (Lindens) in the same way if you were visiting a foreign country and went to a currency exchange. Just because its virtual doesn't mean you shouldn't be careful with your money. It all has value both in Second Life and outside it.

Virtual Wall Street: The LindeX

The *Linden Dollar Exchange, or LindeX,* is a currency exchange run by Linden Lab (see Figure 10-2). This means that you can use real (First Life) money to buy Lindens or to sell Lindens in return for US dollars. The purchase of Linden dollars is charged to the payment method you set up in your account settings (probably a credit card). If you have no payment methods associated with your account, you'll be asked to enter a credit card or PayPal account information. Linden Lab charges a fee for buying or selling Lindens. Consult the Second Life Web site for current fees. At this time there is no fee for buying Linden, and when selling Linden you pay a fee of 3.5% per transaction.

The price per Linden is set by market forces. That is, if someone sells a large number of Lindens for a low price, the price of Lindens goes down. It's about supply and demand.

Even though SL is a very free market, limits are placed on how many Lindens you can trade. These limits protect the LindeX from fraud. How much you can trade depends on whether you are a regular resident, business owner, or day trader.

The current LindeX limits are listed at

```
www.secondlife.com/currency/describe-limits.php
```

To request a change to your limits, contact Linden Lab at

```
http://secondlife.com/currency/request-review.php
```

Figure 10-2: The LindeX is run by Linden Lab.

Buying Linden dollars via the Web

One of the ways you can increase your virtual wealth is buying Lindens from Linden Lab. They offer a currency exchange where you can use a credit card or PayPal to purchase Linden to use in Second Life.

1. **In your Web browser, go to www.SecondLife.com.**

2. **Click the Buy and Sell Lindens button on the left side of the screen, as shown in Figure 10-3.**

   This opens a secure connection to the Linden Lab servers and allows you to buy or sell Lindens.

   If you haven't logged on to the SL Web site with your resident name and password, you are required to do so before any transaction can occur.

3. **To buy Lindens, click the Buy L$ button, as shown in Figure 10-4.**

   This takes you to a page that allows you to use your account settings to purchase Linden dollars.

   If you have no payment information associated with your account, you can't buy or sell Linden dollars.

The Buy and Sell Lindens button

Figure 10-3: Begin buying and selling Lindens on the SL home page.

Click here

Figure 10-4: The Buy L$ button.

4. **Enter the Linden dollar amount you want to buy, or the US$ amount you want to spend, as shown in Figure 10-5.**

   When you enter one amount, the other amount is automatically calculated. For instance, if you enter 1000 (no comma needed) Linden dollars, the equivalent amount and cost in US dollars is calculated and displayed.

5. **Click the Buy Now! Button.**

   This initiates your buy order.

6. **After your purchase is confirmed, click the Place Buy Order button.**

   Your order is made and charged to the payment method you provided with your account. The next time you're in SL, you see that amount of Linden dollars added to your total.

Figure 10-5: Buy Linden dollars with US dollars.

Buying Linden dollars within Second Life

You have finally found the perfect pair of shoes in Second Life and you don't have enough money and you want to buy them NOW! The simplest way to buy currency in Second Life is to do it from within the world.

1. **Click the Buy L$ icon beside your Linden dollar total at the top-right of your screen, as shown in Figure 10-6.**

   The Buying Currency screen appears, which is where you buy Lindens while in SL.

   The Buy L$ icon

   Figure 10-6: The Buy L$ icon appears beside your Linden total.

2. **Enter the Linden dollar amount you want to buy.**

   The Buying currency screen (as shown in Figure 10-7) shows you how many Lindens you have, how many you're buying, and what your new total will be. It also shows you how much approximately the purchase will cost in US dollars.

   When you enter one amount, the other amount is automatically calculated. For instance, if you enter **1000** as Linden dollars, the equivalent amount and cost of those Linden dollars in First Life currency is calculated and displayed.

3. **Click the Purchase button (refer to Figure 10-7).**

   This initiates your buy order. A confirmation screen appears.

4. **After your purchase is confirmed, click OK.**

   Your order is made and charged to the payment information you provided with your account. The amount is added to your SL total.

Selling Linden dollars

To sell Linden dollars, follow these steps:

1. **In your Web browser, go to www.SecondLife.com.**

2. **Click the Buy and Sell Lindens button on the left side of the screen (refer to Figure 10-3).**

   This opens a secure connection to the Linden Lab servers and allows you to buy or sell Lindens.

Figure 10-7: Purchasing Lindens in SL.

If you haven't logged on to the Second Life Web site with your resident name and password, you are required to do so before any transaction can occur.

3. To sell Lindens, click the Sell L$ button (refer to Figure 11-4).

This takes you to a page that allows you to use your account settings to sell Linden dollars.

If you have no payment information associated with your account, you can't buy or sell Linden dollars.

4. Enter the Linden dollar amount you want to sell.

When you enter a Linden dollar amount, the estimated proceeds amount is automatically calculated. For instance, if you enter 1000 Linden dollars, the equivalent amount and return on those Linden dollars is calculated and displayed.

You must sell enough Lindens to equal more than one US dollar, which is around L$300.

5. Click the Sell button.

This initiates your sell order.

6. After your purchase is confirmed, click the Place Sell Order button.

Your order is made and credited to your Second Life account. When you have enough funds, over 100 Linden to make the transaction worthwhile, in your Second Life account, you can cash them out.

Cashing money out of Second Life

Each SL resident account can have money associated with it. This is like money in the bank. This credit can be applied to your fees in SL or cashed out.

When you want to cash out your credit you have three choices:

- ✔ PayPal
- ✔ Domestic check (USA)
- ✔ International check

For each of these options, you might have to accrue a minimum before Linden Lab will send you a check. Each method also requires a few days to be processed.

If you're expecting to make money fast in Second Life, think again. Processing payments and acquiring money takes some time. Read all the information carefully and see how to set up regular payments from your SL proceeds to your bank account to ensure an even cash flow.

Earning Linden Dollars

One of the most common questions asked in Second Life is, "How do I make money?" Unlike a game where you complete a mission to get paid or stumble upon treasure, money in Second Life doesn't come from the environment (unless you buy it) — it comes from the other residents. So, how do you get other people to pay you? Check out the following sections.

Camping

Camping is the easiest (albeit the most boring) way to make money. In Second Life, when residents congregate at a location, its traffic value goes up, making it appear higher in the search rankings. Businesses (dance clubs, malls, bars, and so on) want their locations to look busy and crowded — you know, popular. *Camping* occurs when a business pays residents to basically loiter at their business. This is usually done by sitting in chairs, dancing, or being animated to look like you're cleaning, as shown in Figure 10-8. All you need to do is search for "Camp" to find hundreds of camping locations.

Spending Linden dollars

Money burns a hole in any pocket, be it your jeans pocket or your virtual pocket in Second Life. After you have some cash in SL, a whole new way to interact with the world opens up to you. You can buy a fancy dress or new shoes, or you can hire a builder to build your dream home. For more on spending your Lindens, check out Chapter 11. Like in the real world, though, spending money is a whole lot easier than earning it.

Figure 10-8: Enjoy some time (and make some L$) in camping chairs.

Camping is boring. Most times, you "park" your avatar in a chair in exchange for L$2 every ten or so minutes. It's no way to make a living, but if you plan to just sit and chat with a friend, why not make a little dough while you do it?

Getting a job

Ever want to be a DJ in a club for hundreds of people a night? Or be a security guard? Would you like to be a writer or a dancer? Second Life allows you to have any Second Life job. You can also search for a job in Second Life. Jobs include dancers, escorts, DJs, hosts, party planners, and anything someone else is willing to pay for. You can look in the classified for people offering employment or make friends with someone who hires people. For more information on getting a job and earning money in Second Life, see Chapter 17.

Running your own business

We bet that someone could write an entire book about starting and running a business in Second Life. Your business can be anything from services to unique objects you create from using third-party tools. For more information on starting a business and earning money in Second Life, see Chapter 17.

Getting Your Weekly Stipend

If you have a Premium account in Second Life, you get a signup bonus and weekly stipend.

A Premium account is one in which you pay a monthly fee of US$9.95. Currently, the signup bonus is L$1,000, and the stipend is L$300 weekly. This stipend is automatically deposited into your account, so it's kind of like getting paid. The stipend is paid on the day of the week when you started your account. There is no stipend for any other type of account.

Because Linden Lab occasionally tweaks the economy of Second Life, these bonus and stipend amounts can change. Don't depend on them.

If you assign a credit card to a free Basic account, you are given a one-time bonus of L$250 45 days after you join.

Referring a Friend

You can receive a L$2000 bonus if you refer a friend who signs up for a Premium account. You can refer people by

- **Sending postcards:** Sending postcards from within the game to friends. To send a postcard in world hit Ctrl+Shift+S.

- **Building a Second Life URL:** Using a SLURL to direct people to a part of Second Life from the Web.

- **Using the Refer-a-Friend form:** A form that sends a direct message from you to your friends inviting them to Second Life. The URL is `http://secondlife.com/community/referral_form.php`.

- **Create your own URL:** Placing a URL on your Web site that has people sign up for Second Life.

For more information go to the Refer-A-Friend! Program page - `http://secondlife.com/community/referral.php`.

After your friend passes certain milestones, you get a bonus totaling L$2000. Some of the milestones include

- The beginning of the referee's second billing cycle

- One month after first payment

- One month after second credit

Spending Your Cash in Second Life

In This Chapter

▶ Spending Linden dollars

▶ Finding the best stuff to buy

▶ Going virtual bargain shopping

▶ Leaving tips for services

▶ Cover charges

▶ The service industry

▶ Importing files into SL

*T*he creative nature of Second Life is one of its defining qualities. Your ability to create an avatar, customized to your every whim — or owning a virtual home, complete with your every heart's desire — isn't mere fun. It's what makes the Second Life economy go 'round. Without the need to drive from store to store, pay shipping, or compete for limited quantities of goods, shopping in Second Life has all the fun of real life — with none of the hassles. So, go on — shop 'til you virtually drop!

This chapter covers how to spend your money by finding the best places to shop, giving others tips, or paying for services. IT also covers uploading files in Second Life that will also cost you a small fee.

What Should I Buy?

The short, sweet, and simple answer to the question of what an avatar needs to buy is this: Nothing. You're not required to buy anything in Second Life. However, you won't know what you might be missing until you see what's for sale, so do some browsing. Window shopping is free, and you never know what you might find. Most SL residents spend a majority of their cash outfitting their avatars. Your avatar is how you are known — how you primarily express who you are — and dressing in crazy ways is just plain fun. Explore and experiment. After all, in SL, everything fits, nothing needs to be dry-cleaned, and not even the worst haircut is permanent. For more on customizing your avatar, see Chapter 5.

Buying Things

The most common way of purchasing things in Second Life is at a store. Like at a typical mall, these stores (see Figure 11-1) sell a huge range of products that appeal to all tastes and budgets.

Most stores operate on the same principle: using a large open area with signs on the walls. These signs, as seen in Figure 11-2, advertise the products that the stores sell. These signs also act as points of sale: That is, the sign itself sells the product. By touching the sign and selecting from the radial menu that appears, you can buy items. These signs are sometimes called *vendors:* in this context, an object that sells other objects.

Figure 11-1: GuRL 6, one of the largest stores in Second Life.

Finding stores and vendors

You find stores in SL the same way you find anything else — with the powerful Search function. Just enter what you are looking for and the most popular stores will show up. For more information on searching, see Chapter 4.

A vendor sign

Figure 11-2: A vendor sign.

Buying an item

After you find a store, browse its merchandise, and decide on a product, it's time to purchase the item. To buy an item in a store, follow these steps:

1. **Find the item you want to buy.**

   For instance, say you want a hair style. Try a shop like Gurl6 and find the sign with the hairdo you like, as shown in Figure 11-3.

2. **Right-click the sign and choose Buy from the radial menu.**

   Before you buy, always inspect what you are about to get:

   a. *Right-click the vendor.*

   b. *Choose Edit.*

   c. *Click the Contents tab.*

      This will let you see exactly what you're going to get for your money.

3. **The contents of the vendor are displayed (see Figure 11-4), and you are asked whether you want to buy it or cancel the transaction.**

Figure 11-3: This looks like a good hairstyle.

Selecting the Wear Clothing Now option allows you to wear the clothes instantly. On the surface, this sounds like a good idea because you don't have to search through your Inventory to find the items you just bought. But (and this is a big but), sometimes this can lead to wearing the box the item comes in rather than the item itself, leading to a situation more embarrassing than your average dressing room snafu.

Under the contents description, you can see the item price. Be sure to pay close attention to how much you're paying for an item.

4. To buy the item, click the Buy button.

You see a message that the person selling the item received payment and that the item is now in your inventory.

Not a lot of consumer protection is available in Second Life. In fact, there is no system in place for it. If you purchase something and get nothing in return, double-check your inventory and then contact the seller to see whether the vendor (the sign) is malfunctioning. In most situations, the seller will provide you with the item and fix the vendor. If you end up being out a lot of money, try contacting the seller before contacting Linden Lab about the situation. Also, know that item delivery can be delayed if SL is particularly busy or if the system has just been updated. Be patient and don't assume the worst.

Whom am I paying?

All transactions in Second Life take place between two residents. So, even if you buy a new car from a vendor sign with no one near, the transaction is still between you and the owner of that object. The owner of the object doesn't even need to be online. Whenever you do any transaction, Second Life tells you whom you are paying and how much you paid. The seller sets the price, you click the Buy button, and SL takes care of the rest. No standing in line, no credit cards, no shipping, and no exact change needed.

Figure 11-4: Check what you're getting before you pay.

Finding the Best Stuff to Buy

Don't you just hate it when you see someone else wearing the jacket you've been trying to find for months? The pursuit to find the best things for yourself is always happening. And with new things constantly appearing in SL, keeping track of the latest and greatest is sometimes difficult. Here are some things you can do to stay on top of (and ahead of) the latest trends:

✔ **Just ask.** If you see another avatar with a hairdo, a piece of clothing, or an object that you want, just ask her where she got it. Most people are happy to give you the landmark of the shop where they purchased things. If no one is around and you want to know where to buy the cool car you found, right-click it, choose Edit, and then find the creator of the object. (You might not be able to do this, depending on permissions.) Figure 11-5 shows an object's Properties with the Owner listed. Click the Profile button next to the creator's name and check out the Picks tab. Often, a retailer will list his own store in his picks. If you don't see a store in the picks, IM the creator and ask for a landmark to the store.

✔ **Join the group.** Some stores in Second Life have groups associated with them. For instance, if we ran a tattoo shop, we would have a group for people who liked our products. We would make it free to join. And, when we had sales or new releases, we would send out a group notice so that people would know that new merchandise was available. If your favorite shop doesn't have a group, suggest it to the owner. For more about groups, read Chapter 7.

The object's Owner

Figure 11-5: Finding the Owner of an object.

✔ **Read about it.** Second Life has several shopping magazines. These include fashion, car, and programming magazines that give you reviews of products. Flipping through the pages of one of these magazines should give you tons of ideas of what would interest you. Or, better yet, try to get a job working for one of these magazines to help you learn where the best products are before anyone else does. Use your Search function to look for magazine locations.

Bargain Shopping

What is the best cost for a pair of shoes? Lots of people in Second Life spend a great deal of time looking for the best bargain they can get. The best price is, of course, free. Tons of free items abound in Second Life. They aren't the latest fashions, gestures, or scripts, but they are free — and who doesn't like free?

How do you find free things? The simplest answer to this question is to look around. The best places to find free stuff are sometimes called *junk yards,* as shown in Figure 11-6. Junk yards offer boxes and boxes of tons of free items of every sort. Each box usually contains many items of a certain type. For instance, you might find a box of furniture to decorate with. It might have 5 couches, some chairs, and 15 different lamps in it. You "buy" the box like any other purchase, but it usually costs only L$0 or L$1. Junk yards usually contain objects made by designers who weren't exactly happy with their results or who removed the item from their store to make room for other merchandise.

Figure 11-6: YadNi's junk yard, one of the best in Second Life.

If you're a new resident with very little L$, junk yards are the way to go. We've met lots of people who have amazing outfits, animations, and objects that they found for free. You just need to take the time to look around and see what's available. Also try searching for "Newbie" in the All tab.

Be wary of listings for Garage Sales or Yard Sales. Although these events can offer some good deals, they're often gimmicks posed just to drive traffic to a store or dance club. Buyer, beware!

Paying for Things Other than Items

You don't always have to buy something in Second Life to spend money. You can also tip people or pay for other services. There is no regulation of this activity in Second Life so be careful.

Tip jars

Most clubs with dancers or performers have tip jars, as shown in Figure 11-7. The money paid to these jars might go to one performer or to the "house" to be shared by everyone. A tip jar allows you to pay people through an object. All you need to do is right-click the object and choose Pay — it acts like paying a resident.

Tip jars are a good way for you to express your appreciation of an art gallery, a musical performance, or other service that you might not be required to pay for.

When you tip a person, he might not get the full amount. The establishment he works for might take a cut of what's put in the tip jar. If this is the case, most times, you will be told that you're not directly paying the person you're tipping. If you have any questions, ask the performer or club owner.

Cover charges

Cover charges are rare in Second Life, but they do occur. Essentially, when you enter certain areas, you're asked to pay a cover charge. If you pay the charge, you can enter the area. If you don't want to pay, that's your choice.

If someone comes up to you and just asks for a cover charge without warning, don't pay it! Also, beware of excessive cover charges. Anything over L$300 or so is too steep for club admission. However, don't let the cover charge put you off. Often times, really great environments have a cover charge to prevent the space from becoming overcrowded or attracting the wrong crowd.

A tip jar

Figure 11-7: A DJ might set out a tip jar.

Paying for services

Second Life is full of experts in all kinds of fields. Maybe you'd like someone to give you a tour, teach you a skill, be a personal shopper, or even be your date for the night. Paying other residents for a service is easy. Like with any transaction, use caution when hiring services.

To pay someone directly for a service, follow these steps:

1. **Go to the person's profile by right-clicking on their avatar and choosing Profile from the menu, and click the Pay button.**

   This opens the Pay Resident window, as shown in Figure 11-8. Here, you can choose a preset amount or enter your own amount.

   You can also get to the Pay Resident screen by right-clicking an avatar and choosing Pay from the radial menu that appears.

2. **Enter or select the amount to be paid and then click the Pay button.**

   After you give someone a payment, you can't reverse it. If you give someone a larger amount of money than you intended, you're stuck.

Figure 11-8: Pay for services here in Second Life.

Importing files

When you import images, sounds, or animations into Second Life, you're charged L$10 for the file upload. This helps Linden Lab offset its storage costs. You can upload the files one at a time or use the bulk loader to bring several files at once. See Chapter 13 for more information on uploading files. You use these files as graphics and textures while building items.

Staking Your Claim in Second Life

In This Chapter

▶ Renting a house or apartment

▶ Setting Land Permissions

▶ Finding and decorating a house

▶ Dealing with unwanted guests (freezing, banning, and ejecting)

*E*verybody needs a home. A place to call your own is important to giving you a sense of belonging in Second Life. It also gives you another opportunity to be as creative as you want to be. You can rent an apartment or a house, rent land and build your own house, or buy your own island and make your own world. In this chapter we show you how to do all of this.

Finding a Place to Rent

You can rent space in SL, either for your own personal use or for your business. Renting space is not done through Linden Lab but as an agreement between two avatars. There is no formal lease policy or contract. Most landlords prefer you to pay for a month ahead of time, but some let you pay by the week. You are given access to a locked home or apartment and allowed to drop items there. After you stop paying rent, it is between you and the landlord as to what happens to your stuff.

 Before renting any property, ask the landlord for referrals from other tenants so you can see what kind of person you are doing business with. Always be cautious and ask many questions.

To find a rental property, follow these steps:

1. **Click the Search button on the bottom of your screen.**

2. **Select the Classifieds tab, and select the Land Rental category from the drop-down list, as shown in Figure 12-1.**

Figure 12-1: Rental properties are listed.

3. **Click the Browse button and start looking for your new rental property.**

4. **Once you have found something you like, contact the owner of the property and ask about rental policies.**

Buying Land

Buying land in SL is completely different from renting. You can buy land from other SL residents, but you can also buy land from Linden Lab directly. Both have different benefits and limitations. Before you buy land, ask yourself a few basic questions:

🠒 Do I really need to buy land, or can I rent something that meets my needs?

🠒 If I buy empty land, who will do the building on it? Will I do the building, someone I hire, or will I buy a finished building?

🠒 Should I own the land by myself or with a group?

🠒 Who should I allow onto my land?

🠒 Can I afford the costs to buy and maintain the land?

As we go through the following sections we will answer these questions and give you the tools to make the best of your land owning experience.

Land types

Second Life has a few different land types that have some specific rules applied to them. The types are:

- ✔ **Mainland Land:** This land is owned and run by Linden Labs. If you want to buy land here you need to deal with Linden Labs or someone who has bought from Linden Labs.

- ✔ **Private Estates:** This land is private islands purchased by individuals or companies from Linden Lab and is separated by water from the main land.

Should I buy from a resident or from Linden?

There are benefits and limitations in buying land from a resident or from Linden Lab. If you buy land from a resident, you can get a custom-sized piece of land and possibly a non-standard rate. There is no set amount to pay for land purchased from another resident, so you should shop around to find the best deal. You can also pay the resident directly so you don't have to use your account payment method. The problems can be that people sell you land at inflated prices, put neighbors beside you that you might not like, and disappear leaving you in the lurch. If you are looking to buy an entire island or wish to access educational discounts, you need to purchase land through Linden Lab.

To buy land from another Second Life resident, follow these steps:

1. **Click the Search button on the bottom of your screen.**

2. **Click the Land Sales tab, shown in Figure 12-2.**

3. **Select a type of land from the Type drop-down list. The types are**

   - **Auction:** Land that is being auctioned off.

   - **For Sale – Mainland:** Land that is being sold from the Linden Lab mainland servers.

   - **For Sale – Estate:** The sale of land from a private island.

   - **All Types:** This searches for all types of land.

4. **Select a rating for the land from the Ratings drop-down list. The ratings are PG Only, Mature Only, and PG & Mature.**

5. **Enter the price lower or equal to the Linden dollars you are willing to pay for land.**

6. **Enter the size in square meters you want to buy.**

7. **Click the Search button to find land that matches your criteria.**

8. **If you find land you like, contact the estate owner and buy from them.**

Figure 12-2: The Land Sales tab.

Purchasing land from Linden means you will be paying a set rate for a set plot of land. You also have to pay a monthly land use fee that is determined by how much land you bought. This is charged to the payment method associated with your account. You get access to Linden Lab support, but you also get the headache of having to call them if something goes wrong. Purchasing islands can only be done through Linden Lab. If you are purchasing an island for an educational institution, Linden Lab offers an educational discount. Also, to buy land through Linden you must have a Premium account, which is an additional monthly fee.

To buy land from Linden Lab, follow these steps:

1. **Go to** www.secondlife.com.

2. **Click the Get Virtual Land link.**

   This link is located on the left-side of the SL homepage, just below the Buy and Sell Linden Dollars link.

3. **From here, follow the links to buy land or islands/regions.**

Read over the Linden Lab land ownership page (http://secondlife.com/whatis/land.php) and talk to some folks selling land. Ask lots of questions and don't spend any hard-earned cash until you are sure it is what you want.

How much land should I buy?

Determining how much land you need is really dependant on what you are going to use the land for. If you just want a small place to call home, something like a 512 meter squared plot should work just fine. If you have bigger plans like your own shop or entertainment complex, you should consider larger plots of land. Also, if you are concerned with security and neighbors, you might consider buying an island. An island gives you a huge amount of space (more than 65,000 square meters) and up to 15,000 prims.

The number of prims you can use on any given area of land is limited. Though the number of prims might sound like a lot at first, you can quickly use up all of them, making it a pain to do anything new. Practice low prim building and prim conservation whenever possible. For more on building, see Chapter 13.

Caring about the neighbors

It's easy to think you don't need to care about neighbors in SL, but they can have a huge effect on your land-owning experience. For instance, say you buy a nice plot of land for your business in SL. You didn't pay much attention to the rating on the island because it was empty, but as you keep logging in stores near yours start selling things of a nature you don't like. Or worse, someone just builds an ugly, touristy building right by your work of art. Pay attention to the rating of your land and ask the person you are buying the land from what policies they have.

Owning land as a group

You can own land as an individual or as a group. Group ownership means anyone in that group has the same land permissions as any other member in the group. This can make it more affordable for people to own land, but it also means you are not the only one making decisions about the land. Additionally, you can donate (deed) land to a group but remain the person responsible for paying for it.

When you have a group and decide to share land it is a very complicated process. It differs between mainland and estate land, and if your group has a mix of both, some tools may not be available to you. Land ownership and permissions involving groups shouldn't be entered into lightly. Do your research on the SL Web site and the SL wiki.

Setting your Home location

One of the benefits of owning or renting land is being able to set a spot as your Home. Setting your spot as *Home* means you can quickly return to that spot by using a shortcut key (Ctrl+Shift+H) or selecting Teleport Home from the

World menu. To do this, infohubs are a holdover from the old teleportation system and are welcome areas on the mainland. Search for "infohub" to find one.

Setting Land Permissions

So now that you've bought a piece of land, what are you going to do with it? Well, pretty much whatever you want. One thing you have to decide on is your *land permissions.* This defines who can access and build on your land.

You can use two tools to control your land: the About Land tool, which sets access, permission, and object limits on your land, and the Region/Estate tool, which controls what your land looks like and some of the same permissions as the About Land tool. Through effective use of these tools, you can obtain the setting on your land that you want.

To make things easier, for this section we assume that you own the entire region (sometimes called an island or sim). If you purchase a parcel of land from Linden Lab or a resident, you may not have access to all these features.

Using the About Land tool

The About Land tool is used by a land owner to control their land. This includes controlling access, permissions, bans, and other things. If something is grayed out on your About Land tool, you haven't been given permission to use it when you bought the land.

To open the About Land tool, follow these steps:

1. **Find a portion of the ground on the area you own.**

   This sounds simple, but it can be difficult. The floor of a building doesn't count, so we suggest you look for grass.

2. **Right-click on the ground and select About Land from the radial menu.**

   This opens the About Land tool.

The About Land tool has several tabs, covered in the follow sections.

The General tab

The General tab (shown in Figure 12-3) shows you the most basic information about the land. This includes the name of the land, description, and who owns it. For instance, if you find a great building but there is no one around and you want to know where to get one like it, look on this tab to see who owns the land and message them. If the land is for sale, you can also buy it through this tab.

Figure 12-3: The About Land tool's General tab.

The Covenant tab

If you want to sell your land to other people, you can set up what is called a *covenant.* The Covenant tab (shown in Figure 12-4) helps you set up rules and zoning on the land you sell. You can also keep or give privileges to the next owner. A covenant on your land gives prospective buyers an idea of how your land sales work and what rights they will retain. After you have decided on a covenant, it is a good practice to keep as close to the original as possible. You should definitely include the rating of the area and any themes that the area has.

If you are thinking of including a covenant on your land, look around at other covenants and research them online.

The Objects tab

The Objects tab (shown in Figure 12-5) shows you how many prims or objects are on your land. It gives the total number of prims that are on the parcel of land and the maximum amount of prims available. There are also prim numbers for the parcel owner, a group if one is associated with the land, and ones owned by others. This tab also shows you how many items are currently selected.

This tab also allows you to set a number of minutes to autoreturn other residents' objects. Autoreturn means that after a set period of time objects dropped by people in an area, like a sandbox, are returned to them automatically. Always remember to clean up when you are building things to minimize autoreturns. You can turn it to 0, which means no objects are auto returned or enter a number of minutes.

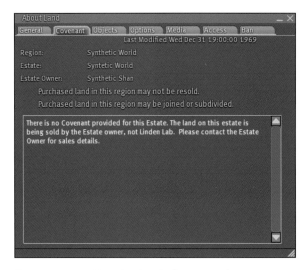

Figure 12-4: The About Land tool's Covenant tab.

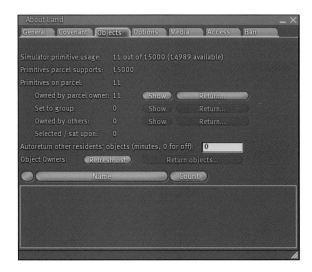

Figure 12-5: The About Land tool's Objects tab.

The bottom of the screen shows all owners of objects on the sim and how many they have.

The Options tab

The Options tab (shown in Figure 12-6) allows you to make a number of settings that allow or prohibit certain behaviors on your land. These settings include

- **Edit Terrain:** This allows other residents to change the shape of your land. Unless the sim is for the training of how to change land, you should keep this off.

- **Create Landmarks:** This allows other residents the ability to create landmarks on your land.

- **Fly:** This allows residents to fly or not on your land.

- **Create Objects:** This allows other residents or groups to create objects on your parcel of land.

- **Object Entry:** This setting allows you to stop anyone from bringing any object onto your land. Unless you are worried about griefing or trash, you should not turn this off.

- **Run Scripts:** This setting allows other residents to run scripts. Unless you have some reason to do so, we would turn this off or restrict it to a certain group.

- **Land Options – Safe:** This means avatars can't take damage. *Damage* is based on a health point system. Certain objects like weapons can do damage to you if this option is on. If you loose all your health you are returned to your home location and all your health is restored.

- **Land Options – Show in Search:** This shows the land when a search for it is run. You will need to pay L$30/week for this service.

- **Land Options – Mature Content:** This marks the land as having mature content so people can include or exclude it in searches.

- **Land Options – Restrict Pushing:** This stops people from being able to use weapons or scripts to push people around on the land.

- **Land Options – Publish listing on the web:** This publishes a listing about the land on the SL Web site.

- **Snapshot:** Add a picture here to represent your land.

- **Landing Point:** If defined, the landing point is where people appear on the island when they teleport to the island from the map. If none is defined people can teleport anywhere on the island. You should set this to a focal point of your land, like the front door of a shop or in front of a navigation teleport board. This is a board that has several teleport points in an area on it and lets you click on them to go there.

- **Teleport Routing:** You can block all teleportation to the island or allow people to teleport anywhere on the island or only to the landing point.

The Media tab

The Media tab (shown in Figure 12-7) controls the multimedia of your land. You can set the media stream texture to use when streaming videos in. You can also set the music URL for sim music. This section also includes settings for voice.

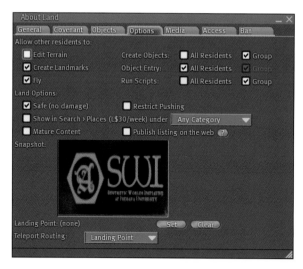

Figure 12-6: The About Land tool's Options tab.

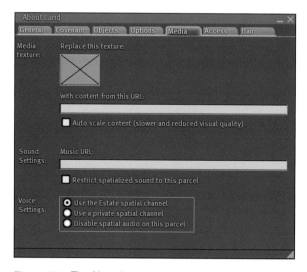

Figure 12-7: The About Land tool's Media tab.

The Access tab

The Access tab (shown in Figure 12-8) limits access to your land. If you are planning to restrict access, form a group (it is much easier to maintain a group than to list the avatars individually) and use that to control access. You can also sell temporary land passes here. A land pass allows you to charge for temporary access to your land.

Figure 12-8: The About Land tool's Access tab.

The Ban tab

The Ban tab (shown in Figure 12-9) allows you to permanently ban certain avatars from your land. You can also deny people access based on the payment method (or lack of one) associated with their account.

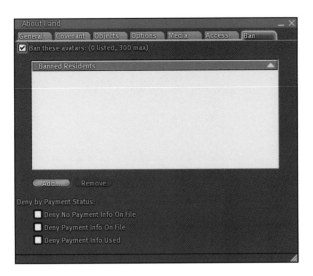

Figure 12-9: The About Land tool's Ban tab.

Using the Region/Estate tool

The Region/Estate tool is a more advanced type of tool for land management. To open it, select World➪Region/Estate. There are a number of items exactly the same as the About Land tool, so we only cover the differences. The Region/Estate tool also has several tabs, covered in the follow sections.

The Region tab

The Region tab (shown in Figure 12-10) has many similar parameters as the About Land tool. You can teleport users or everyone home and also message the entire region from this screen.

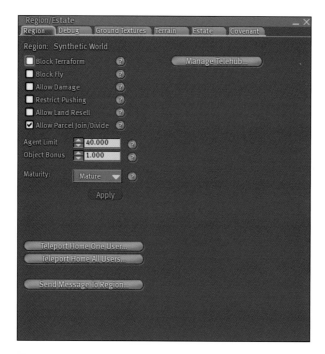

Figure 12-10: The Region/Estate tool's Region tab.

The Debug tab

The Debug tab (shown in Figure 12-11) is the most technical of the tabs on the Region/Estate tool. Its purpose is to give you high-level control over scripts and objects on your sim. Nothing should be changed here unless you are experiencing problems with scripts, colliders, or physics. Colliders and physics are related to objects that move and interact with avatars. Finally, you can *restart* your region here. This means the server that runs your sim will be automatically restarted. Everyone will be kicked off the sim and moved to the next available one. All objects will remain. The time it takes to restart can vary wildly, so only do this as a last resort of problems.

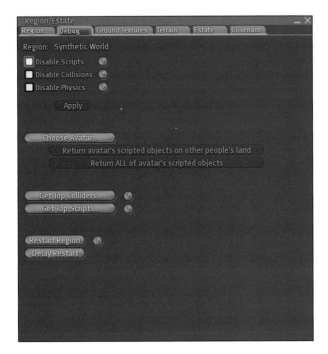

Figure 12-11: The Region/Estate tool's Debug tab.

The Ground Textures tab

The Ground Textures tab (shown in Figure 12-12) allows you to define the textures of the land based on its elevation. This gives the land a natural feel.

The Terrain tab

The Terrain tab (shown in Figure 12-13) allows you to set water levels and where the sun is. You can specify the sun's position or let it change based on the estate time. Also, you can import a raw file here to make custom land, as seen in Figure 12-14.

The Estate tab

The Estate tab (shown in Figure 12-15) reproduces information from the About Land tool. It also puts some commonly changed functions, like access and time, in one spot for you to use.

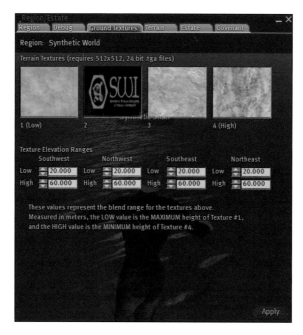

Figure 12-12: The Region/Estate tool's Ground tab.

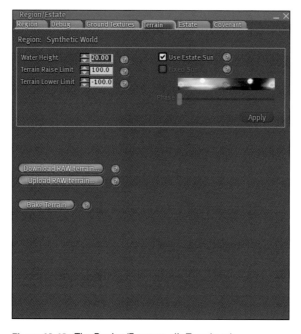

Figure 12-13: The Region/Estate tool's Terrain tab.

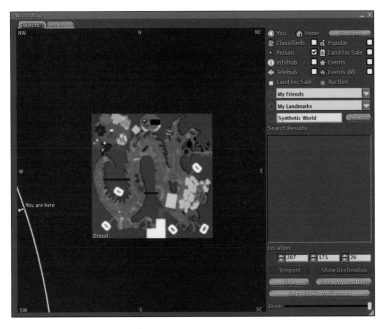

Figure 12-14: An example of custom-created land.

Figure 12-15: The Region/Estate tool's Estate tab.

The Covenant tab

This is the same as the Covenant tab on the About Land tool.

Dealing with Unwanted Guests — Freezing, Ejecting, and Banning

Sometimes you may have some unwelcome guests on your sim. Don't panic! You have a wealth of tools you can use to control the situation. You can freeze them, eject them, or ban them.

- **Freeze:** This stops the person from moving or interacting with other people on the sim for 30 seconds.

- **Ejecting:** Ejecting an avatar makes them leave the sim entirely. They can return right away but they have to come back to the sim.

- **Banning:** Banning an avatar doesn't allow them to return. To allow people back on the sim, you have to remove them from the ban list.

All of these should be used with caution, but if you have someone on your land who you don't want, make sure they are out of there.

To freeze a resident, follow these steps:

1. **Right-click an avatar and choose More from the radial menu.**
2. **Click Freeze from the radial menu.**

To eject or ban a resident, follow these steps:

1. **Right-click an avatar and choose More from the radial menu.**
2. **Click Eject from the radial menu.**

   You are then given the choice to eject or to ban a resident. If you ban someone, they have to be removed from the ban list before they are allowed to return to the sim. To remove someone from the banned list, open the About Land dialog box and click the ban tab. Then select their name and click remove. They are no longer banned.

Part IV
Building and Customizing

The 5th Wave   By Rich Tennant

"Sometimes I feel behind the times. I asked my 11-year old to build a Second Life store for my business, and he said he would, only after he finishes the one he's building for himself."

What makes Second Life better than many other virtual spaces is the ability to create content. Whether it's your dream house, that dress you can't afford in the real world, or a fly dance move from the latest music video, you can create your world — in Second Life.

Chapter 13 starts you off with basic building skills. Building is a little tough, but we take you through each and every menu to get you on your way. In Chapter 14, you see how to augment the objects you build with scripts to add interactivity. Lamps that turn on when touched, talking signs, working elevators . . . your imagination is the limit, and you don't have to be a programmer to figure out how it all works.

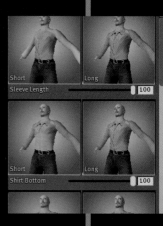

The clothes make the man, right? But who is the (wo)man making the clothes? You, that's who. Chapter 15 gets you started making the custom clothes of your dreams. Why settle for the fashions you can buy in stores when you can express your own personal style? Then, to show off your creations, why not create some custom poses and animations so you can flaunt them? See how in Chapter 16.

Building Basics

*W*ith the exceptions of the oceans and land, and basic avatars everything in Second Life (SL) — every beach, every mansion, every car, and every boat — has been built by residents just like you. Yes, you can make your own pirate ship, castle (see Figure 13-1), or luxury loft. Anything is possible with just a few skills.

If You Build It, They Will Come

Building in SL is one of the most amazing parts of SL. It's as if you have an unlimited box of customizable building bricks and blocks that you can use to build anything. You are limited only by your imagination and where you are building things.

Who made all this?

The first thing you need to realize about building in Second Life is that everything you see — except for basic avatars — was created by users. The amazing cityscapes, the cars, and the fantastic clothes and hair are all user-created. So what the heck are all these things made from? The answer is primitives, or *prims*.

Figure 13-1: Build yourself a home like this.

What are prims?

A *prim* is the most basic building block in Second Life. It can come in a number of basic shapes that can be modified on a prim-by-prim basis. When combined with other prims, you can build a near-infinite amount of combinations and creations. When you click a prim, you see faint blue lines around the individual prims. Prims can have color, texture, and different luminosities. Prims can also be linked to make more complex shapes.

Because everything is made from prims, start by understanding the basic shapes (shown in Figure 13-2). Right-click a piece of land and choose Create from the radial menu.

Table 13-1 lists the basic SL prim shapes.

Table 13-1	Basic Prim Shapes
Shape	**Image**
Cube	
Prism	

Shape	Image
Cylinder	
Sphere	
Torus	
Tube	
Ring	
Sculpted	

Combined and modified, these eight shapes make up every prim in Second Life.

Figure 13-2: Viewing the basic prim shapes.

Where can I build?

Sure, you can build any*thing* you want in Second Life, but you might not be able to build it any*where* you want. If you see the No Build icon (as shown in Figure 13-3) on the top of your screen, the region you're in has turned off your ability to build. This is set by the owner of the region. For more information on land permissions go to Chapter 12.

The No Build icon

Figure 13-3: This icon means you can't build on this land.

Mastering Prims

Building begins by seeing how to create basic prims, change their shape, and combine them. To build and work with prims, you need to be in Edit mode, where you can create and modify prims.

To turn on Edit mode and create a prim, follow these steps:

1. **Click the Build button on the bottom of the screen.**

   The Build Tool appears, and your cursor becomes a wand.

   You can also open the Build tool by choosing Tools⇨Select Tool⇨Create.

2. **Click the ground.**

   Your first prim appears. The default shape is a cube.

3. **To make different shapes, select the Shape button.**

4. **Now click on the ground with the Wand tool.**

   The shape you selected now appears.

Public sandboxes are spaces made just for builders. If you want an open place to build, search for Sandbox and teleport to one of these open spaces. For more on teleporting, see Chapter 4.

Using the Build Tools

The Build tool is what you use to move, rotate, stretch, and configure prims. This section examines each of the five aspects of the Build tool.

Mastering the camera controls while building is essential. This allows you to see the prim that you're creating from many angles as well as how it relates to other prims around it. To get a better look at a prim, turn on your camera controls (choose View⇨Camera Controls) and look around a bit. For more on camera controls, see Chapter 4.

Focus

Use the Focus tool (as shown in Figure 13-4) to change your camera focus with your mouse. When you use this tool, your cursor turns into a square magnifying glass with a plus sign in it. Clicking your screen changes focus to that area of the screen. This is similar to the camera controls but the object is always the central focus while the camera controls have no central focus.

The three Focus modes are

- **Zoom:** Use the slider or your mouse scroll-wheel to zoom in or out.

- **Orbit:** This mode allows you to orbit the camera around the focus point. Be careful; this ride can be a bit wild, so don't eat first.

- **Pan:** This mode pans the camera back and forth based on mouse movements.

Figure 13-4: The Focus menu of the Build tool.

Move

The Move tool (as shown in Figure 13-5) allows you to move a prim with your mouse. When you use this tool, your cursor changes to a white hand. The three modes for this tool are

- **Move:** This mode moves this prim based on mouse movements on the X and Y coordinates. This means you don't move the prim up, down, forward, and back.

- **Lift:** This mode moves the prim up and down on the Z axis.

- **Spin:** This mode spins (turns the prim on an axis) the prim in three dimensions.

Edit

Use the Edit tool (as shown in Figure 13-6) to edit a prim. When this tool is selected, the selected prim highlights in a light blue color, and three arrows appear. The red, blue and green arrows move and shape the prim. The X, Y, and Z coordinates of the prim appear at the top of the screen. The following sections discuss the five Edit modes available to you when using the Edit tool.

Figure 13-5: The Move menu of the Build tool.

Figure 13-6: The Edit menu on the Build tool.

You're working in three dimensions here. This means that you can move a prim forward or back, right or left, and up or down. These are represented by the X, Y, and Z coordinates, respectively. You might get a little frustrated at first, but the more you build, the more you get used to working in three dimensions.

Position

In Position mode, you can move your prim in three dimensions. This gives you more information about the exact location of the prim than the Move mode of the Move tool. To use Position mode to position a prim, follow these steps:

1. **Right-click a prim and choose Edit from the radial menu.**

   The Edit tool appears, with Position mode selected by default. The prim's positioning arrows are displayed as well, as shown in Figure 13-7.

2. **Click one of the colored arrows running through the prim and then drag the prim to its new position.**

   Note the arrows (sometimes called *handles*) that are close to each other, like corners. These handles allow you to move two dimensions at once.

Rotate

Use Rotate mode to rotate your prim in three dimensions. This gives you more information than using Spin mode of the Move tool. To use Rotate mode to rotate a prim, follow these steps:

1. **Right-click a prim and choose Edit from the radial menu.**

   The Edit tool appears.

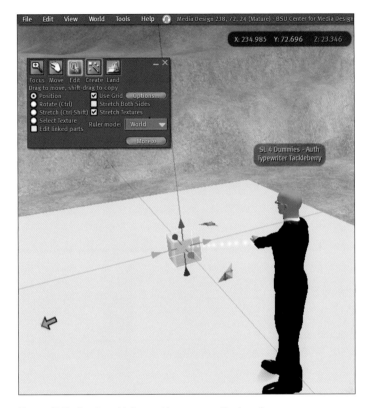

Figure 13-7: A prim with its position arrows displayed.

2. Select the Rotate radio button.

Colored arcs appear around the prim, as shown in Figure 13-8.

3. Click one of the colored arcs running around the prim and then drag the prim to its new rotation.

Stretch

Use Stretch mode to stretch the size of your prim in three dimensions. Here's how:

1. Right-click a prim and choose Edit from the radial menu.

The Edit tool appears.

2. Select the Stretch radio button.

Colored points appear around the prim, as shown in Figure 13-9.

Figure 13-8: A prim with its rotation lines displayed.

3. **Click one of the colored points running around the prim and then drag the prim to its new size.**

   By dragging the white stretch points, you can stretch the shape equally in three directions.

Select Textures

Use Select Textures mode to assign textures to the prim as a whole or on each of its faces. The exact method of adding textures is covered later in this chapter in the section, "Selecting Colors and Textures."

Edit options

Five edit options are also available via the Edit tool. These options are check boxes (instead of radio buttons) and allow you to customize your edit environment to your liking. The five edit options are

✔ **Edit Linked Parts:** Use this to edit linked prims as if they were one large object. For more on linked prims, see "Linking prims" in this chapter.

Figure 13-9: A prim with its stretch points displayed.

✔ **Use Grid:** Using this option turns on a grid while you're editing a prim so you can see how much change is taking place.

✔ **Stretch Both Sides:** Use this option to move both sides of a prim when you're stretching it. This way, you can keep a uniform shape.

✔ **Stretch Textures:** Use this option to stretch the textures on a prim when you stretch the prim. This matches the new size of the prim.

✔ **Ruler Mode:** The ruler has three setting.

- *World:* Use this to set the coordinates in relation to the *sim* (island or region) the prim is on.

- *Local:* Use this to set the coordinates in relation to the prim.

- *Reference:* Use this to set the coordinates in relation to another prim you've defined.

Create

Use the Create tool (as shown in Figure 13-10) is the tool/mode you will use the most. You create and edit prims in this mode and it gives you the most control over their appearance. The five aspects of the Create tool are

Figure 13-10: The Create menu of the Build tool.

- ✔ **Shape Selection:** Select the shape of the prim you wish to create. See Table 13-1, earlier in this chapter, for a list of the prim shapes.
- ✔ **Keep Tool Selected:** Select this check box to keep the Create tool selected after you place the new prim.
- ✔ **Copy Selection:** This option copies the current selection when you click to create the prim. You have two options available to you when copying a prim:
  - *Center Copy:* This option makes a copy and centers it relative to the selected prim.
  - *Rotate Copy:* This option makes a copy and rotates it relative to the selected prim.

Land

This mode is for advanced land building. Once you own land, experiment with these features but they are not meant for beginners.

Dissecting Prim Properties

To see the properties for a selected prim, click the More button on the Build tool palette. This gives you the exact location, dimensions, contents, and textures applied to a prim.

The General tab

The General tab (see Figure 13-11) shows general information about the prim, such as who created and owns the prim. This tab contains great information and is used for setting permissions on a prim.

Figure 13-11: The General tab of the prim properties displayed.

The Object tab

The Object tab (see Figure 13-12) shows the exact size, location, and rotation measurements for the selected prim. It tells you whether the prim is locked or is *physical* (affected by physics). It also defines whether the prim has substance or not, such as a door you can walk through. The exact positioning here is useful in advance building to make sure a prim is in the exact location and shape you want it to be.

The Features tab

The Features tab (as shown in Figure 13-13) shows advanced settings for the selected prim.

The Texture tab

The Texture tab (as shown in Figure 13-14) is used to set and modify the texture applied to the prim. A *texture* is a graphic element laid on top of the prim. This can be on the whole prim or on a specific face. This is how beautiful brick buildings or tartan skirts are created in Second Life. You don't have to set any of these options, but they allow more precise texture mapping on your prims. The options on the Texture tab are

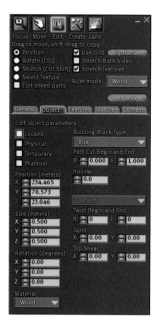

Figure 13-12: The Object tab of the prim properties displayed.

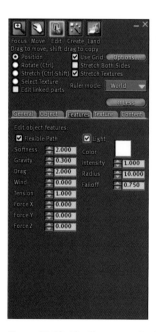

Figure 13-13: The Features tab of the prim properties displayed.

✔ **Transparency:** This controls the transparency of the prim. For example, at a setting of 0, a prim is opaque. At 90, a prim is invisible. Somewhere in the middle gives you different levels. This affects both color and texture.

✔ **Full Bright:** This setting allows the prim to appear the same in darkness and light. If you select Full Bright to be on even at midnight, the texture appears as it would in full sunlight.

✔ **Mapping:** This defines the type of mapping on prims. *Mapping* is how textures are displayed. Beginners should keep this set to Default. Planar mapping is an advanced method of applying textures as if you were projecting them onto the prim.

✔ **Shininess:** This allows you to select the reflectiveness, or shininess, of a prim. You can choose from None, Low, Medium, and High.

To get a chrome effect, choose a white color and high shine.

✔ **Bumpiness:** This allows you to give a prim the appearance of texture. You can choose different building materials, such as bricks, siding, or stucco.

✔ **Repeats Per Face:** This area allows you to define how often a texture is repeated on each face of the prim regardless of how big it is. The lower the number, the bigger the texture will appear.

✔ **Rotation (Degrees):** This allows you to define the rotation of the texture in degrees.

Figure 13-14: The Texture tab of the prim properties displayed.

✔ **Repeats Per Meter:** This area allows you to define how often a texture is repeated per meter of the prim.

✔ **Offset:** This allows you to vertically and horizontally slide the texture along the side of the prim until it's lined up how you like.

✔ **Align Media Texture (Must Load First):** If you're using a media texture (like a movie), this aligns it to the prim.

The Content tab

The Content tab (see Figure 13-15) shows the contents of the prim, including other prims and scripts. The contents are stored in a folder under the contents folder displayed on this tab. Depending on permissions, you might not be able to see the scripts contained here. For more on scripting, see Chapter 14.

Figure 13-15: The Content tab of the prim properties displayed.

Selecting Colors and Textures

Colors are flat colors applied to the entirety of a prim. *Textures* are image files that cover the face of a prim. Each face can have a unique texture, or the prim as a whole can have texture applied to it.

Applying colors

To apply a color to a prim, follow these steps:

1. **Right-click a prim and choose Edit from the radial menu.**

   The Edit tool appears.

2. **Click the More button.**

3. **Click the Texture tab.**

4. **Click the Color box.**

   The Color Picker appears, as shown in Figure 13-16.

5. **Choose a color and then click the Select button.**

   The Apply Immediately option (that is on by default) shows the texture or color on the prim as soon as you click on it.

Figure 13-16: The Color Picker lets you pick from a huge number of colors.

Applying textures

To apply a texture to a whole prim, follow these steps:

1. **Right-click a prim and choose Edit from the radial menu.**

   The Edit tool appears.

2. **Click the More button.**

3. **Click the Texture tab.**

4. Click the Texture box.

The Pick: Texture window appears, as shown in Figure 13-17.

Figure 13-17: The Texture window lets you pick from a huge number of options.

5. Choose a texture from your inventory and then click the Select button.

You can apply both a color and a texture to the same prim. The color you choose is applied as a tint to the texture.

You might not want the same texture on every face of your prim. For instance, dice understandably sport different things on each face. You can add a different texture to each face of your prim by dragging the texture from your Inventory to the side of the prim where you want it to appear instead of setting the texture in the Edit menu.

To apply a texture to a face of a prim, follow these steps:

1. Select the prim you want to edit by right-clicking it and choose Edit from the radial menu.

2. Click your Inventory button and find the texture you want to use.

3. Drag the texture onto the face you want to apply it to.

The texture appears only on that face of the prim, as shown in Figure 13-18.

To make one-way glass, apply an opaque texture to one side and a transparent texture to the other side. Now you can see through one side but not the other.

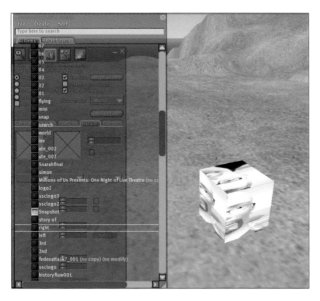

Figure 13-18: A prim with different textures on different faces.

Working with Multiple Prims

Using one prim is great but almost everything you see in Second Life is made of multiples of prims. When building it is essential to learn how to work with multiple prims at the same time.

Making copies

So you have one prim perfect. It's the right size and shape, but you need an exact copy. No one wants to do all the steps over again to create a copy. Second Life has an easy way to copy an existing prim you own. To copy a prim, follow these simple steps:

1. **Select the prim you want to copy by right-clicking on it and choosing Edit from the radial menu.**

2. **Hold down the Shift key.**

3. **Drag one of the arrows.**

   A copy of that prim is created as you drag, as shown in Figure 13-19.

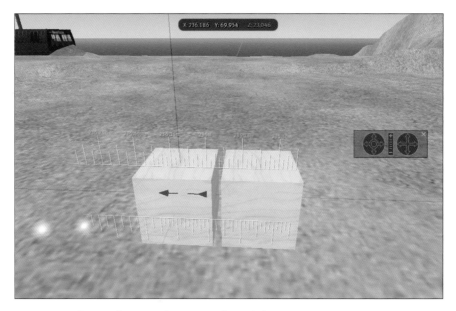

Figure 13-19: A new prim created as a copy of an existing one.

Selecting multiple prims

After you have more than one prim, you might want to select several of them at the same time to change something about them. Maybe you want to move two walls higher simultaneously so they stay at the same level. To select multiple prims, follow these steps:

1. **Select one prim by right-clicking on it and choosing Edit from the radial menu.**

2. **Hold down the Shift key and select the other prim by clicking on it.**

   Now you can move or configure the prims together, as shown in Figure 13-20. Notice how the arrows appear between them. This means the objects are linked.

Linking prims

If you want to collect a bunch of prims and make them act like a single prim, link them. Just select all the prims you want and then link them so that they act as a single prim. To link prims, follow these steps:

1. **Select a group of prims by right-clicking on them while holding the Shift key.**

2. **From the Tools menu, choose Link.**

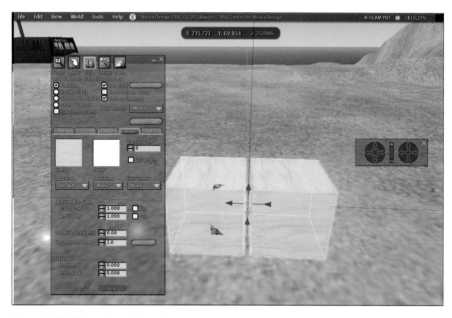

Figure 13-20: Two prims selected.

The first prim you selected before linking appears in blue when you link the prims.

The prims now act as one big prim, as shown in Figure 13-21.

Although they act like one prim, the prims contained in a linked prim still count individually to prim counts. An area is only allowed so many prims so it might seem like one thing to you but a linked object can add to a high prim count.

Sometime you might want to change one part of a linked prim. You don't want to unlink the prim, but you need to change the color or texture on one small part. By selecting the Edited Link Parts mode check box from the Edit tool, you can do just that. Each prim can be individually edited and stay linked with the other prims.

On the other hand, you might want to take apart that linked prim. The process is basically the reverse of linking prims. To unlink prims, follow these steps:

1. **Select the linked prim by right-clicking on it and choosing Edit from the radial menu.**

2. **From the Tools menu, choose Unlink.**

   The prim is reverted to individually selected prims.

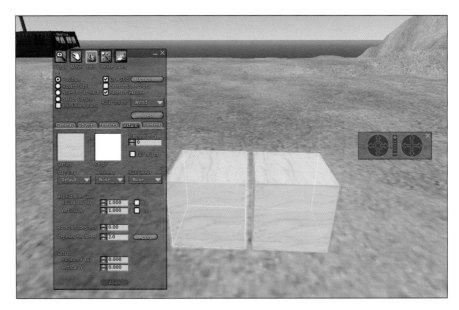

Figure 13-21: Two linked prims. The prim outlined in blue is the first prim selected.

Cleaning Up

Sure, building is fun. It's one of our favorite things to do in Second Life. We experiment and build and twist and link all sorts of prims. But just like in your First Life, when you're done with a project, you need to clean up when you finish working. No one likes a bunch of garbage prims littering up their sim or sandbox. Be kind and clean up any mess you make. You can clean up by right-clicking on a prim and clicking Take (it is stored in your inventory) or pressing Delete to put it in your trash.

Taking Your Building Skills to the Next Level

In This Chapter

▷ Working in groups

▷ Building with scripts

▷ Open sourcing your Second Life

*A*fter you master the basics of building, a whole new aspect of Second Life (SL) opens for you. Remember that everything in SL was created by other users like you. The advanced building options allow you to expand to build an infinite amount of things and store them in your Inventory. And, you don't have to go it alone in this endeavor, so we discuss working in groups. You can build and share objects with others, working collaboratively. Second, we look at how you can add scripts or programming to your objects so they can perform dynamic interactive actions. Finally, we talk about the open source elements of Second Life that might just change the whole world.

Building with Groups

One the biggest sources of confusion about building is how to build with groups of people. Who owns the objects and how do we share them are common questions. This section covers how a group of people can work together on a great project.

Sharing objects with a group

Sometimes you might want to share building objects with others. Say that you're working with a group on a large building, and you need help. By allowing the objects to be edited by group members, you can have multiple people working on the same project at the same time.

To share objects with a group, follow these steps:

1. **Form a group.**

   For more information on groups, see Chapter 7.

2. **Select the object you want to share and then choose Edit from the radial menu.**

   This opens the Build window.

3. **On the Build window, click the More button.**

4. **Select the Share with Group check box, as shown in Figure 14-1.**

5. **Click the Set button next to the group listing for the group to which you want the object to belong.**

   Anyone in that group can now edit the object.

This also works for linked objects. This is handy because when you want to share a larger, more complex object, you don't have to enable sharing for each linked object.

Select this box.

Figure 14-1: Enable an object to be shared.

Setting permissions on objects with groups

If you share an object with a group and a group member takes it, the object then becomes owned by that group member. What does that matter? If you don't set the Next Owner permissions correctly on that object, the new owner won't be able to modify it and neither will the original creator. Sounds complex? Here's an example.

Tom makes a lamp. He links all the objects and shares them with the group named Lamps'r'Us. Sally is a member of this group, so she can edit the lamp. Tom leaves, and Sally wants to take the lamp to clean up the area they're working in. After she takes the lamp, the Next Owner permissions are applied to her. Because Tom left the permissions set at the defaults, the next owner can't modify or copy the object. So, when Sally pulls the object from her Inventory to work on it again, she can't edit it — and Tom, who created the object, can't modify it. The object is essentially now *unmodifiable* (a *dead object*) by anyone.

To correctly set the Next Owner permissions so that an object can be modified by a group member, follow these steps:

1. **Select the object you want to set permissions on and edit it.**
2. **On the General tab you find the next owner permissions at the bottom of the tab.**
3. **Click Modify to allow the next owner to modify the prim,**
4. **Click Copy to allow the next owner to copy the prim.**
5. **Click Resell/Give Away to allow the next owner to sell the prim.**

When creating objects to share with a group, always take a copy for yourself. That way, if someone takes the object and creates a dead object, you can take another one from your Inventory, change the permissions, and *voilà!* That person has a modifiable copy of the object.

Deeding objects

If you want the profit from the sale of objects to go to a group, you need to deed it to the group. To do so, follow these steps:

1. **Follow the steps to share an object with a group listed in the earlier section, "Sharing objects with a group."**
2. **After you assign the object to a group, click the Deed button next to the Share with Group check box.**

When the object is sold, the funds are placed in the group's money account. For more on groups see Chapter 7.

Debugging permissions

If you're having problems with group permissions, you can check the exact permissions of an object from the Debug menu. The Debug menu is a menu you can turn on and off, and it gives you access to some techie features. To view the debug permissions on an object, follow these steps:

1. **Press Ctrl+Alt+D.**

   This gives you two new menus: Client and Server.

2. **From the Client menu, choose Debug Permissions.**

   It will look as if nothing happened.

3. **Look at an object.**

   You see more text on the General tab, right below the Group listing.

   You see some crazy codes (as shown in Figure 14-2), but Table 14-1 and Table 14-2 explain them.

Permissions

Figure 14-2: Debug permissions of an object.

Table 14-1		Types of Debug Permissions
Code	*Permission*	*Description*
B	Base	The basic permission the object has.
0	Owner	The permissions the owner has.
G	Group	The permissions the group has.
E	Everyone	The permissions everyone who is not an owner or in a group that owns the prim.
N	Next Owner	The permissions the next owner receives.
F	Full or Folded	This includes all the objects included in the linked objects.

Table 14-2		Types of Debug Rights
Code	*Right*	*Description*
V	Can Move	The permission allows you to move the prim.
M	Can Modify	This permission allows you to modify the prim.
C	Can Copy	This permission allows the owner to copy the prim.
T	Can Transfer	This permission allows the owner to transfer the prim.

These codes might seem like gobbledygook right now, but as you work with permissions, they will show you exactly what rights you have for certain objects.

Writing Scripts in Second Life

When you want to build something in SL that actually does something, you need to attach a script to the object. *Scripts* are text programs that can run based on what users do around them. Have you ever clicked an object and received a landmark or notecard? That is a script working.

The first thing to understand is that you don't have to be a programmer to use scripts. If you've managed to find your way into SL, built a few objects, and linked them, you can create a script. This is not to say that writing scripts is easy, but with practice and knowing where to find help, you can usually figure it out. The biggest thing to remember is that someone probably has done it before, and you can learn from that person.

Writing scripts in LSL

Scripts are created in the Linden Scripting Language (LSL) proprietary scripting language. It's similar in structure to other higher-level scripting languages, such as C# or visual basic. It doesn't require you to compile anything, but the editor will help you with the right syntax.

How do I program in LSL?

Essentially, creating a script means telling a particular object what to do based on what residents do. You have to define the actions the object can do, based on a set of actions that a resident can take. For instance, if a resident clicks a box, it rings like a telephone. Sounds easy enough.

The best places in the world to discover more about LSL are

- **The LSLWiki**

    www.lslwiki.net/lslwiki/wakka.php?wakka=HomePage

- **The LSL Portal**

    http://wiki.secondlife.com/wiki/LSL_Portal

These two sites offer a ton of information on everything you need to use LSL, including basic scripts and better tutorials than we could put in these pages. They also have tons of example scripts that can help you get started making objects interactive.

To view a script for an object, follow these steps:

1. **Select an object whose scripts you want to view.**

2. **Click the Content tab.**

3. **Click the item under the Contents folder to view its scripts.**

    The object's scripts appear in the Script window, as shown in Figure 14-3.

```
Script: Kart                                              _ ×
File    Edit    Help

// Kart with Scripted Camera
//
// by Ben
// Some help from Casval and Dave


//
// This is a simple, fun vehicle meant for offroading.
//
// It is meant as an example to use in making your own vehicle.
//
//
rotation rot;
key owner;

// Defining the Parameters of the normal driving camera.
// This will let us follow behind with a loose camera.
list drive_cam =
[
        CAMERA_ACTIVE, TRUE,
        CAMERA_BEHINDNESS_ANGLE, 0.0,
        CAMERA_BEHINDNESS_LAG, 0.5,
        CAMERA_DISTANCE, 3.0,
        CAMERA_PITCH, 10.0,

        // CAMERA_FOCUS,
        CAMERA_FOCUS_LAG, 0.05,
        CAMERA_FOCUS_LOCKED, FALSE,
        CAMERA_FOCUS_THRESHOLD, 0.0,


Line 0, Column 0
  Insert...                ▼              Save

  ☑ Running                              Reset
```

Figure 14-3: A SL script.

Second Life Open Source

The Second Life *viewer,* or the program you use to interface with the world, has an open source version. This is code available for download from the Linden Lab Web site (http://secondlifegrid.net/programs/open_source) and allows you to modify the code of the viewer, recompile it, and then run it. This is for advanced programmers and should not be entered into lightly. Like when mastering LSL, a number of people are available who can help you. Search the Web for "SL open source browser" and ask in second Life for more help.

15

The Clothes Make the Avatar: Creating Your Own Clothing

In This Chapter

▷ Altering clothes

▷ Making clothes from scratch

▷ Designing accessories

▷ Adding prims to make clothing more realistic

▷ Hairdos from scratch

*H*alf the fun of Second Life is dressing up your avatar. In a world where everything fits and you can be as outrageous as you want to be, why not learn to make your own clothes to express your own sense of crazy style? Plus, maybe you'll make something so unique that others want to wear it and — even better — be willing to pay you for it.

Because of the flexibility of appearance in Second Life, folks around you will "read" your avatar as an expression of your personality even more than they might assume things about you based on the fashion you choose in real life. So why not go all out and really express yourself? There's no better way than to make your own clothing. In this chapter, we walk you through making small adjustments to clothes you might have purchased from others, making clothing from scratch in Adobe Photoshop, crafting accessories (such as hats and flirty skirts), and even how to create a great hairdo. Get ready to go couture!

Haute Couture: Using Adobe Photoshop to Make Your Own Clothes

You can use a less-expensive graphics programs to create clothing, but Adobe Photoshop is what the best designers in Second Life swear by. It's a pricey program (US$75 – US$800) but worth every penny if you want to become a serious fashion designer in SL. However, any graphics editor that supports Targa file formats (TGA files) and can handle layers in an image will work. *Targa* is widely used as the standard graphics file format for high-end graphics output.

For this section, we'll assume you're fairly friendly with Photoshop. If not, go grab a copy of *Photoshop CS3 For Dummies* by Peter Bauer (Wiley Publishing, Inc.). If you use another graphics editing program, the tools in Photoshop might prove similar enough to what you use that you can still follow along.

To make clothes in Second Life, start by downloading the body templates on top of which you "paint" clothing. To download the free body templates, follow these steps:

1. **Aim your Web browser to www.secondlife.com.**

2. **Click the Downloads link in the bottom-left corner of the screen.**

3. **Scroll down the page and then click the Templates link in the Free Downloads section.**

4. **Click the Entire Template Collection in One Download link to download all the templates.**

   You need all these templates to show you where on your avatar's body your clothing will appear.

   You download these templates as Zip files. If you decide to become serious about making clothing, you'll want to save these Zip files in an easy-to-find place because you'll be using these them often.

After you have all the body templates at your disposal, you're ready to start making your own clothes.

Creating a custom t-shirt

Get started creating your own clothing with an easy project: a t-shirt. This will cost $L10 to upload the image we're going to make. Who doesn't love a pithy t-shirt? Rather than starting from scratch, start with a template:

1. **Go to Robin Wood's great SL tutorial Web site to download her pre-made t-shirt template:**

   http://www.robinwood.com/Catalog/Technical/SL-Tuts/SLPages/RSWTShirt Start.html

Look for the Click Here to Download link and download the PSD file.

2. Save and unzip the file.

If you don't have a program installed to open Zip files, go to www.winzip.com and download the free version of WinZip.

3. Open RSW T-shirt.psd **in Photoshop.**

You see a template like the one in Figure 15-1.

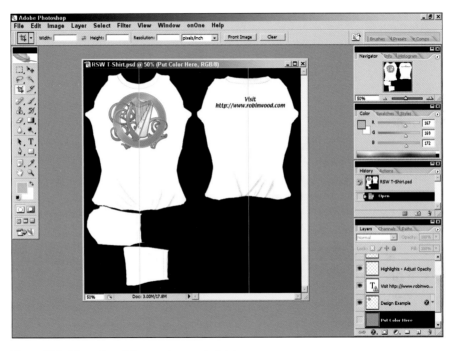

Figure 15-1: These templates can be very helpful.

4. Be sure to have your Photoshop Layers tool open by clicking View⇨ Layers.

You'll see that the template has seven layers. They are, from the bottom: Texture, Put Color Here, Design Example, a Text Layer, Highlights, UVs, and Cover.

5. Hide the Cover layer by clicking its eye icon.

This reveals the background of the template.

6. Decide what color you want your t-shirt to be.

The second layer from the bottom — the Put Color Here layer — determines the color of the t-shirt. You need to make the layer visible. You'll see when you make the eye icon visible on the layer that the whole template turns blue. Use your Bucket tool to paint this whole layer with the background color of your shirt. The shirt in this example will be orange. See Figure 15-2 to see this layer painted.

7. **Choose a design for your t-shirt.**

The Design Example layer is the design for the front of our example t-shirt. You can put whatever design you want on the front of your shirt, but be sure it has enough contrast with the background color of your shirt so that it's visible, as shown in Figure 15-3. You can also add something to the back of the shirt or hide the layer with that text on it. You may want to save the shirt in a variety of colors to try on later.

Think about your design in terms of how it will wrap around the avatar anatomy. The chest area (okay, cleavage) on female avatars tends to eat the design on the front of a shirt as it wraps around her shape. You might want to make a male version with the image on the front and a female version with your image on the back.

8. **Turn the top layer, the Cover layer, back on (by clicking the eye icon on the layers) and black out the background of the file (by turning the eye icon off on the layers).**

9. **Save your file as a Targa (`.tga`) file in 32-bit resolution using the Save As function under the file menu.**

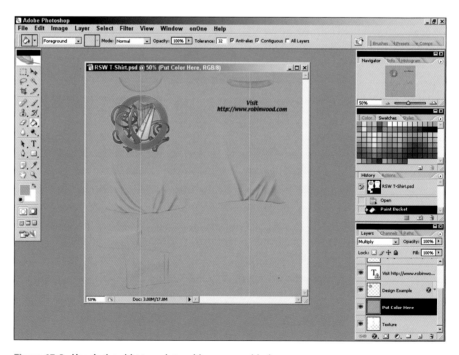

Figure 15-2: Here's the shirt template with orange added.

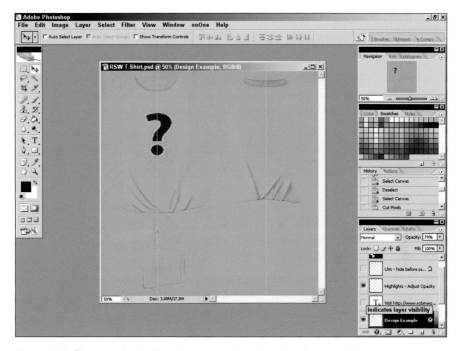

Figure 15-3: Choose a design that shows up well on the color of your t-shirt.

Don't bother to click the box to compress it. The file won't be large anyway.

10. **In Second Life, choose File➪Upload Image and navigate to your saved t-shirt Targa file.**

11. **From the Preview Image As drop-down menu of the dialog box, choose Female Upper Body or Male Upper Body (depending on the version of your t-shirt) to see how the t-shirt will look (as shown in Figure 15-4) before you pay the L$10 to upload the image, and then close the dialog box.**

12. **Open your Appearance menu and select the Shirt tab.**

13. **Take off the shirt you're wearing by clicking the Take Off button. Then click the Create New Shirt button.**

14. **Click the Fabric box and navigate to the shirt texture you just uploaded, as shown in Figure 15-5.**

You might want to choose a private place to do this because you'll be momentarily topless. Even though avatars without custom skins look like Barbie dolls, it can still be embarrassing to be caught topless, especially as a woman.

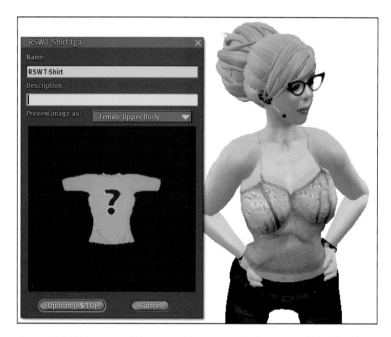

Figure 15-4: Save yourself the money by previewing how your shirt will look before you pay to upload the file.

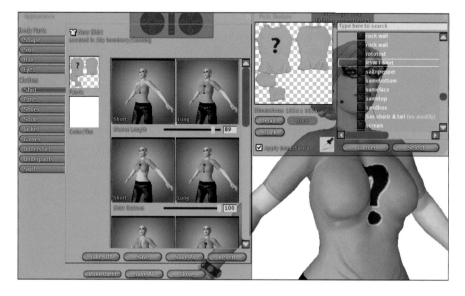

Figure 15-5: You might want to choose a private place to do this since you'll be momentarily topless.

15. **Adjust the t-shirt by using the options on the Shirt menu until you like how it looks. Adjust its wrinkles, length, and so on until it's just how you want.**

16. **Click Save.**

If you want to save the t-shirt so you can give away copies, simply right-click it in your inventory, choose Copy, right-click again in your inventory, and choose Paste. If you selected that it's transferable, copyable, or modifiable, the folks you give it to will be able to make changes and give away copies as well. For more information about the properties of objects, check out Chapter 13.

Making clothes from scratch: A baseball jersey

After you get a bit of experience using clothing templates in Photoshop, make something from scratch. Baseball shirts with contrasting raglan sleeves are perfect for men or women and offer something a little different from the standard t-shirt. Here's how to make one:

1. **In Photoshop, open the upper-body template.**

   Use the template from the Second Life Web site, as we describe in the earlier section, "Haute Couture: Using Adobe Photoshop to Make Your Own Clothes."

   For more detailed templates with better marks for tank top lines, waistlines, and so on, go to Robin Wood's Web site and download her body templates:

   ```
   www.robinwood.com/Catalog/Technical/SL-Tuts/SLTutSet.html
   ```

   They're a bit more complicated, but after you get used to creating clothes, you'll be grateful for the additional guidelines they offer.

2. **Make all the layers on the sample images invisible by clicking the eye icons on the layer tool.**

   The Second Life body templates have sample images on layers. You'll want to make all those layers invisible so you're looking at just the base template. It should look like Figure 15-6. The guidelines on the template will help you line up straps, stripes, and waistlines.

3. **Create a new layer by clicking Layer>New Layer (call it Layer 1) on top of all the existing layers.**

   This is the layer you paint on to create the new shirt.

   It's okay to do a quick Google search for baseball shirts if you need design inspiration. Just remember that you shouldn't re-create any copyrighted material in Second Life — your shirt needs to be an original design.

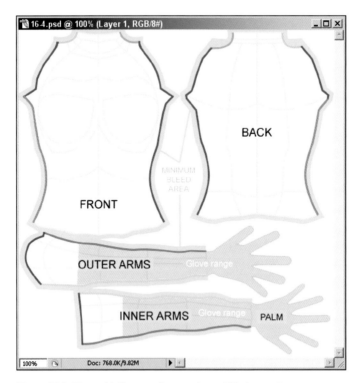

Figure 15-6: The guidelines on the template will help you line up straps, stripes, and waistlines.

4. **Start with the body of the shirt by making sure that the only image layers visible are the bottom-most layer — called** *Background* **— and your new layer called Layer 1.**

5. **On this top empty layer, using whatever Photoshop tool you like best, outline the body of the shirt with the color you want.**

   Be sure to fill in enough to cover the Minimum Bleed Area on the template, which is the pale-green outline around the body. You'll also want to choose where the shirt neckline will stop by painting only up to the second rounded line around the neck. In Figure 15-7, you can see the outline that we created for the body of the shirt. The edges don't have to be perfect because they fall into the bleed area. We tend to use the brush tool set to a size 10 or so brush.

6. **Fill in the body of the shirt with the same color. We use the Bucket tool.**

7. **To create the contrasting sleeves of the shirt, create a new layer on top of your existing layer called Layer 2.**

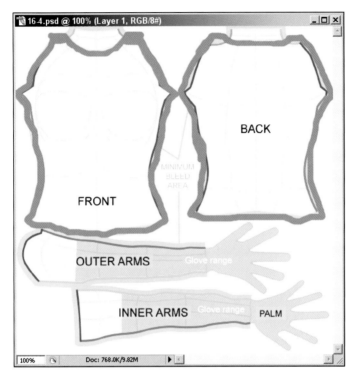

Figure 15-7: The edges don't have to be perfect since they fall into the bleed area.

8. **Outline and fill in the arms using whatever paint tool and color you prefer.**

   Again, be sure to fill in at least to the outside of the Minimum Bleed Area. Be sure to extend the sleeve fabric a bit past the wrist so you can use the appearance editor to crop them to a uniform length later. Check out Figure 15-8 to see what it should look like after your sleeves are filled in.

9. **After you have the basic shape, you can start adding some realism to your shirt by using shadows and so on.**

   Our example shirt has a contrasting neck band, some small gray stitching along the neck and wrists, and a logo on the back, but you can add whatever you'd like with the Photoshop tools you're most familiar with. See Figure 15-9 to see the finished shirt texture.

   When you add effects, use a new layer each time. This will make it easy to undo elements of the clothing that you decide you don't like.

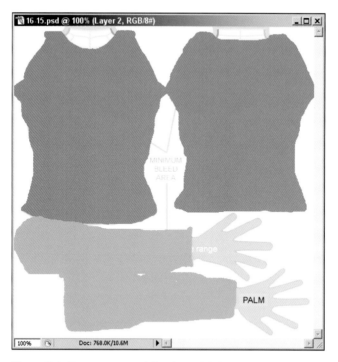

Figure 15-8: Be sure to extend the sleeve fabric a bit past the wrist so you can use the appearance editor to crop them to a uniform length later.

10. **Flatten all your visible layers (Apple +E or Ctrl +E), flatten all the layers of your shirt, and then hide the template layer so that you only see your shirt.**

11. **Right-click the shirt's visible layer (probably Layer 2) in the Layers palette and choose Select Layer Transparency.**

12. **Press Q on your keyboard to create a quick mask (a quick mask creates an alpha layer for the background of the image, which SL will see as being transparent). Select the whole image, copy it, and paste it all into a new layer called finished shirt.**

13. **Move the finished shirt layer below Layer 2.**

    You'll have something similar to Figure 15-10.

    The black area you see now will end up as transparent in Second Life when you wear the shirt.

The *alpha layer,* that black layer that blocks out the background of the template, is handy to know about. If you want to make a keyhole shirt, put a hole in some pants, or create some other kind of open area on a piece of clothing, you'll want to be sure that the open area shows up as black on your alpha layer.

14. **Save the file as a 32-bit Targa (.tga) file, and you're ready to upload it into Second Life and try it on.**

    Follow Steps 9–14 in the previous "Creating a custom t-shirt" section to upload the graphic, test it, and adjust it. See Figure 15-11 to see how our finished shirt turned out.

Don't be afraid to experiment. Make lots of different versions of a piece of clothing until it's just right. Save your Photoshop files often as different versions, and use the Upload preview in Second Life to see how they look.

You can also use photographs of real clothing applied to the template for super-realistic clothing, but beware of copyright infringement.

Figure 15-9: The finished texture looks a bit like fabric laid out and ready to sew.

Figure 15-10: Be sure to move the black alpha layer below your painted layer before saving or you won't be able to see your shirt.

Figure 15-11: This shirt might not be high fashion, but it's an easy way to express yourself.

Editing Clothes Made by Others

In Chapter 13 we discuss setting permissions on objects. Now it's time to combine that knowledge and apply it to clothing. In this section, we just look at modifying the length and color of clothing. However, the editing possibilities are endless — as long as the maker of the clothes allows modifications.

Adjusting sleeve length

Say you bought a great shirt, but it has long sleeves, and you prefer short ones. If the maker of the shirt made it modifiable, you can easily shorten them.

You can tweak any article of clothing *as long as it's modifiable.* Here's how to check:

1. **Choose a clothing item from your Inventory by right-clicking it and choosing Properties.**

   The Inventory Item Properties dialog box appears, as shown in Figure 15-12.

   For an article of clothing to be editable, the Modify check box of the You Can section of the Properties menu must be selected (marked). If the Modify box isn't enabled, you're done — you can't edit the article of clothing.

2. **Assuming that the shirt is modifiable, close the Inventory Item Properties dialog box and keep going.**

Modify box

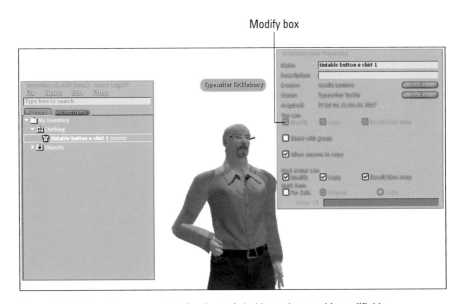

Figure 15-12: Check the properties of a piece of clothing to be sure it's modifiable.

Here's how to modify the sleeves, making long sleeves shorter:

1. **Put on the shirt:**

   a. *Right-click it in your Inventory.*

   b. *Choose Wear, as shown in Figure 15-13.*

2. **Right-click your avatar and choose Appearance from the radial menu, as shown in Figure 15-14.**

3. **From the Appearance menu, click the Shirt tab and scroll to the Sleeve Length adjustment slider, as shown in Figure 15-15.**

4. **Adjust the Sleeve Length slider to make the sleeves the desired shortened length.**

   Your shirt has shorter sleeves.

5. **Be sure to click the Save button (or agree to save when the menu asks you to) or you'll lose the changes you made to the item.**

You can take away fabric from clothing, but you can't add it. For example, if you buy a short-sleeved shirt, you can't make the sleeves longer. Likewise, if you buy shorts, you can't make them into trousers. You can, however, make long sleeves or long pants shorter — that is, as long as the clothing creator made them modifiable.

Figure 15-13: Put on the article of clothing you want to modify.

Figure 15-14: The appearance editor.

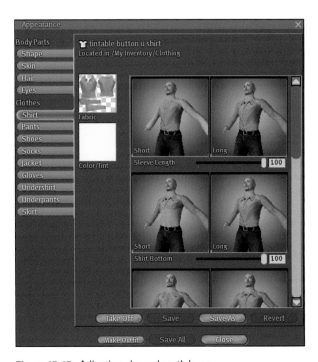

Figure 15-15: Adjusting sleeve length here.

You can also raise and lower the waistband and neckline of a shirt. If a shirt shows off too much midriff, consider making a pair of system underwear (underwear made using the Second Life menus rather than uploading a texture made outside of Second Life) to match it and making that garment as tall as possible. If the color of the shirt and the underwear match (see Figure 15-16), no one will see a seam, and you won't show anything you don't want to.

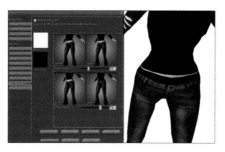 

Figure 15-16: The before and after of the modified shirt.

Changing the color of a garment

Changing the color of a modifiable piece of clothing is simple. Follow these steps:

1. **Put on the shirt you want to edit by right-clicking it in your inventory and choosing Wear.**

2. **Right-click your avatar and choose Appearance from the radial menu.**

3. **In the Appearance menu, click the Shirt tab.**

4. **Click the Color/Tint box and select the desired color from the pop-up, as shown in Figure 15-17.**

5. **Click the Save button or say yes when you're asked if you want to save or you'll lose the changes you made.**

If you want to own the same piece of modifiable clothing in different colors, check the Properties menu to see whether you're allowed to copy it (refer to Figure 15-12). If you can, make a copy of it in your inventory and change the color of one. Now you have two versions of the garment, in different colors.

Changing the color won't always turn out just as you want because you're really tinting the fabric that the original garment is made of *and* combining the old color with the new color. This might result in a shade other than what you really wanted. Experiment with different shades until you like the outcome.

Figure 15-17: The range of colors is nearly infinite.

Creating Accessories by Using Clothing Layers

Clothing layers don't have to cover you up. With the alpha layer, you can mark areas of a template to remain clear. Because of this, creating jewelry, tattoos, and other body modifications as clothing layers is easy. In this section, we show you how to make a pearl bead necklace that you wear on an Underwear layer. You can also use this technique to create a simple tattoo. Be aware, though, that wearing such accessories on a clothing layer means you can't wear anything else on that layer, such as actual underwear.

1. **Open the Upper body template downloaded from the Second Life Web site and draw a circle, as shown in Figure 15-18.**

   We used the circle selection tool and then traced using the Stroke command.

2. **Resize the circle to the size of bead you would like (Edit>transform, scale) and copy/paste it over and over to make a necklace.**

3. **Merge the layers to put all the beads on the same layer (Cmd+E or Ctrl+E), as shown in Figure 15-19.**

   These beads are a subtle off-white color, but you can use any color you'd like.

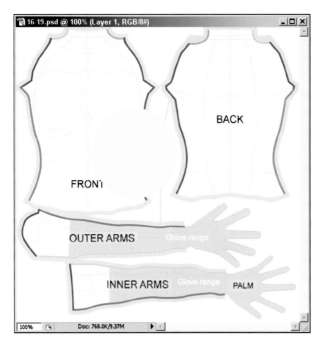

Figure 15-18: A simple circle starts off the bead design.

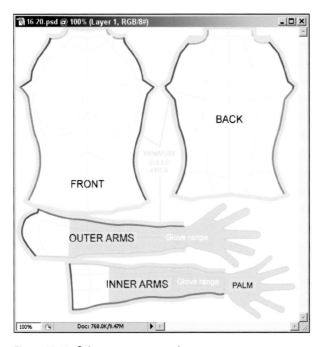

Figure 15-19: Culture your own pearls.

4. **On another layer below the beads, draw a line (using the brush tool set to a small brush) connecting them to make it look as if they're on a chain or cord, as shown in Figure 15-20.**

5. **Apply bevel/emboss (in the Layer style) to the bead layer to make the beads look rounded.**

   Adding the bevel to the layer makes the beads look round and gives them a bit of a shine; see Figure 15-20.

6. **Merge the bead and cord layer; then hide the other layers.**

7. **Press Q to create a quick mask. Then select the whole image, copy it, and paste it all into a new layer.**

   The black area you see will end up transparent in Second Life when you wear the necklace.

8. **Save the file as a 32-bit Targa (TGA) file.**

   You're ready to upload the file into Second Life and try it on.

   Follow steps in the earlier section, "Creating a custom t-shirt," to upload the graphic, test it, and adjust it.

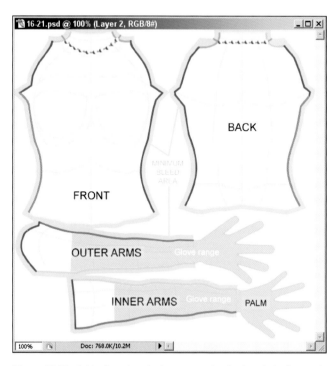

Figure 15-20: Add a bevel to the layer to make the beads look round and shiny.

9. The finished necklace should look similar to Figure 15-21.

Even though this necklace is simple and without much detail, you can let your imagination run wild after you get the basics down.

Figure 15-21: This necklace is simple and without much detail, but now that you know how to make it you can let your imagination run wild.

You can use these same techniques to create tattoos, makeup, or skin details. Just use a template, paint on your tattoo or makeup (leaving the rest of the template blank with an alpha layer), and upload it.

Using Prims in Clothing

If you've seen folks wearing belts and skirts that swirl in the wind, or collars that stand up, you've seen clothing made of prims. *Prims* are the basic building blocks used to create objects in Second Life. We discuss attaching objects to your avatar in Chapter 5, and we use the same approach here. First, though, you have to build the clothing that you'll attach.

Skirts are perhaps the easiest and most common prim clothing because the skirts made with the Appearance tool just don't look like real skirts. The same skills you use here can be used to make any kind of prim clothing, so guys shouldn't feel left out — you can make some tails for your tux, or even a tail for your avatar.

Decide what kind of skirt you want to make. This example shows how to make a knee-length, lace skirt. To make a skirt from prims, follow these steps:

1. **Start with a hollow tube (hollow set to 95.0 on the Hollow setting). It's one of the basic shapes available on the building menu.**

2. **Set the size from the knee to the waist.**

   For this example, use size set to X=0.500, Y=0.500, and Z=0.495.

   You can eyeball the skirt by standing next to it. Make the width of the tube about the width of your body.

   To test whether your initial tube is wide enough, switch it to Phantom in the Object tab on the Edit menu so you can walk into it and see whether it goes around you. Be sure to turn Phantom off afterward.

3. **Use the Cut Path options on the Object tab of the Edit menu to cut away most of the tube.**

   For this example, use B=0.750 and E=1.000. To set the beginning and ending cuts.

4. **Use the Taper settings to angle the top end of the shape to form the gathers of the skirt.**

   This example uses X=–0.85 and Y=–0.65. This little wedge will become the individual pleats of the skirt.

5. **Copy and rotate this shape so that it makes an oval at the top approximately the size of your waist.**

   You'll need about 15 objects to make a full skirt. For a fuller skirt, use more.

6. **Change the texture of all the prims by holding down the control button as you click on each object, and then use the Texture tab of the Edit menu.**

   This example uses a lace texture that we got from a free stock photo site, but you can use any texture you'd like.

   You have lots of free textures in your inventory already. Look in your Library folder for the Textures folder. Even textures for rock and grass can be cool on clothes if you tint them with other colors. Who knew pink marble could look just like satin?

7. **Select all the prims selected and then click the Flexible option on the Features tab in the Edit Objects menu box.**

   This makes the sections of your skirt flow as you walk, which looks more realistic. To test it, select the whole skirt and move it. You can't tell that it's flexible until you move it. You'll see it flow and swing as you move it.

8. **Select all the objects in the skirt by highlighting them all and then link them by clicking Tools (at the top left of your screen) and selecting Link.**

   All the parts become one object.

9. **Name your skirt with the Edit tool on the General tab.**

   If you don't do this, you'll bury the skirt in your Inventory as just another generic object.

10. **Right-click your skirt and choose More⇨Take Copy.**

11. **Open your Inventory, click the Recent Items tab, and find your skirt.**

12. **Right-click the skirt and choose Attach To⇨Pelvis.**

    Your skirt will probably attach to you upside down or in some other strange way. Use the Edit tools to rotate it and position it correctly.

We pair the skirt with a simple, gray tank top and gray underpants with knee-length legs both made with the Edit Appearance tools. Then we made a short jacket using the lace texture used on the skirt prims and put the skirt off-center just a little for an asymmetric waist line. This full dress cost only L$10 for the template upload. Now that's a bargain.

Don't be frustrated if your first efforts don't turn out exactly how you'd like them to. Sometimes mistakes create the best innovations. Try on your creation, experiment with combining it with other clothing. Above all, have fun.

Making Hair

By far, hair is by far the toughest accessory to make in Second Life. It has to look like real hair and fit your head, which isn't always easy to do. Expect to look silly when you try it on and expect to make some horrible hair before you make your first really great do. In this section we make a very simple, Gibson Girl hairdo. It's not nearly as stylish as many that you'll find in the Second Life shops, but it will show you the basics that you'll need to start creating your own unique looks.

To create a basic hairdo, follow these steps:

1. **Make a torus using the building tool. It's the hollow ring shape at the top of the tool with the other basic shapes**

2. **On the Object tab, enter the following settings:**

Size X	0.450
Size Y	0.250
Size Z	0.200
Pathcut V	0.350

Pathcut E	1.000
Hole Size X	0.30
Hole Size Y	0.35
Taper X	1.000
Taper Y	1.000

It's a funny little shape, but most of it will be hidden inside your head.

3. **Copy the object over and over again, rotating each of them to create a crown.**

   For help with copying and rotating of objects, see Chapter 13.

   It should take about nine pieces. For a finer look, use a more-narrow torus and more copies.

4. **Select all the prims by holding down the Ctrl button and clicking on each one and create a copy by then holding shift and dragging the group.**

5. **Rotate the copy 180 degrees below the first object.**

   This will look a little like a plywood pumpkin, but don't worry. When finished you will get a shape which is beginning to look like the Gibson Girl style that we're going for.

6. **Select the new do and link all the objects by pressing Ctrl+L.**

7. **Give you hair a name in the General tab — something like Hair Test 01.**

8. **Right-click the hair and choose More⇨Take Copy.**

9. **Find the hair in your inventory (probably on your Recent Items tab), right-click it, and choose Attach⇨Skull.**

   The hair won't know how to attach, so you'll have to do some editing to rotate and position it on your head. You will notice there is something missing — bangs.

10. **To add bangs, copy one of the original prims and make it sweep across the forehead like bangs by rotating it.**

   This is a good time to save and copy the hairdo again. Be sure to rename each version of the hair so you can keep your separate drafts of your hairdo.

11. **To soften the hairdo, add some wisps at the front of the face. Start by making a new torus with these settings:**

Size X	0.144
Size Y	0.283
Size Z	0.140
Pathcut V	0.770

Pathcut E	1.000
Hole Size X	0.30
Hole Size Y	0.35
Taper X	1.00
Taper Y	1.00

This smaller shape can also be used around the neck or twisted to be added to the bun to make loose curls.

12. **Use this new prim to add some detail around the face to your taste.**

   Try it on often to make sure you are framing your face. Save copies of it often.

13. **Put on a copy of the final style.**

14. **After you have the hairdo positioned, edit the texture, experimenting with different ones until you find one you like.**

   We used Atoll Wood Endcut (which is in your Library already), tinted orange. We also rotated the texture zero degrees.

15. **Save a copy of the final version of your new hairdo.**

16

Making a Statement with Poses, Animations, and Gestures

*E*veryone in Second Life (SL) has the same basic poses and animations. For example, your hands go up and down when you type, your feet shift a bit when you stand still, and you primly put your hands on your knees when you sit. But why be like everyone else? Why look like a stiff robot when you can move naturally, give people a thumbs up when you approve of an idea, or flip a cartwheel when you're excited?

In this chapter, we go over the difference between a pose, an animation, and a gesture. We show you how to try out one of each (you can buy one or use one from the Library in your Inventory), and then create your own. Before you know it, you'll have your own distinct style for expressing yourself physically.

Understanding the Terminology

Before you begin, time to lay out some of the terminology to help differentiate between a pose, an animation, and a gesture:

✔ **Pose:** *Poses* are stationary, frozen positions. Your avatar will strike the pose and stay in it until you turn off the pose.

✔ **Animation:** *Animations* are short sequences of movement, such as a dance step, cartwheel, or hand wave. They might or might not loop to repeat until you stop the animation.

Animation Override: You can purchase a *HUD* (*Heads-Up Display,* see Chapter 4 for more info) that automatically overrides the default animations (the ones given to you by SL when you created your account) your avatar will use while standing, sitting, and talking.

✏ **Gesture:** *Gestures* are combinations of animations, sound effects, and poses. For example, you can buy a complete gesture that makes you wave, say "Hi," and then stop waving. You can also combine your own sounds and animations to make your own custom gestures. Gestures are typically *hot–keyed* (setting up a custom keyboard shortcut to make the gesture easier to use) to be used from the keyboard rather than searching for them in your Inventory each time you want to use them. They can also be associated with words that you might use in chat. For example, when Sarah (co-author) types **LOL** in her chat window, her avatar automatically laughs while clutching its stomach.

You can upload sounds just like you upload an image, using File⇨Upload Sound. It will cost you $L10 to bring a sound into SL. Clips must be in Wave format (.wav) files, and must be 10 seconds or less in length.

Some folks confuse animations and gestures. When you search for premade ones, you might want to try both search terms.

Creating and Using a Pose

You can, of course, buy poses premade in Second Life, but we start by showing you how to make your own. If you want to discover how to use a pose you already have in your Inventory, you can skip to later in this section.

To make a pose, you need a 3-D posing program, such as Poser (www.e-frontier.com/go/poser), but this can be expensive. Look for a great, free alternative — Avimator (www.avimator.com) — and its updated version, QAvimator (www.qavimator.org). Both are free and easy to use. Avimator has a much simpler interface than the updated QAvimator, but the Q version will give you more control over your animations and poses.

To start, visit the QAvimator Web site, download the software for your operating platform, and install it.

After you install the software and open the application, you see the QAvimator interface, as shown in Figure 16-1. Lots of options are available in QAvimator for you to play with, but for this example, we focus on the basics — the timeline, the Avatar tab, and the Keyframe tool (key frames mark important changes in the position of the avatar). Movements will be cued to transition smoothly from one keyframe to another at the bottom.

Avatar tab

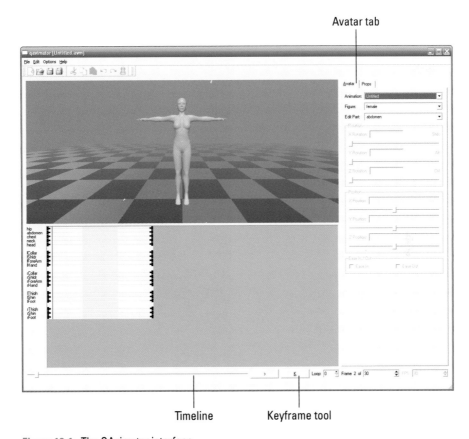

Timeline   Keyframe tool

Figure 16-1: The QAvimator interface.

Start by making a yoga position. This one is called Sraddha Vrisikasana (or Devotion Scorpion), and is truly a position we could never achieve in real life (although in Second Life, it's easy). To create the Sraddha Vrisikasana, follow these steps:

1. **Change the number of frames to 2 in the Frame box at the bottom-right of the screen.**

   To make a pose, you need only two frames.

2. **Move the frame slider at the bottom of the screen to the right.**

   The slider moves all the way over to the right because we have only two frames in this animation.

   This (the second frame) is the frame that will contain your pose.

3. **Click the K button to mark this as a keyframe.**

   You're ready to strike a pose.

4. **Choose Options⇨Joint Limits.**

   After all, most yoga positions require a bit of unnatural bendiness.

   The bottom half of the screen shows a timeline with each poseable body part listed.

5. **Click each and make the following adjustments by using the X Rotation, Y Rotation, and Z Rotation tools on the right side of the program window.**

   You end up with a position that looks like Figure 16-2.

Body Part	X Rotation	Y Rotation	Z Rotation
Hip	167	0	0
Abdomen	−20	0	0
Chest	−55	0	0
Neck	0	0	0
Head	−65	0	0
lCollar	0	0	0
lShldr	0	−92	0
lForeArm	0	0	90
lHand	0	0	0
rCollar	0	0	0
rShldr	0	96	0
rForeArm	0	0	−90
rHand	0	0	0
lThigh	65	0	0
lShin	78	0	0
lFoot	78	0	0
rThigh	65	0	0
rShin	78	0	0
rFoot	78	0	0

6. **Save the pose.**

   Choose File⇨Save As and name your pose. We call ours `scorpion.bvh`.

   Be sure to change the file extension to `.bvh`, or Second Life will not recognize the pose.

7. **Fire up Second Life and choose File⇨Upload Animation, as shown in Figure 16-3.**

   Yes, uploading your pose will cost L$10. Still, the L$10 is worth it to have your very own crazy yoga pose!

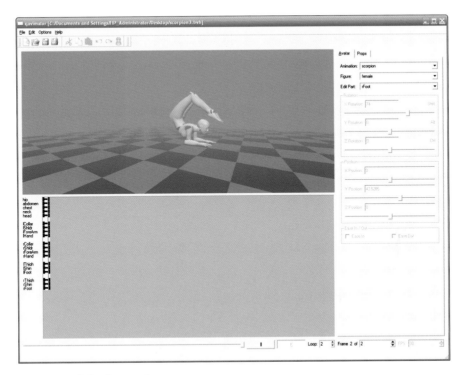

Figure 16-2: Quite the amazing yoga pose.

8. **Navigate to the `scorpion.bvh` file and choose Open.**

   An upload menu (as shown in Figure 16-4) appears with some really important options.

9. **Fill in these definitions andmake these settings for your pose:**

   - *Name:* Give your pose a name you can remember so you can easily find the pose in your Inventory.

   - *Description:* If you intend to sell your poses, you'll want to be sure to put in a clear description so others will know what the pose is.

   - *Priority:* This field dictates whether your pose will be overridden by typing animations, default shifting around while your avatar stands and so on. If you make it the highest priority (4), you will hold the pose no matter what else you are doing.

   - *Preview While:* For this pose, we'll preview it Standing. If this were a sitting pose, you'd want to select Sitting from this list so you can preview how your new pose will transition from the basic sitting pose. However, we will add that previewing this one in Walking is pretty funny.

   - *Loop:* Select this check box so your avatar will stay in the pose rather than just doing it once and standing back up.

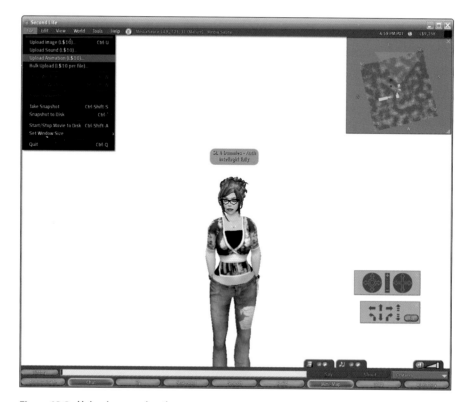

Figure 16-3: Upload your animation.

- *In% and Out%:* These percentages control the speed at which the loop happens. Because we don't want this to visibly loop (thereby giving a still appearance), we put both settings at 0.

- *Hand Pose:* You can't control how your fingers look in QAvimator, so this is where you choose whether you want your fingers to point, be relaxed, or even make a Peace sign. We chose Relaxed so our fingers are spread to look like they're supporting us better.

- *Expression:* This is a fun one. We're setting ours to None, but if you want it to look like you're particularly enjoying your yoga (or maybe it's causing you pain), go ahead and choose a different expression.

- *Ease In (sec) and Ease Out (sec):* These settings dictate how long it takes your avatar to reach the final pose and how long it takes to go back to a normal standing position. We set them both to 0 to get a sudden pose that will stay.

10. **Click the blue Play button to preview your pose.**

   The gray avatar in the blue screen should strike the scorpion pose and stay there. If it does, click the Upload (L$) button.

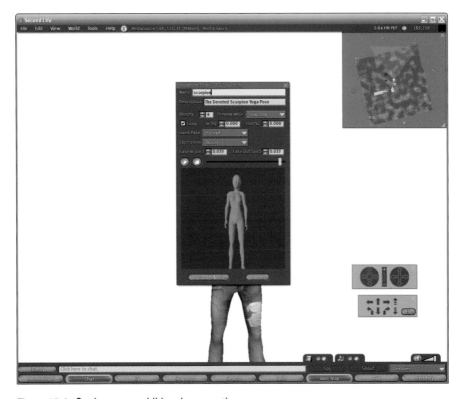

Figure 16-4: Setting some additional pose options.

Your new pose is saved in your Inventory in the QAnimations folder with the name you gave it in Step 9.

Now it's time to try out the pose you just made. Although the following directions are for the pose we showed you how to make in the first part of this chapter, they will work for any pose in your Inventory, including premade and purchased poses. To perform the pose, follow these steps:

1. **Click the Inventory button on the bottom-right of your screen and find the pose in the Animations folder of your Inventory.**

   You'll know it's a pose because it will have a little yellow dancing man next to it, as shown in Figure 16-5.

2. **Double-click the pose to prompt a pop-up window (as shown in Figure 16-6) asking you how you'd like to perform the pose.**

   • *Play in World:* If you click the Play in World button, everyone around you can see you perform the pose.

   • *Play Locally:* If you click the Play Locally button, only you will see the pose on your screen.

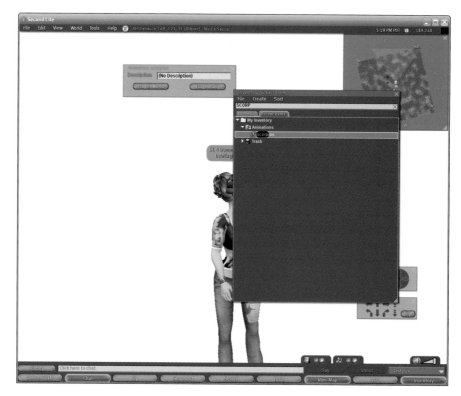

Figure 16-5: Here is the scorpion pose in my Animations folder.

If you're unsure about your new pose and don't want to look silly in front of other people, choose Play Locally so that no one else can witness your contortions.

Figure 16-6: Decide whether you want others to see you striking a pose.

Your avatar performs the pose, as shown in Figure 16-7.

Making an Animation

Animations are just like poses except that instead being frozen in a position, your avatar moves through a serious of movements and then stops or repeats them. Most animations that you see in SL are dance steps, so we'll do something different. Hmmm, how about "raising the roof?" Here's how:

Figure 16-7: Tah-dah! You're a virtual yoga master!

1. **In QAvimator, start a new project by choosing File⇨New.**

2. **Set the number of keyframes to 6.**

   The default setting gives you 30 frames to work with, but you won't need that many for this example.

   When you "raise the roof," you pump your arms from a bent position to a straight position over and over, so each arm pump is two movements (up and down). You also need to get into the position and then back out again.

   To accomplish this, set the following:

   - *Two arm pumps:* Two keyframes each
   - *The initial position:* One frame
   - *The transition back to normal:* One frame

     That's a total of six keyframes.

   a. *Click the hip timeline at six equal distances.*

   b. *Click the K button to create a keyframe at each one.*

3. **Make the animation. Set the X, Y, and Z rotations for each of the parts for each keyframe to match the following tables.**

✓ **Keyframe 1**

Body Part	X Rotation	Y Rotation	Z Rotation
lCollar	65	0	0
lShldr	−4	−88	0
lForeArm	0	0	146
lHand	0	0	62
rCollar	53	0	0
rShldr	0	85	0
rForeArm	0	0	−149
rHand	0	0	−52

✓ **Keyframe 2**

Body Part	X Rotation	Y Rotation	Z Rotation
lCollar	0	−1	−7
lShldr	−2	−89	0
lForeArm	0	0	87
lHand	0	0	41
rCollar	0	0	0
rShldr	0	85	0
rForeArm	0	0	−90
rHand	0	0	−34

✓ **Keyframe 3**

Body Part	X Rotation	Y Rotation	Z Rotation
lCollar	46	4	−11
lShldr	0	−92	0
lForeArm	0	0	59
lHand	0	0	28
rCollar	−46	0	0
rShldr	0	92	0
rForeArm	0	0	−59
rHand	0	0	−28

✓ **Keyframe 4**

Body Part	X Rotation	Y Rotation	Z Rotation
lCollar	−69	0	0
lShldr	0	−91	0

lForeArm	0	0	17
lHand	0	0	12
rCollar	−69	0	0
rShldr	0	91	0
rForeArm	0	0	17
rHand	0	0	−28

🗸 **Keyframe 5**

Body Part	X Rotation	Y Rotation	Z Rotation
lCollar	90	0	0
lShldr	0	−92	0
lForeArm	0	0	17
lHand	0	0	0
rCollar	90	0	0
rShldr	0	92	0
rForeArm	0	0	−17
rHand	0	0	0

If entering all these numbers feels tedious now, when you get used to how to pose the figure in QAvimator, this will all be easy. The numbers become less important and more intuitive.

4. **Save the animation as `raisedaroof.bvh` or whatever filename you like.**

5. **Upload the animation with the following settings for the upload preview:**

   - *Priority:* 2.
   - *Preview While:* Standing.
   - *Loop:* Select this only if you want your avatar to repeat the animation over and over again.
   - *In% and Out%:* These aren't important here because you're not looping the animation in this example.
   - *Hand Pose:* Relaxed.
   - *Expression:* We chose a happy face for the animation. You have several to choose from.
   - *Ease In (sec) and Ease Out (sec):* Leave these set at 0.300.

6. **Click the Upload (L$10) button and then find the animation in your Inventory under the Animations folder. Enjoy!**

   Now you can raise the roof when you want to celebrate, as shown in Figure 16-8.

Figure 16-8: SL rocks! Raise the roof!

Animations and poses can be placed in poseballs very easily. *Poseballs* are used to imbed poses into furniture, to provide dances on a dance floor, and so on. For sample poseball scripts you might want to look at, check out

www.netstartel.com/~walton/sl/poser.txt

For more on building poseballs, see Chapter 13.

Creating a Gesture

To make a *gesture,* such as waving hello or shaking your head, Gestures can be combinations of poses, animations, and sounds. In this example, we show you how to combine a few animations and sound effects to create something that really announces a party. It's easy and fun, so jump right in!

To create a gesture, follow these steps:

1. **Open your Inventory by clicking the Inventory button on the bottom-right of the screen.**

2. **Choose Create⇨New Gesture.**

   The new gesture appears in your Inventory's Gestures folder and is called New Gesture.

3. **Double-click New Gesture to open it and then give your gesture a name.**

We call ours Celebrate.

The default for the new gesture has the avatar wave and say, "Hello," but we're going to change that.

4. **Start by removing the steps in the right-hand box by clicking each one and then clicking the Remove button until the right-hand box is empty.**

5. **Add the elements you want by clicking Animation in the Library box on the left and then clicking the Add button.**

   You see Start Animation: None in the Steps box. Now you have to tell the gesture what animation to play.

6. **Click the Animation to Play drop-down list, below the Steps box, and scroll down until you see "Celebrate" (or whatever you called your animation in Step 3).**

7. **(Optional) Add a sound to your gesture:**

   a. *Click Sound in the Library box.*

   b. *Click the Add button.*

8. **(Optional, if you use Step 7) Click the Sound to Play drop-down list, below the Steps box, to see some of the sound options.**

   We opt for Comedy 1, which is in the Sounds folder in your Library (found in your Inventory). Here's how:

   a. *Go into your Library and find Comedy 1.*

   b. *Right-click Comedy 1, copy it, and paste it into your Sounds folder under My Inventory.*

      This makes it become an option on the Gesture screen.

   At this point, you have the hand raising and a sound. Continue with the remaining steps to add one more gesture.

9. **Click Animation in the Library box again, click the Add button, and then choose Clap from the Animation to Play drop-down list.**

   Your gesture menu looks something like Figure 16-9.

10. **Click the Preview button to see what your gesture will look like.**

11. **If you're happy with your gesture, click the Save button to save it in the Gestures folder in your Inventory. If you're not happy you can continue to make changes using the menus.**

12. **Select the Active check box at the bottom of the New Gesture window.**

    The gesture is available from the Gestures drop-down menu on the far right of your SL screen.

After you create a few animations and gestures, you'll either want to create more, or, well, have a better appreciation for really great ones you find in SL. Here are a couple of good places to find animations in SL. You'll see the

Figure 16-9: Reviewing the New Gesture window.

region name and coordinates for each location. Use these on the Map so you can teleport right to the spot.

Most stores will have pose stands you can use to preview how the animation or gesture will look when your avatar performs it. Expect to pay anything from $L1 to $L100 for each animation.

- ✓ **Bits and Bobs (Resolution; 155, 69, 24; PG):** Here you can find a HUGE selection of animations of mostly couples, ranging from dancing to, well, more "adult" behaviors.

- ✓ **Pose Paradise (Pose Paradise; 158, 117, 21; Mature):** Go here for lots of cute couple's poses, but you can also find great Kung Fu moves as well as sitting, walking, and other animations.

- ✓ **Animation Warehouse (Animation Island; 147, 26, 322; Mature):** This is a huge warehouse of animations from many different vendors.

- ✓ **M&P Shop (The Puppeteer; 142, 144, 31; Mature):** Here you can find a castle with a tower for each kind of animation, furniture with built-in animations, and HUDs for animation override.

Many animation stores sell mature animations. If you're worried about having to look past sexual animations to find sitting, dancing, and other innocent animations, then visit only those animation stores that are marked PG.

Part V
Real Life Opportunities in Second Life

The 5th Wave   By Rich Tennant

"For thirty years I've put a hat and coat on to make sales calls and I'm not changing that now just because I'm doing it on Second Life from my living room."

In this part . . .

Not everyone in Second Life is lounging by the beach taking in the virtual rays. Some folks are hard at work, and you can be, too. Besides, you probably need some income for that shoe addiction.

Chapter 17 outlines how to become gainfully employed in Second Life in ways that are probably more fun than your real-life job. In Chapter 18, we explore a bit about the big businesses that are in Second Life, how they're using Second Life, and what your business can gather from their successes and failures.

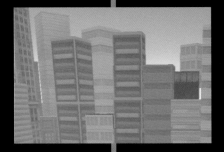

Chapter 19 delves into the fastest growing use of Second Life — education. Find out where the campuses are, what kinds of classes are being offered, and why Second Life is so big with educators.

Getting Paid in Second Life (It's Not Easy)

In This Chapter

▶ Choosing your field: services or products

▶ Using SL to test product ideas

▶ Getting a job

▶ Setting a salary

▶ Understanding the job market

▶ Running your own business

▶ Making money from real estate

Many people join Second Life (SL) after reading some news report touting SL as a way to make easy money. These stories remind us of press coverage of the Wild West during the Gold Rush. Promises of free cash flowing like water had folks piling into wagons and traveling across country with a pie plate and pick axe in hand, intent on striking it rich! All too soon, pioneers found out making a fortune would require hard work and luck. Second Life is no different, as you can see in Figure 17-1. It is a pioneer town with lots of opportunity, but it takes smarts, ingenuity, and a lot of effort to cash in. In this chapter, we get you headed in the right direction to avoid common mistakes and increase your chances of striking it rich.

Here are the two ways to earn money in Second Life: Provide a product or a service. Both approaches have been very successful in SL, and both have been huge failures. The best advice is to pick what you are good at and exploit that talent. For example, if you make amazing furniture, open a furniture store. If you're an excellent scripter, set up shop as a scripter.

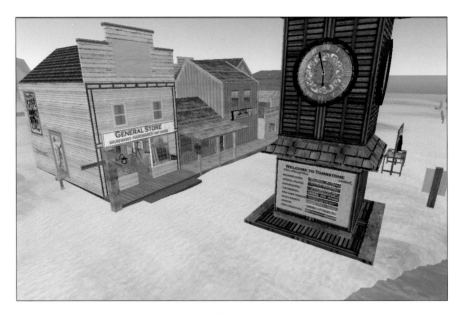

Figure 17-1: Second Life can be like the Wild West.

Finding Your Niche

The best products in the real world succeed because they fill a need. They solve a problem, entertain, or make the purchaser's life easier or better in some way. Finding a niche in SL is tough until you live there for a while, shop around a lot, and get a feel for what's already available. You won't make money selling a product or service that someone already offers for less. So, be sure that whatever you plan to offer is desirable to a SL resident (no one needs a better mousetrap in a world where the only mice are people dressed up like mice) and that yours is noticeably better or less expensive.

Selling Things in Second Life

Anything you can make you can sell in Second Life. Something as simple as a box can be sold — that is, if you can convince someone to buy it. (Doubtful, of course.) Usually, you sell products that are uniquely designed collections of objects or pieces of clothing. There is no magic formula for a successful product, but try to make what you sell the best work you can do.

Second Life has a lot of places where you can sell your product, as shown in Figure 17-2. If you created something that you believe will sell in SL,

If you make an item that you'd like to sell you'll have to set the properties of the object so that others may click on it and purchase it. See chapter 13 for information on how to set a price on an object in its properties. Once you've got something to sell, you'll need to find a place to sell it. You can either start your own store (as we'll discuss later in this chapter) or you can seek out a store owner who will let you sell your objects in their store. The best way to find such a store is to look in the Search menu's classified ad listings for stores asking for merchandise.

Figure 17-2: One of the many malls in Second Life.

The ultimate testing ground

Second Life can act as an excellent business incubator. You can start selling products as soon as you make them and never even have to have a store. Explore and create bold new products and offer any service you want. You might even consider giving your product away to a few key people to get interest piqued.

Say you try a product in SL, and it fails. Guess what happens? Nothing. Not a thing. You don't have to declare bankruptcy or fill out complicated IRS forms. You just try something else. Challenge yourself to be as creative as you can be. You never know what t-shirt or hair design might just take off.

In addition to selling products, the other thing you can sell is your time or skill. This would include things such as selling your scripting skill or your building skill (like an independent contractor). Again, you can sell any service that you can convince people to buy. Try to provide quality services for a reasonable price. Also, take advantage of the social network to add word-of-mouth advertising. To sell your time or skill, check the classified ads on the search menu for job advertisements. You can also place your own advertisement to announce that you're looking for a job.

Finding and Landing a Job

Think of being unemployed, sitting at your kitchen table with the newspaper circling Help Wanted ads. Second Life isn't much different. Second Life provides classifieds you can search through, complete with a category for employment. After you find someone looking for employees, you still have to get the job. Be professional and honest, and you might get lucky and find some work.

The first thing you should do in any job search is figure out what you want to do. Sure, you can do some menial job, but you won't make much money; or, you might get a high-paying job but doing something you don't like. Also, you need to consider your time commitments. Do you want this to be your career or just something you do to make a few virtual bucks to buy some cool new furniture?

Looking in the classifieds

Use the classifieds to search all the ads listed in the employment category. Start by figuring out what keywords might apply to the job you want. For instance, if you want a job scripting vendor objects, keywords such as *script, scripting, scripter,* and *vendor* might populate a fruitful search.

How much money can I make?

In Second Life, how much you can make is really dependent upon two things: How much time you're willing to work and how good you do your SL job. If you spend a lot of time working in SL and perfect your craft, the chances are good you will make some decent money. How much money is *good* for you really depends on your needs and wants. If you don't buy a lot of expensive things, maybe working a job isn't the best thing for you.

Remember: Decent money in SL is not a living wage. Don't be surprised if people aren't willing to pay you an hourly wage anywhere close to the minimum wage when translated to US$.

Some job listings might sound a little strange. For instance, some people employ other people in SL to play the role of their virtual children. Keep an open mind and have fun.

To search for a job, follow these steps:

1. **Click the Search button on the bottom of your screen.**

   This opens the Search window.

2. **Select the Classifieds tab.**

3. **Select the Employment category from the drop-down list, enter one of your keywords, and then click the Search button.**

   The results show all the employers looking for work that match your keyword, as shown in Figure 17-3.

Finding a good job is only the beginning. You have to meet with the employer, confirm that the employer is still looking for help, and then apply for the job. Most employers in Second Life are concerned that you're dedicated, that you'll show up on time, and that you know enough about the environment to actually do the job. Unlike in the real world, a SL employer can't call you at home to make you come into work so they'll want to be assured that you're dedicated to the work

Figure 17-3: Employment search results.

Placing your own classified

In addition to looking at the classifieds, you might want to try advertising yourself as seeking a job. To place your classified ad, follow these steps:

1. **Open the Search menu and click on the Classifieds tab, as in Figure 17-4**

2. **Clicking the Place an Ad button will open up the Classified tab on your profile where you can begin to create your ad (or delete an ad if you've already placed one), as shown in Figure 17-5.**

   The Classified tab on your profile can also be accessed by right-clicking on your avatar, choosing Profile, and clicking the Classified tab.

3. **Once you've clicked the New button you'll be able to start entering text on your new ad, as shown in Figure 17-6.**

4. **The pull down list below the text box will let you pick what kind of ad you're placing. Choose Employment if you're placing a job ad.**

5. **Click the gray image box at the top of the ad page to insert a picture for your ad. Be sure to use an image that will get the attention of potential employers.**

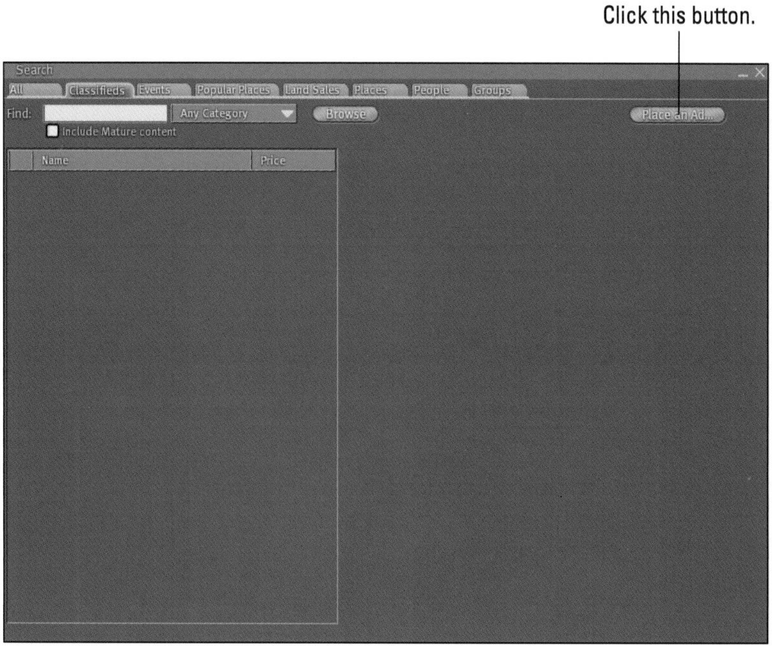

Click this button.

Figure 17-4: Click the Place an Ad button to begin placing your own ad.

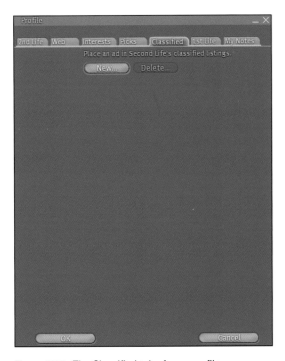

Figure 17-5: The Classified tab of your profile.

6. **When you're finished creating your ad, click the Publish button.**

   This will officially place your ad for others to find on the Classifieds tab of the Search menu.

7. **Before your ad goes live you'll be asked to pay to place the ad. The more you pay per week, the higher your ad will appear in the Classifieds screen. L$50 a week will put you around the middle of the listings. If you want to ensure you'll be at the top of the list, you'll want to pay at least a few hundred L$ a week.**

Asking around

A common way to find employment in SL is to find a place where you want to work and ask whether that establishment is hiring. In fact, some places even have signs posting open jobs. Say you want to DJ at your favorite club: Talk to the DJs and managers there to find out what you need to do to get hired. You might have to volunteer for a while, but you will learn a lot and make tons of new friends.

Figure 17-6: Be sure that you provide descriptive, confident text for your ad.

Apprenticeships

Another way of finding work is to apprentice for someone. If you find a builder whose buildings are amazing to you, ask whether he needs any help. Again, you may have to do some work for *gratis* but consider it a learning experience. You might also find a friendly shop owner willing to let you sell a few products in her store in exchange for a share of the profits.

Kinds of Jobs Available

One of the most common questions asked in SL is what kinds of jobs are available. The answer is really up to you. You can find easy jobs that don't pay all much as well as difficult, high-skilled jobs (that also sometimes don't pay all that well). Some jobs are also dependent upon your creativity. For example, we know an individual who makes good money giving guided tours for executives new to SL. Be brave and find something you love doing in SL. The following sections examine a few of the different types of jobs available in SL.

Hundreds more types of jobs are available than the ones we have space to discuss here.

Camping

Camping is the easiest, yet most boring, way to make money. In SL, when residents congregate at a location, its traffic value goes up, and it appears higher in the search rankings. As you can imagine, this is a good thing for a businessperson. *Camping* happen when a business person pays people to basically loiter at his business. This is usually done by sitting in chairs, dancing (as shown in Figure 17-7), or being animated to look like you're cleaning. All you need to do is search for Camp to find hundreds of camping locations.

Sounds like easy money. Well, it is, and it isn't. Camping doesn't pay much. In fact, it pays so little that it's very nearly not worth doing. Not to totally dismiss camping, though, it can have some benefits. If you're just talking to someone in SL and don't need to be near them to hold the conversation via instant message, why not sit in a chair and get paid for it while you're talking to them?

You just can't walk away from the computer when you're camping. When you're inactive for too long, Second Life logs you out. To make money by camping, you need to remain in one place and remain active in SL.

Figure 17-7: People dance-camping for money.

Entertainment industry

Bars and clubs are always looking for people to help out. They love dependable people who show up on time and contribute to the experience of the event or club. There is also a whole Event Planning industry. Jobs such as DJs, security, concierge, and host/hostess are usually available for those willing to put in the time.

You can also find adult entertainment occupations. Some folks make Lindens as exotic dancers or escorts. If you're comfortable with this work, talk to people in the industry and find out as much as you can before you consider it.

Fashion industry

What people wear in SL is a huge business. Fashion and all the jobs around it are very big in SL, and are a great way to make money. You can design clothes and stores, model the clothing, or even be a virtual photographer. Several fashion magazines (see Figure 17-8) in SL are always looking for quality people to work with them.

Some fashion magazines include

- Second Style Magazine
- Aspire
- OMG
- FM For Men
- Linden Lifestyles

Being a landlord

Another way you can make money in SL is by being a landlord or a real estate agent. You can buy land and then rent or sell parts of it. For more information, consult Chapter 12.

Being Your Own Boss

This is how you can end up becoming your own boss. You search all over SL to find a hair style you like. Nothing is perfect. You have a picture from a magazine of what you're looking for, but no one in SL makes that hairstyle. So you read up on hair styles and how to make them, and you start experimenting. You work one solid night on the hair, and finally it starts to look right. You wear it around, and someone asks you where you bought it, whether it comes in green, and how much it costs. Bam! You're in business.

Figure 17-8: A news stand selling Second Life magazines and newspapers.

If you can't find the right job or you think you have a product or skill that you can market on your own, the answer to your empty bank account just might be starting your own business.

Starting a business

In SL, you don't need any pesky legal documents or tax forms to start a business. All you need to do is start charging for objects that you make or for services you provide. Sounds simple? Well, it might involve less paperwork, but it's just as difficult to make money in Second Life as it is in Real Life (RL). You should do market research, design testing, and customer care — all the things that will help you make a successful business.

Planning

Just because your product or service might be virtual doesn't mean that you shouldn't follow good practices for setting up your business. How do you envision your business? Will you be selling a product from your own store or offer it for sale in other stores?

Part of business planning should be identifying your own unique niche in SL. If you want to be a clothes designer, look around at clothes you like and find out where you could offer something different. Also, look at how much those products cost when pricing your own products.

Marketing a business

There is no prescribed way in SL to market your business. You can advertise in industry magazines, place classified ads, use billboards, create groups, or just use word of mouth. Be as creative and original as possible, and you will attract people to your business. You can't do anything wrong, and marketing shouldn't cost you all that much, so feel free to experiment.

To create a classified ad for your business, follow these steps:

1. **Click the Search button on the bottom of your screen.**

   This opens the Search window.

2. **Select the Classifieds tab.**

3. **Click the Place an Ad button.**

   This opens up the Classifieds area in your profile. You can also get to the same location going to your profile and clicking the Classifieds tab.

4. **Click the New button, as shown in Figure 17-9.**

   SL tells you that your ad will be displayed for a week and that it will be listed higher on the list, depending on how much money you spend.

   The classified ad is tied to your present location, so make sure you are at your business' location When you create the ad.

5. **Enter a title and description for your ad.**

   Make your ad as clear and compelling as possible. Give people a reason to use your business.

6. **Select the category for the ad.**

   Make sure this fits your ad perfectly so that people can find what you're advertising. You can choose only one category per ad.

7. **Select the check box to identify whether your business is mature (or not).**

8. **Select the Auto-renew check box to automatically renew your ad once per week.**

   This might not be a good option for your first ad. Make sure that people are seeing your ad first before you sign up to automatically renew; otherwise, you're just wasting money.

9. **Click the Publish button.**

10. **Enter how much you want to spend on the ad.**

Click to create an ad.

Figure 17-9: Enter a new ad.

The more you spend, the higher it appears in search results. The price of your ad depends on the competition in your area of business. Ads for adult content, builders, and dance clubs are at a premium of at least $L5000 a week. In other lower demand businesses $L50 might get your ad near the top of the search results.

11. Click the Publish button again.

The fee is deducted from your account, and your ad appears in the classifieds listing.

If you're serious about making a go of it with your business, you might want to consider hiring a marketing firm in SL to help. Check out their clients and see what successes they have had. A quick search for "marketers" in the search menu will yield a huge host of companies who can help your business grow.

Setting up shop

Location is as important in SL as it is in RL. In SL, you can buy land and build your own shop, set up a booth in a mall, or just sell your product or service by word of mouth. You might also want to list your products on Web sites, such as OnRez (www.onrez.comx), to make more sales.

Managing your business and hiring help

If you start a business and need help, consider yourself lucky. Most SL businesses are run solo. If you do well enough to have to hire other people, you should be pleased. Hiring people in SL should start with advertising, either at your business or in the classifieds.

Check out people's experience and references, and pay employees on time.

18

Bringing Big Business to Second Life

In This Chapter

▶ Understanding the state of the Second Life economy

▶ Discovering Second Life business strategies

▶ Finding out the truth about business in Second Life

▶ Studying current industries in Second Life

*T*hroughout this book, we cover the person-to-person business in Second Life (SL), but one of the things that gets SL lots of press coverage is big business within SL. By big business, we mean multinational conglomerates, such as IBM and Toyota, that have a presence in SL. When major players in the real-world business markets begin virtual spaces, people who might never have seen or thought about SL begin to take notice. With big business entering a frontier like SL, things are bound to be shaken up a bit both for the environment of Second Life and the businesses that enter it. In this chapter, we distill what we know about big businesses in SL and hopefully make it easier for a big business to fit in.

Even though Second Life is one of the most dynamic, exciting virtual worlds in existence, it's not for everyone — and not for every business. Companies who sell products that are difficult to reproduce in Second Life, or who sell products/services to a demographic different from the demographic in Second Life, might find a presence in Second Life ineffective.

If you're a small business owner Second Life can be a powerful marketing tool. Not only might you be able to garner some PR from your company's presence in SL, but you might also be able to make use of Second Life to create a community around your product such as a good web presence might do as well. For very little investment, Second Life can provide some dramatic marketing results.

State of the SL Economy

Summing the entire state of the SL economy is difficult. Like the real world, so many factors affect how the SL economy does. Factors such as population growth, downtime, software bugs, and nefarious folks can all affect the economic situation in SL. Also, like any economy, SL has its ups and downs. We recommend that you keep up with a number of Web sites and blogs that center on virtual economies if you're interested in bringing a big business into SL. These Web sites and blogs are the best way to keep track of things and stay up-to-date on the latest changes that affect the SL economy. We recommend the following Web sites and for staying on top of the SL economy:

- ✔ `http://secondlife.com/whatis/economy_stats.php`: Linden Lab's page of recent economic activity in Second Life.

- ✔ `http://blog.secondlife.com/2007/08/14/the-second-life-economy/`: Linden Lab's official explanation of how the Second Life economy functions and is maintained.

Current Big Business Strategies in SL

One of the common questions that we're asked is, "What works for business in SL, and what doesn't?" The easy answer is, "Anything," but that doesn't really give you what you need to know. Corporations aren't making gobs of money in SL. It's not a huge revenue stream for major companies. Some people make a decent living or supplement their real world income from SL, but if you're a company looking to strike it rich in SL, you need to look very hard at what you doing. Based on knowing SL and its economy, these are the business strategies we've seen work the best in SL.

Marketing

Second Life provides an excellent spot for you to market real-world products. How is that possible? Say, for instance, that you're a car manufacturer with a hip, sporty car you want to market to hip, sporty people. You build the car in SL and have a huge event to announce it and give away a bunch of the SL cars. You have hired a great builder, so the SL car (see Figure 18-1) looks exactly like the real car, and the SL resident can begin to see herself in the car. Liking how the car looks in SL, the resident goes out and test-drives the real car (because the car manufacturer's SL store told the resident where its local real-world dealer was and what time it was open) and ends up buying a real life car. *Voilà!* This is exactly what Toyota did with its Scion line of cars.

Figure 18-1: The author's SL Toyota Scion. She liked it so much that she owns a real one!

Virtual meeting and training space

Second Life can offer a major corporation space — a lot of space, for a very inexpensive price, in which it can build just about anything. A business can build a meeting space where its remote employees can meet, show videos and Power Point presentations, and even talk by using the voice feature, all for a significantly lower cost. A business can also do training sessions and show off new products to employees. A business can section off parts of land it owns to be especially for employees. This allows the business to control who comes in and out, so they can discuss internal company business.

Information and support

Another strategy that some large companies practice is using their presence in SL as a way to release new products and get information from the customers. We know of companies that have weekly customer meetings and also show off their newest products in SL before introducing them in the real world. Sometimes, businesses even offer a prototype for people to comment on before the product or the next version of the product is released. Second Life is a huge marketplace that's eager to contribute ideas and information, and a company shouldn't be afraid of what SL residents might say. A business should put its best product out there and ask the SL community to help improve it. The company might just get some awesome suggestions.

Top Five Second Life Business Myths

As Second Life hit the mainstream media in 2007 magazines, newspapers, and television jumped on the bandwagon to talk about business in Second Life. As with any over-night hype, there were some misconceptions released about the potential to make money in Second Life. In this section we'll try to address some of the common myths around business in this virtual world.

Bringing your business into SL is a way to get rich quick

If you've been in business any amount of time, you realize getting rich quick anywhere is very difficult, and SL is no exception. There's no huge, untapped source of gold or anything like it in SL. For your business to grow in SL, it'll take time and work. If you want to get rich quick, you've been watching too many infomercials.

Every business will work in SL

Some things work in SL, and others don't. For example, a company that sells scooters to the elderly might have a tough time connecting with the SL audience, but that's not to say you can't — or shouldn't — try. Before you bring your business into SL, do lots of research to see how — and whether — you should set up a virtual shop. Be sure to walk around the shops listed in Chapter 20 to see how a successful business operates.

You can't make any money in SL

Although SL is primarily a marketing tool for large companies outside Second Life, you can make money. Again, this is no gold rush, but it is possible. *Playboy,* for instance, has a very classy island to promote its publications and Web sites, but also sells in-world clothing that matches its real-world clothing. If you buy a logo shirt in SL you like, you can buy the same shirt in the real world.

You have to invest a lot of money in SL to be successful

Anyone who tells you that you have to spend millions of dollars to have your business succeed in Second Life is after your millions of dollars. Setting up a good presence in SL isn't free, but it shouldn't break your bank, either. If you're looking to establish the presence for a large business in SL, shop around. Find out who created the business area you like and do research on companies who want to work with you. A small business can establish an impressive space for a few hundred dollars (or much less if you build it yourself). Bigger companies might want to pay for multiple regions to be developed. Great developers can charge from hundred to thousands to create really incredible spaces.

Second Life is so vast and empty that no one will buy my products

For the uninformed or uninitiated, SL can look a little empty at first — but this isn't the case. If you take away all the real-world food, transportation, and housing-related businesses you see, your world would begin to look a little sparse as well. In SL, the population tends to migrate together and create communities around a space they find engaging and comfortable. There are hotspots of activity. The key is making your business one of them.

Industries with a Second Life Presence

The businesses that are coming into SL are always changing. It's difficult to tell you who the major players are because by the time you read this book, things might have changed completely. Because of this, we're going to tell you about the industries that are already in SL. If you're in one of these industries and your company is thinking about creating a presence in SL, look around at what some companies in your industry have done and then carve out your own niche. If your industry isn't here, you might have found a new niche all by yourself. Get in-world, look around, and see whether it's the spot for your big business.

Computer software and hardware

Certainly, computer software and hardware is a perfect fit for SL because it's full of early technology adopters who already love advanced technology and broadband connections and who are eager to learn more about your product. Sounds like a dream audience to us. Companies in this area sometimes have multiple islands they use as showcases, marketing tools, and places for their customers to meet. Some of these businesses already in SL include Dell (see Figure 18-2), IBM, Intel, Sun, and Cisco.

Figure 18-2: Dell's presence in SL — Dell Island.

Automobiles

When you can build a life-like version of your vehicle and allow customers to drive around on your own test track for a fraction of the cost of doing it in the real world, what car company wouldn't be looking to buy land in SL? An automobile company can set up a virtual show room with detailed scale models of its cars that people can buy and ride in, allowing the consumer to place themselves inside the product. SL also allows car companies to show off vintage and concept cars to a wider audience. Some of the automotive businesses already in SL include Scion, Pontiac, and Mercedes-Benz.

Media and entertainment

Media companies are also an excellent fit for SL. Reuters, the news agency, has a bureau in SL to provide real-world news in SL and to provide SL news to the real world (see Figure 18-3). Major studios create whole islands or groups of islands for their TV shows and movies. The latest *Transformers* movie island includes avatars based on the robots in the movie. With so much creativity available and an audience hungry for media, SL is a perfect fit for these kinds of companies. Some of these businesses already in SL include Reuters, Showtime, NBC, and BBC.

Figure 18-3: Reuters headquarters in SL.

Clothing

Second Life is at times a clothing-shopper's dream. With are so many outfits, styles, hairdos, and accessories to try on, your head can spin. Now, large clothing companies are starting to make SL versions of their real-life clothes. If you buy a shirt from a designer you like in SL, you might think it will look good on you in real life. Some of the clothing companies already in SL are Nike, Reebok, and Playboy.

Education in Second Life

In This Chapter

▷ Learning and teaching in Second Life

▷ The Teen Grid: Education fun for younger folk

▷ A tour of Second Life campuses

> *Anyone who tries to make a distinction between education and entertainment doesn't know the first thing about either.*
>
> —Marshall McLuhan

Imaging ditching your old college lecture hall, the heavy books, and the droning lectures to escape into a space where you can fly, teleport, and build the classroom you want to learn in. Hundreds of universities have moved parts of their campuses into Second Life (SL) to explore the possibilities of learning in a virtual world. In this chapter, we discuss why SL is so appealing for education, introduce you to the Teen Grid, and highlight some great examples of how education can take up roots in a virtual world.

Learning and Teaching in Second Life

The Second Life Educators (SLED) mailing list (https://lists.secondlife.com/cgi-bin/mailman/listinfo/educators) details thousands of active members from campuses all over the world. From the individual renegade educator forging his or her way in the virtual world to an entire campus rebuilt from pixels and textures, there's been a rush of teaching and learning efforts into SL over the past two years. Education doesn't have to be boring, and these teachers and institutions are showing the way to make it fun and interactive. By using role playing, simulations, building, social events, and other approaches, higher education in Second Life makes use of the flexibility of the space to allow students to have hands-on experiences with topics that might be difficult to teach in the classroom.

Similar to SLED, an academic researchers mailing list — the Second Life Researchers List (SLRL) — is available. More information can be found at http://list.academ-x.com/listinfo.cgi/slrl-academ-x.com.

Simulations

Learning to run a business can be difficult. Budgets, payroll, profits, and marketing — on top of developing a great product or service — can drive you bonkers and bankrupt except in SL. Teaching students to function as entrepreneurs is easy and inexpensive in SL. Given a small budget and some guidance, students can start a *real* business that can make *real* profits without breaking the bank. With a budget of a few hundred L$, a team of students can start a thriving SL company. And if they make a profit, they just might get to keep it!

Role playing

Campuses have limits. As much as educators might like to, it's often difficult to really put students into positions where they can get some hands-on learning. Imagine trying to get a room full of students to understand gender issues. What's it really like to live as a woman? How do men see things differently? You could bring in a trunk of clothes and have students cross-dress and traipse around campus, but chances that are someone is going to get arrested. In SL, though, not only is taking on a new role easy, but it's fun! Dress up and take on a new persona for powerful insights into a new life style, a profession, or a totally new way of life. It's as easy as playing dress-up and trying out something new.

Building

As an architecture student, why build a scale model of a new building in foam core or cardboard when you can build the actual building, walk around in it, ask other people to do the same, and really see how your design would work with people living in it? Don't like that wall there? Move it! Got a controversial new home design? Try it out in SL before trying it in the real world. Though you might be able to build a design in another tool, only Second Life allows you to invite thousands of people to explore the space, provide feedback, and even buy it, move into it, and make it their own.

Building doesn't have to be related to architecture, though. Students reading literature, exploring history, or even studying biology can benefit from building models of what they're learning about. Read *Romeo and Juliet* and then build a set, dress in costume, and act it out all without hammers and sewing machines.

Social events for learning

Learning doesn't have to happen in isolation, and study groups in the library basement can be narcoleptic experiences. No more. Holding study groups and other social learning events in SL can add back the spice into hitting the books. Learning groups can happen 24/7 from anywhere. They can be attended by students from all around the world, and group leaders can be anyone from a local instructor to a world expert.

Conferences are often streamed into SL. To extend the reach of the presentations via video on the Web, video presentations can be displayed on a screen in SL. No matter how far away the conference is being held or how overbooked the event, SL always has room. And you don't need to buy a plane ticket to attend, either! Streaming content into Second Life is free and there are lots of public meeting spaces available for educators to use for such events.

The Teen Grid

In a parallel universe run by teenagers, SL offers the *Teen Grid,* which is a safe haven for 14–17-year-olds. In addition to being a crazy, swinging place that offers teenagers a refuge, many excellent educational projects are happening in the Teen Grid. To access the Teen Grid as an adult, you have to be an educator, be background-checked by Linden Lab, and have a designated "home" in SL where your avatar will stay. For more on the requirements, rules, and the Teen Grid in general, visit the Second Life Web site.

Here are a couple of examples to give you an idea of what's possible.

Global Kids

Global Kids (www.globalkids.org), begun by Barry Joseph, creates fun experiences for kids while teaching them about important global issues. Global Kids runs digital day camps (see Figure 19-1) where students learn about issues such as the UNICEF World Fit for Children campaign as well as other world issues related to children.

Global Kids led a distance learning program that met at the U.S. Holocaust Memorial Museum in Washington, D.C., bringing together youth from their after-school program. These students learned about museum tours and curating, and teen developers in SL then created a simulation of a German street the morning after Kristallnacht.

The Robert Wood Johnson is funding the Global Kids partnership with YouthVenture to support 40 groups of teens to develop social, entrepreneurial projects addressing health issues and vulnerable populations.

Figure 19-1: A Global Kids meeting in SL.

PacficRim Exchange (PacRimX)

PacRimX (http://pacificrimx.wordpress.com), founded by Stan Trevena and Chris Flesuras, was created as a way to further strengthen the relationship between Modesto City Schools in California and Kyoto Gakuen High School in Japan. The goal of the project is to use SL to create a constant level of interaction between the students of these schools that otherwise wouldn't exist. Most of the projects focus on four key areas: communication, cooperation, cultural sharing, and creativity. Because the students eventually meet each other in real life through school trips and exchanges, the idea at PacRimX is to build relationships in the virtual world first, in the hope of leading to deeper friendships.

Both Global Kids and PacRimX make the most of the global SL community by bringing together kids from all over the world to learn with and from each other.

Touring Second Life Campuses

You can find as many approaches to learning in SL as there are educators exploring the space. The best approach when considering your educational options is to tour of some of the best educational spaces in SL.

To find out more about educational efforts in Second Life, check out SimTeach (www.simteach.com) for links, discussion boards, a wiki, and more.

Here is a brief list of some of the SL campuses that we think are worth touring. After each campus name, you can find the region name and coordinates to use with the map in Second Life so you can teleport right to the spot.

This list touches only on the presence of education in SL. We could write a whole book about what educators are creating in SL and how this effort is changing higher education in a global way. Go check it out and be prepared to become jealous of the fun ways students get to learn nowadays!

Ohio University without Boundaries

```
Ohio University (45, 92, 25)
```

This double-island campus might sport traditional architecture, but the ideas here are anything but "old school." When you visit, be sure to take the tour so you won't miss any of the super-smart things that Ohio University built into its space. The best bit of this virtual campus is that it simultaneously works as a marketing tool for the university by giving visitors a real sense of what the brick-and-mortar campus looks like (see Figure 19-2) while integrating innovative technology to break some of the limits of a land-based campus.

Figure 19-2: Ohio University in SL.

Glidden, Northern Illinois University

```
Glidden (84, 166, 27)
```

If you want to see a beautiful campus, you can't miss Glidden. These buildings (as shown in Figure 19-3) not only foster learning but are the epitome of detailed buildings, down to the accurate window casings. Smartly, most of the land is left wide open to encourage students to build, collaborate, and fill the space with activities instead of congested buildings. On Glidden, quality beats out quantity.

Figure 19-3: The Glidden SL campus.

Literature Alive

```
Montclair State CHSS (184, 193, 22)
```

You might remember reading "Young Goodman Brown" or "The Fall of the House of Usher" in high school, but you've never seen them like this. Hear the raven call to you, find the body bricked in the wall from "The Cask of Amontillado" (as shown in Figure 19-4), and more. Why just read literature when you can live it?

Figure 19-4: Discover the body bricked into the wall to receive a clue and explore more of Poe's creepy imagination.

Massachusetts Institute of Technology (MIT)

```
MIT (44, 230, 31)
```

MIT is known for its super-smarts, and even in SL, these folks excel. The best part of this island is this discussion tool (as shown in Figure 19-5), which is made to facilitate debates and to gauge student opinions during class. As you move from Agree to Disagree, the gameboard keeps track of where you've been and for how long. It's really amazing to see when a group of people is having a discussion and moving on the board to express how they feel about the topic.

Angel Learning Isle

```
Angel Learning Isle (232, 94, 29)
```

Angel Learning is a well-used learning management system in higher education — and the first one to venture into SL. This island is unique in that it's created and controlled by the educators who live there. Constantly growing and changing, it's a great place to meet with other educators to collaborate, build, and discuss. The gazebo on Angel Learning Isle (as shown in Figure 19-6) offers teleports to many of the best education spots in SL. Be sure to check it out.

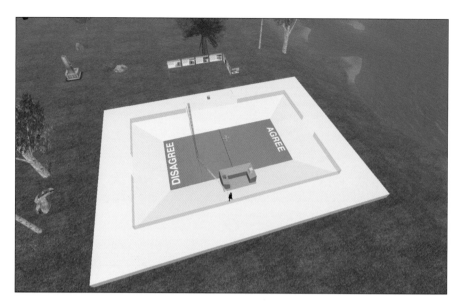

Figure 19-5: Moving across the voting floor shows others how you feel about the topic being discussed.

Figure 19-6: The Angel Learning Isle gazebo of knowledge.

Info Island

```
Info Island (97, 128, 33)
```

This is the home of all that is library in Second Life. Several libraries, a mystery mansion, a genealogy library, and a teaching tool repository will keep you busy for hours. Be sure to use the map (as shown in Figure 19-7) to teleport around so you don't miss anything.

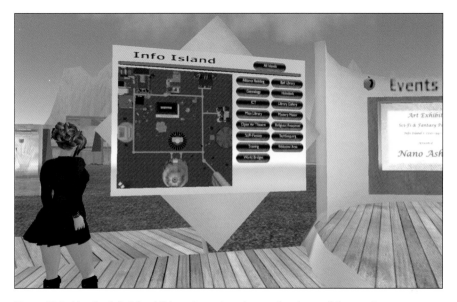

Figure 19-7: Use the Info Island Teleport map to get around and see all the great resources.

New Media Consortium

```
NMC Campus (128, 128, 0)
```

The New Media Consortium (NMC) is the powerhouse for education in SL. With dozens of islands filled with meeting spaces, libraries, collaborative spaces, and other resources, the NMC continent of islands offers some of the best examples of learning spaces in SL. The NMC often hosts exciting speakers and streams in video feeds from conferences all over the world, as shown in Figure 19-8.

Figure 19-8: Attending an educational video conference at the NMC.

Part VI
The Part of Tens

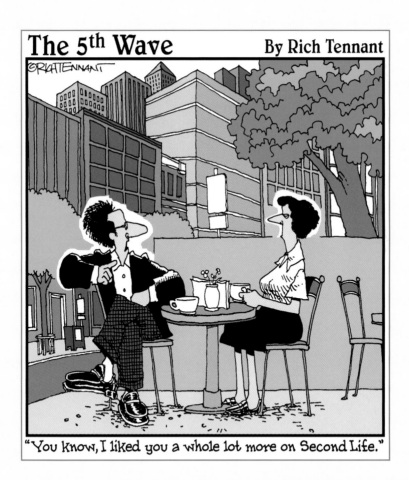

The 5th Wave   By Rich Tennant

"You know, I liked you a whole lot more on Second Life."

In this part . . .

When all else fails, turn to the trusty Parts of Tens at the back of a *For Dummies* book. These chapters give you the quick lowdown on the places you should consider shopping at and the places you shouldn't miss in Second Life.

If you need quick references, this is your part. Not that you shouldn't read the rest of the book. Because it's all good. Really. Bah. Just skip to the end like you always do.

Ten (Or So) Great Places to Shop

Shopping is a huge part of Second Life (SL), and trying to contain it to a single list of ten is crazy. So, for your consumerism pleasure, we provide three lists for you of the best places in Second Life for hair, men's clothes, and women's clothes. Shop 'til your avatar drops!

The Top Ten Places to Shop for Hair

Finding a great hair stylist is tough in real life but in Second Life it doesn't have to be. We've done the footwork (or teleport work) for you and found some of the best hairstyles in the virtual world. In Second Life you can experiment with radically different hairstyles without worrying about whether you'll be hiding under a hat for the next few months thanks to a bad cut.

For each listing we've provided you with the name of the store and the info you'll need to teleport to the store. Use the region name and coordinates to find each location using the world map. For more help using the map check Chapter 4.

We apologize that we, the authors, are the models throughout this chapter, but it was just too much fun to try on everything we found!

Gurl6

```
GurlyWood (110, 109, 22)
```

Gurl6 is a huge hair store for men and women. Be ready to be overwhelmed. If you take your time in this store, not only will you find great hairstyles but some great deals here as well. Be sure to check out the free and newbie hair as well as the hair separates that allow you to mix and match bangs and backs, as shown in Figure 20-1.

Figure 20-1: Intellagirl models her new hair.

Calla by Tigerlilly Koi

```
Callatropia (124, 194, 24)
```

Calla, the creation of Tigerlily Koi, is a multiple-floor hair store with men's and women's styles. Calla also carries detailed hair accessories, such as chopsticks and combs.

Vixen by Verikai Vargas

```
Vixen Island (213, 92, 31)
```

Vixen has a small but great inventory of women's hairstyles. Don't be put off that all the hair is displayed in blond. Every style comes in a wide range of colors.

Calico Creations by Calico Ingmann

Calico Kitty (124, 70, 36)

Like with many hair stores, Calico stacks its men's and women's styles high up on the walls. Be sure to use your camera controls (View⇨Camera Controls) to pan up and around to see them all. Also, be sure to check out the discount styles. Calico marks down some really great hairdos. Calico specializes in crazy punk styles but also carries classic styles

Bryce Designs by Bryce Tully

Illusion (34, 132, 38)

Hair is about the toughest thing to make in SL, and men's hair must be the toughest. It's darned hard to find a decent male hairstyle, but Bryce does a great job with men's and unisex hair. Some of the styles are a little Fabio, but others are punky and fun.

Adimu by Rubina Stanwell

Marmela (85, 197, 24)

Adimu specializes in braids, dreadlocks, and fantastic Afros for men and women. This is the only SL hair store specializing in culturally diverse styles. Grab some kickin' corn rows (as shown in Figure 20-2) and hit the clubs in style.

Sirena by Natalia Zelmanov

West Sunset (159, 49, 21)

Affordable prices and great subtle styles make Sirena a must-stop shop for male and female hairstyles. Natalia Zelmanov makes shiny, flowy hair with pretty styles.

Tekeli-li! by Tekelili Tantalus

Asunder (111, 131, 39)

Tekeli-li doesn't carry many styles, but the ones that are in the store are must-haves for anyone who roleplays in SL. Most of the female-only hair styles come with elaborate head dresses, like the one in Figure 20-3. They're truly works of art.

Figure 20-2: Typewriter shows off his new corn rows.

Figure 20-3: This style comes complete with flexi braids and a scripted head dress with effects.

Casu Capra

    Plush River (II 211, 152, 23)

Casu Capra has a nice selection of men's hair in messy, modern styles. This
vendor carries only natural colors, but all styles are modifiable, so you can
change them to a shade you like.

Hair Solutions

    Elite Island (66, 64, 22)

These male and female hairstyles are just plain fun. Try something different —
something you can't pull off in your real life. Go ahead. You know you want to!

The Top Ten Men's Clothing Stores

The clothes make the man, right? Whether you're club kid, an executive, or
the rugged outdoors type you'll need some duds to make your statement in
Second Life. Women's clothing stores outnumber men's by about ten fold so
we thought we'd help you dudes out there by sifting through the hundreds of
stores and offering up the best bets for great clothes.

For each listing we've provided you with the name of the store and the info
you'll need to teleport to the store Use the region name and coordinates to
find each location using the world map. For more help using the map check
Chapter 4.

Blaze by Blaze

    CColumbia Blaze (71, 74, 23)

In one of the best-designed stores in SL, you can find the formal wear you
need for that job interview or wedding. Blaze has it all in a friendly, open
environment, as shown in Figure 20-4. There is also an excellent casual section that is dominated by interesting stylish looks.

House of Zen by Zen Deledda

    HHinode Shima (142, 33, 29)

This shop offers some of the best designer, casual men's clothing. Come here
when you need to get a new shirt to go dancing in. You can also find fantastic
suits, classic men's clothing, and some female clothing. Typewriter (Mark's
avatar) wears House of Zen Clothes almost exclusively.

Figure 20-4: Dress smart for an interview.

Tonktastic by Tonk Tomcat

```
Rrhododendron Island (190, 246, 22)
```

If you're interested in hanging out in a darker part of the urban jungle, check out this grungy, urban store. Leather, cammo, and sharp urban designs make up this shop's cool clothes. Don't step on a rat!

Nyte'N'Day by Nyte Caligari

```
CCouture Isle (142, 125, 48)
```

This store has some excellent casual and more collegiate-feel clothing for the Big Man on the SL campus. There isn't a huge selection of men's clothes, but what is here is excellent. There is also a small selection of women's clothing.

sf designs by Swaffette Firefly

```
LLotus (231, 228, 142)
```

Ever want to dress up like the lord of the manor or Robin Hood? This shop offers great period-piece costumes (as shown in Figure 20-5), suits, and contemporary club wear. This shop also has a great selection of boots and shoes. Although not for everyone, take a look.

Figure 20-5: Typewriter of Sherwood Forest.

D & A Designs

```
IIsabella (251, 52, 123)
```

This shop contains excellent sportswear (see Figure 20-6). If you need a white satin shirt for club-in or a polo to hang out in, come to D & A Designs where the clothes are as fun to look at as they are to wear.

STELLAR DESIGNS by Lex Morgan

```
SStellar Isle (62, 215, 23)
```

Swim trunks and well-made casual clothes are the order of the day here. STELLAR brings you some great clothes that are fun to wear and make you look great. Don't forget a swimsuit!

DE Designs

```
DDE Designs (204, 132, 29)
```

If leather or a Gothic look is more your style, try DE Designs. Two floors of very creative and innovate outfits will bring your fantasies to life and let you play what ever role you want. This shop also includes lots of excellent mainstream clothes.

Figure 20-6: Typewriter is ready for the dance floor.

Dan Senyurt's

```
TTe Wharau (234, 77, 53)
```

If you need a shirt, this is the place to go for the best understanding of male shirts in Second Life. The clothes look and hang in a life-like manner and look great (see Figure 20-7). If you need a shirt to get some service, come to this shop!

Romance by Corwin Vargis

```
MMoonstone (51, 234, 29)
```

Another shop that is a little off the beaten track, Romance offers some truly unique and creative clothing. Have fun dressing up and showing your masculinity.

Figure 20-7: Typewriter shows off a Canvass green shirt.

The Top Ten Women's Clothing Stores

Women in Second Life suffer from abundance. There are just too many darn choices of great clothes at great prices and since everything fits, it can be nearly impossible to know what to wear. In an effort to make your head spin a little less we've hunted down our best ten choices for well made, well priced clothes in Second Life. Shop til you drop!

For each listing we've provided you with the name of the store and the info you'll need to teleport to the store. Use the region name and coordinates to find each location using the world map. For more help using the map check Chapter 4.

Midnight City

```
MMidnight City (117, 135, 26)
```

Midnight City has it all. The best designers, such as Torrid Midnight and Aimee Weber, sell their wears here. Set aside some serious shopping time and take a look in every shop.

Canimal

```
CCanimal (210, 61, 26)
```

The beautiful thing about Canimal is that most designs come in a variety of colors (see Figure 20-8). If you find an outfit you like, chances are that you can get it in several colors and that elements of other outfits in the store will be made in matching colors.

Figure 20-8: Showing off a Canimal blue top and a pair of black capris.

LittleRebel by Jonquille Noir

```
GGallinas (144, 101, 58)
```

LittleRebel carries everything from business wear to bikinis. Most outfits are affordable enough to splurge on without a second thought. Like many other designers, Jonquille is prolific, so be ready to spend some time browsing.

Nicky Ree

```
DDeco (86, 96, 33)
```

Nicky fills this store with a mix of casual, business, and mix-and-match coordinates. Nicky even has ball gowns, as shown in Figure 20-9. It's tough not to find something you'll like in this store.

Figure 20-9: Ball gowns with flowing skirts aren't easy to make, but Nicky gets it right.

Coconut Ice by Andromeda Raine

```
BButterfly Island (132, 161, 25)
```

Andromeda makes ultra-feminine gowns and fantasy wear. From dresses fit for Cinderella's ball to Tinkerbell-like fairy dresses, everything is here to make you feel very, very girly.

DiamonX Studios by Raudf Fox

```
FFushida (233, 167, 117)
```

Find some flat-out, amazing historic dresses here. Complete with feathered hats and bustles, if you want to dress up Victorian-style, there's simply no better place to go than DiamonX.

Indira Bekkers

```
Our Virtual Holland3 (107, 160, 22)
```

Indira is the closest thing to true *haute couture* in Second Life. She makes custom clothes, but even the conservative and well-made clothing available off the rack in her store will make you feel like a millionaire (see Figure 20-10).

Figure 20-10: Intellagirl couldn't resist putting on pink sneakers with this perfect black suit and gray silk tie.

Pizazz by Lynour Richelieu

```
LLaothoe (205, 39, 491)
```

Pizazz is great for bargain shoppers who want to look put together without big price tags. For about L$500, you can buy a box of 13 matching separates and have outfits for days. All the clothes are drawn well, and the flexi skirts twirl just like the more expensive ones you might elsewhere.

Escape by Kya Eliot

```
HHex (72, 154, 331)
```

Kya's clothes are perfectly shaded to look ultra-realistic. They're trendy without looking trashy, and most things come in a selection of colors.

Boing Fromage by Elka Lahane

```
OOverdrive Island (162, 139, 37)
```

Elka makes great, quirky, and fun clothing and accessories. Giant sunglass and duct tape t-shirts are just the beginning of her Bjork-like style. When you want fun, you want Boing Fromage.

Ten Great Places to Visit

In This Chapter

▶ Where to find fun

▶ Where to find good buys

▶ Where to find the best of SL

W e'd like to offer special thanks to First Opinions Panel (www.first opinionspanel.com), who conducted surveys of hundreds of Second Life residents to generate this list for us. It was important to us that this list not be our favorite spots in Second Life (SL) but the favorite spots of SL residents. We received hundreds of great spots for this list but had to narrow them down to just ten. Don't limit yourself to exploring just these. Second Life is an ever-changing beautiful place, so get out there and check it out!

What follows is the name of the region, its location rating, and a description.

Luskwood

```
Lusk (218, 168, 61), PG
```

Founded by Michi Lumin, Luskwood (as shown in Figure 21-1) is the oldest furry hangout in Second Life. Don't worry if you're not a furry — all are welcome in this beautifully landscaped region complete with giant trees, dance floors, and playgrounds. Luskwood is very friendly.

Figure 21-1: There are always friendly, furry folk on the Luskwood dance floor.

Spaceport Alpha

```
Spaceport Alpha (128, 128, 0), PG
```

With some of the most detailed models of real object anywhere, Spaceport Alpha (and Bravo, for that matter) are spots that your kids will want to look at over your shoulder. See Russian rockets, American shuttles, and even lunar landing modules. All are in correct scale with every imaginable detail.

Particle Laboratory

```
Teal (180, 74, 21), PG
```

The Particle Laboratory, by Jopsy Pendragon, offers simply some of the most beautiful light effects you'll see in Second Life. From fireworks shows at sunset to mysterious, dimly lit caves with dramatic music and fog, you'll find much to see here. Use the hot air balloon to tour all the best spots at the Particle Laboratory.

The Ivory Tower of Primatives

```
http://slurl.com/secondlife/natoma/210/164/27/Natoma (209,
          163, 27), PG
```

If you want to learn to build objects in Second Life, nowhere is better than the Ivory Tower of Primatives (as shown in Figure 21-2). Lumiere Noir deconstructs every possible shape of primitive object, along with great tutorials and examples of common objects.

Figure 21-2: Discover light effects by playing with the giant light bulb at The Ivory Tower of Primatives.

Isle of Wyrms

```
http://slurl.com/secondlife/limbo/135/119/21/

Limbo (126, 219, 91), Mature
```

Here there be dragons! This is a beautifully built place, full of dragon avatars and fantasy buildings. You'll see some of the best avatars in SL on the Isle of Wyrms. The dragon at the entrance to the Island of Wyrms is alive. He blinks and lashes his tongue around.

Virtual Starry Night

Luctesa (75,1 81, 23), Mature

Milan Brynner and Tressis, a Dutch company, have created simply breathtaking re-creations of Van Gogh landscapes in 3-D forms that you can walk around in, as shown in Figure 21-3.

Figure 21-3: Walk right into "The Courtyard of the Hospital at Alres."

Nakama

Nakama (129, 153, 21), Mature

Nakama is devoted to Japanese anime, in distinct sections: Kawaii Ku is devoted to cutesy anime; Ayashii Ku to future dystopian-style anime; Tonari Ku (neighbor district) to slice-of-life style anime; and Hokenjidai Ku (feudal district) is devoted to anime set in feudal Japan. Well worth exploring.

The Pond

```
The Pond (127, 135, 41), PG
```

The Pond has everything! Shopping, dancing, and scuba diving (as shown in Figure 21-4). You can even take an Australian walk-about around Ayres Rock!

Figure 21-4: Intellagirl gets inspected by a curious squid while scuba diving on The Pond.

Paris 1900

```
Paris 1900 (9, 171, 16), Mature
```

Complete with a scale model of the Eiffel Tower (see Figure 21-5), the Paris subway, street vendors, and loads of French shopping, Paris 1900 will have you shouting, "Oui! Oui!"

Figure 21-5: Be sure to grab a free parachute and jump off the top of the tower. It's quite the ride.

Saijo City

```
Saijo City (140, 45, 109), Mature
```

Spin Martin's post-apocalyptic creation is a role-playing space with an ongoing story you can take part in. The narrative evolves with the players. Even if role playing isn't your cup of tea, you should check out the amazing mood-setting builds on this island. All the elements you need to feel totally "Mad Max" are in Saijo City.

Index

Notes